MISTLETOE & MAYHEM

HORRIFIC TALES FOR THE HOLIDAYS

MISTLETOE & MAYHEM

HORRIFIC TALES FOR THE HOLIDAYS

EDITED BY RICHARD DALBY

CASTLE BOOKS

Published by CASTLE BOOKS, © 1993
a division of Book Sales, Inc.
110 Enterprise Avenue
Secaucus, NJ 07094

First published in 1993 by
Michael O'Mara Books Limited
9 Lion Yard
Tremadoc Road
London SW4 7NQ

Printed in the United States of America

ISBN 1-55521-972-1

CONTENTS

FOREWORD

The Christmas horror story has been a popular and hardy perennial since the days of Charles Dickens. More than any other genre, horror literature continues to reflect the primitive fears extant in our society.

This anthology gathers together thirteen seasonal tales of horror and the supernatural by some of the greatest practitioners in the genre, ranging from a Victorian classic by W. W. Jacobs to memorable modern-day tales of terror by Robert Bloch, Nigel Kneale and Ronald Chetwynd-Hayes, and a new novella by Basil Copper.

A very wide spectrum of 'horror' will be found here in many guises and in many different settings, including Egypt, the Swiss Alps, and America, as well as the more traditional settings of English country houses at Christmas Eve.

Stephen Gallagher's masterpiece of contemporary horror, 'To Dance by the Light of the Moon', rounds off this 'baker's dozen', extending the Christmas season to the last hour of New Year's Eve (and beyond . . .)

R. D.

JERRY BUNDLER

W. W. Jacobs

William Wymark Jacobs (1863–1943)
achieved enormous popularity with his many
humorous short stories and novels (*Many Cargoes,
Dialstone Lane, Night Watches, The Castaways,*
etc.), and his macabre classic 'The Monkey's Paw'
is among the most reprinted horror tales of all
time. Equally effective is 'Jerry Bundler', which
originally appeared in the Christmas Number of
the *Windsor Magazine*, December 1897, and was
adapted for the stage by the author two years
later. (It was revived with a happier ending in
1902, when the play *The Ghost of Jerry
Bundler* ran for 100 performances at
the Haymarket Theatre.)

I t wanted a few nights to Christmas, a festival for which the small
market-town of Torchester was making extensive preparations.
The narrow streets which had been thronged with people were
now almost deserted; the cheap-jack from London, with the remnant
of breath left him after his evening's exertions, was making feeble
attempts to blow out his naphtha lamp, and the last shops open were
rapidly closing for the night.

In the comfortable coffee-room of the old Boar's Head, half a dozen
guests, principally commercial travellers, sat talking by the light of the
fire. The talk had drifted from trade to politics, from politics to
religion, and so by easy stages to the supernatural. Three ghost stories,
never known to fail before, had fallen flat; there was too much noise

outside, too much light within. The fourth story was told by an old hand with more success; the streets were quiet, and he had turned the gas out. In the flickering light of the fire, as it shone on the glasses and danced with shadows on the walls, the story proved so enthralling that George, the waiter, whose presence had been forgotten, created a very disagreeable sensation by suddenly starting up from a dark corner and gliding silently from the room.

'That's what I call a good story,' said one of the men, sipping his hot whisky. 'Of course it's an old idea that spirits like to get into the company of human beings. A man told me once that he travelled down the Great Western with a ghost, and hadn't the slightest suspicion of it until the inspector came for tickets. My friend said the way that ghost tried to keep up appearances by feeling for it in all its pockets and looking on the floor was quite touching. Ultimately it gave it up and with a faint groan vanished through the ventilator.'

'That'll do, Hirst,' said another man.

'It's not a subject for jesting,' said a little old gentleman who had been an attentive listener. 'I've never seen an apparition myself, but I know people who have, and I consider that they form a very interest- ing link between us and the after-life. There's a ghost story connected with this house, you know.'

'Never heard of it,' said another speaker, 'and I've been here some years now.'

'It dates back a long time now,' said the old gentleman. 'You've heard about Jerry Bundler, George?'

'Well, I've just 'eard odds and ends, sir,' said the old waiter, 'but I never put much count to 'em. There was one chap 'ere what said 'e saw it, and the gov'ner sacked 'im prompt.'

'My father was a native of this town,' said the old gentleman, 'and knew the story well. He was a truthful man and a steady churchgoer, but I've heard him declare that once in his life he saw the appearance of Jerry Bundler in this house.'

'And who was this Bundler?' enquired a voice.

'A London thief, pickpocket, highwayman—anything he could turn his dishonest hand to,' replied the old gentleman; 'and he was run to earth in this house one Christmas week some eighty years ago. He took his last supper in this very room, and after he had gone up to bed a couple of Bow Street runners, who had followed him from London but lost the scent a bit, went upstairs with the landlord and tried the door. It was stout oak, and fast, so one went into the yard, and by means of a short ladder got on to the window-sill, while the other stayed outside the door. Those below in the yard saw the man crouching on the sill, and then there was a sudden smash of glass, and with a cry he fell in a heap on the stones at their feet. Then in the moonlight they saw the white face of the pickpocket peeping over the sill, and while some stayed in the yard, others ran into the house and helped the other man to break the door in. It was difficult to obtain an entrance even then, for it was barred with heavy furniture, but they got in at last, and the first thing that met their eyes was the body of Jerry dangling from the top of the bed by his own handkerchief.'

'Which bedroom was it?' asked two or three voices together.

The narrator shook his head. 'That I can't tell you; but the story goes that Jerry still haunts this house, and my father used to declare positively that the last time he slept here the ghost of Jerry Bundler lowered itself from the top of his bed and tried to strangle him.'

'That'll do,' said an uneasy voice. 'I wish you'd thought to ask your father which bedroom it was.'

'What for?' enquired the old gentleman.

'Well, I should take care not to sleep in it, that's all,' said the voice, shortly.

'There's nothing to fear,' said the other. 'I don't believe for a moment that ghosts could really hurt one. In fact my father used to confess that it was only the unpleasantness of the thing that upset him, and that for all practical purposes Jerry's fingers might have been made of cotton-wool for all the harm they could do.'

'That's all very fine,' said the last speaker again; 'a ghost-story is a ghost-story, sir but when a gentleman tells a tale of a ghost in the house in which one is going to sleep, I call it most ungentlemanly!'

'Pooh! nonsense!' said the old gentleman, rising; 'ghosts can't hurt you. For my own part, I should rather like to see one. Good-night, gentlemen.'

'Good-night,' said the others. 'And I only hope Jerry'll pay you a visit,' added the nervous man as the door closed.

'Bring some more whisky, George,' said a stout commercial; 'I want keeping up when the talk turns this way.'

'Shall I light the gas, Mr Malcolm?' said George.

'No; the fire's very comfortable,' said the traveller. 'Now gentlemen, any of you know any more?'

'I think we've had enough,' said another man; 'we shall be thinking we see spirits next, and we're not all like the old gentleman who's just gone.'

'Old humbug!' said Hirst. 'I should like to put him to the test. Suppose I dress up as Jerry Bundler and go and give him a chance of displaying his courage?'

'Bravo!' said Malcolm, huskily, drowning one or two faint 'Nos.' 'Just for the joke, gentlemen.'

'No, no! Drop it, Hirst,' said another man.

'Only for the joke,' said Hirst, somewhat eagerly. 'I've got some things upstairs in which I am going to play in the *Rivals*—knee-breeches, buckles, and all that sort of thing. It's a rare chance. If you'll wait a bit I'll give you a full-dress rehearsal entitled, "Jerry Bundler; or, The Nocturnal Strangler."'

'You won't frighten us,' said the commercial, with a husky laugh.

'I don't know that,' said Hirst, sharply; 'it's a question of acting, that's all. I'm pretty good, ain't I, Somers?'

'Oh, you're all right—for an amateur,' said his friend, with a laugh.

'I'll bet you a level sovereign, you don't frighten me,' said the stout traveller.

'Done!' said Hirst. 'I'll take the bet to frighten you first and the old gentleman afterwards. These gentlemen shall be the judges.'

'You won't frighten us, sir,' said another man, 'because we're prepared for you; but you'd better leave the old man alone. It's dangerous play.'

'Well, I'll try you first,' said Hirst, springing up. 'No gas, mind.'

He ran lightly upstairs to his room, leaving the others, most of whom had been drinking somewhat freely, to wrangle about his proceedings. It ended in two of them going to bed.

'He's crazy on acting,' said Somers, lighting his pipe. 'Thinks he's the equal of anybody almost. It doesn't matter with us, but I won't let him go to the old man. And he won't mind so long as he gets an opportunity of acting to us.'

'Well, I hope he'll hurry up,' said Malcolm, yawning; 'it's after twelve now.'

Nearly half an hour passed. Malcolm drew his watch from his pocket and was busy winding it, when George, the waiter, who had been sent on an errand to the bar, burst suddenly into the room and rushed towards them.

"E's comin', gentlemen,' he said, breathlessly.

[4]

'Why, you're frightened, George,' said the stout commercial, with a chuckle.

'It was the suddenness of it,' said George, sheepishly; 'and besides, I didn't look for seein' 'im in the bar. There's only a glimmer of light there, and 'e was sitting on the floor behind the bar. I nearly trod on 'im.'

'Oh, you'll never make a man, George,' said Malcolm.

'Well, it took me unawares,' said the waiter. 'Not that I'd have gone to the bar by myself if I'd known 'e was there, and I don't believe you would either, sir.'

'Nonsense!' said Malcolm. 'I'll go and fetch him in.'

'You don't know what it's like, sir,' said George, catching him by the sleeve. 'It ain't fit to look at by yourself, it ain't, indeed. It's got the—*What's that?*'

They all started at the sound of a smothered cry from the staircase and the sound of somebody running hurriedly along the passage. Before anybody could speak, the door flew open and a figure bursting into the room flung itself gasping and shivering upon them.

'What is it? What's the matter?' demanded Malcom. 'Why, it's Mr Hirst.' He shook him roughly and then held some spirit to his lips. Hirst drank it greedily and with a sharp intake of his breath gripped him by the arm.

'Light the gas, George,' said Malcolm.

The waiter obeyed hastily. Hirst, a ludicrous but pitiable figure in knee-breeches and coat, a large wig all awry, and his face a mess of greasepaint, clung to him, trembling.

'Now, what's the matter?' asked Malcolm.

'I've seen it,' said Hirst, with a hysterical sob. 'Oh Lord, I'll never play the fool again, never!'

'Seen what?' said the others.

'Him—it—the ghost—anything!' said Hirst, wildly.

'Rot!' said Malcolm, uneasily.

'I was coming down the stairs,' said Hirst. 'Just capering down—as I thought—it ought to do. I felt a tap—'

He broke off suddenly and peered nervously through the open door into the passage.

'I thought I saw it again,' he whispered. 'Look—at the foot of the stairs. Can you see anything?'

'No, there's nothing there,' said Malcolm, whose own voice shook a little. 'Go on. You felt a tap on your shoulder—'

'I turned round and saw it—a little, wicked head and a white, dead face. Pah!'

'That's what I saw in the bar,' said George. "Orrid it was—devilish!'

Hirst shuddered, and, still retaining his nervous grip of Malcolm's sleeve, dropped into a chair.

'Well, it's a most unaccountable thing,' said the dumbfounded Malcolm, turning round to the others. 'It's the last time I come to this house.'

'I leave to-morrow,' said George. 'I wouldn't go down to that bar again by myself, no, not for fifty pounds!'

'It's talking about the thing that's caused it, I expect,' said one of the men; 'we've all been talking about this and having it in our minds. Practically we've been forming a spiritualistic circle without knowing it.'

'Hang the old gentleman!' said Malcolm, heartily. 'Upon my soul, I'm half afraid to go to bed. It's odd they should both think they saw something.'

'I saw it as plain as I see you, sir,' said George, solemnly. 'P'raps if you keep your eyes turned up the passage you'll see it for yourself.'

They followed the direction of his finger, but saw nothing, although one of them fancied that a head peeped round the corner of the wall.

'Who'll come down to the bar?' said Malcolm, looking round.

'You can go, if you like,' said one of the others, with a faint laugh; 'we'll wait here for you.'

The stout traveller walked towards the door and took a few steps up the passage. Then he stopped. All was quite silent, and he walked slowly to the end and looked down fearfully towards the glass partition which shut off the bar. Three times he made as though to go to it; then he turned back, and, glancing over his shoulder, came hurriedly back to the room.

'Did you see it, sir?' whispered George.

'Don't know,' said Malcolm, shortly. 'I fancied I saw something, but it might have been fancy. I'm in the mood to see anything just now. How are you feeling now, sir?'

'Oh, I feel a bit better now,' said Hirst, somewhat brusquely, as all eyes were turned upon him. 'I dare say you think I'm easily scared, but you didn't see it.'

'Not at all,' said Malcolm, smiling faintly despite himself.

'I'm going to bed,' said Hirst, noticing the smile and resenting it. 'Will you share my room with me, Somers?'

'I will with pleasure,' said his friend, 'provided you don't mind sleeping with the gas on full all night.'

He rose from his seat, and bidding the company a friendly good-night, left the room with his crestfallen friend. The others saw them to the foot of the stairs, and having heard their door close, returned to the coffee-room.

'Well, I suppose the bet's off?' said the stout commercial, poking the fire and then standing with his legs apart on the hearthrug; 'though, as far as I can see, I won it. I never saw a man so scared in all my life. Sort of poetic justice about it, isn't there?'

'Never mind about poetry or justice,' said one of his listeners; 'who's going to sleep with me?'

'I will,' said Malcolm, affably.

'And I suppose we share a room together, Mr Leek?' said the third man, turning to the fourth.

'No, thank you,' said the other, briskly; 'I don't believe in ghosts. If anything comes into my room I shall shoot it.'

'That won't hurt a spirit, Leek,' said Malcolm, decisively.

'Well, the noise'll be like company to me,' said Leek, 'and it'll wake the house, too. But if you're nervous, sir,' he added, with a grin, to the man who had suggested sharing his room, 'George'll be only too pleased to sleep on the doormat inside your room, I know.'

'That I will, sir,' said George, fervently; 'and if you gentlemen would only come down with me to the bar to put the gas out, I could never be sufficiently grateful.'

They went out in a body, with the exception of Leek, peering carefully before them as they went. George turned the light out in the bar and they returned unmolested to the coffee-room, and, avoiding the sardonic smile of Leek, prepared to separate for the night.

'Give me the candle while you put the gas out, George,' said the traveller.

The waiter handed it to him and extinguished the gas, and at the same moment all distinctly heard a step in the passage outside. It stopped at the door, and as they watched with bated breath, the door creaked and slowly opened. Malcolm fell back open-mouthed, as a white, leering face, with sunken eyeballs and close-cropped bullet head, appeared at the opening.

For a few seconds the creature stood regarding them, blinking in a strange fashion at the candle. Then, with a sidling movement, it came a little way into the room and stood there as if bewildered.

[7]

Not a man spoke or moved, but all watched with a horrible fascination as the creature removed its dirty neckcloth and its head rolled on its shoulder. For a minute it paused, and then, holding the rag before it, moved towards Malcolm.

The candle went out suddenly with a flash and a bang. There was a smell of powder, and something writhing in the darkness on the floor. A faint, choking cough, and then silence. Malcolm was the first to speak. 'Matches,' he said, in a strange voice. George struck one. Then he leapt at the gas and a burner flamed from the match. Malcolm touched the thing on the floor with his foot and found it soft. He looked at his companions. They mouthed enquiries at him, but he shook his head. He lit the candle, and, kneeling down, examined the silent thing on the floor. Then he rose swiftly, and dipping his handkerchief in the water-jug, bent down again and grimly wiped the white face. Then he sprang back with a cry of incredulous horror, pointing at it. Leek's pistol fell to the floor and he shut out the sight with his hands, but the others, crowding forward, gazed spell-bound at the dead face of Hirst.

Before a word was spoken the door opened and Somers hastily entered the room. His eyes fell on the floor. 'Good God!' he cried. 'You didn't—'

Nobody spoke.

'I told him not to,' he said, in a suffocating voice. 'I told him not to. I told him—'

He leaned against the wall, deathly sick, put his arms out feebly, and fell fainting into the traveller's arms.

MUSTAPHA

Sabine Baring-Gould

Sabine Baring-Gould (1834–1924),
squire-parson of Lew Trenchard, will always be
associated with the great hymns he wrote,
especially the much-loved 'Onward, Christian
Soldiers'. In addition to his *Lives of the Saints*
(1872–7), he produced over a hundred other
volumes including novels, biographies, religious
and travel books, and studies of folklore.
'Mustapha' is taken from Baring-Gould's rare
collection of supernatural short stories,
A Book of Ghosts (1904).

1

Among the many hangers-on at the Hotel de l'Europe at
Luxor—donkey-boys, porters, guides, antiquity dealers—was
one, a young man named Mustapha, who proved a general
favourite.

I spent three winters at Luxor, partly for my health, partly for
pleasure, mainly to make artistic studies, as I am by profession a
painter. So I came to know Mustapha fairly well in three stages,
during those three winters.

When first I made his acquaintance he was in the transition
condition from boyhood to manhood. He had an intelligent face, with
bright eyes, a skin soft as brown silk, with a velvety hue on it. His
features were regular, and if his face was a little too round to quite
satisfy an English artistic eye, yet this was a peculiarity to which one

soon became accustomed. He was unflaggingly good-natured and obliging. A mongrel, no doubt, he was; Arab and native Egyptian blood were mingled in his veins. But the result was happy; he combined the patience and gentleness of the child of Mizraim with the energy and pluck of the son of the desert.

Mustapha had been a donkey-boy, but had risen a stage higher, and looked, as the object of his supreme ambition, to become some day a dragoman, and blaze like one of these gilded beetles in lace and chains, rings and weapons. To become a dragoman—one of the most obsequious of men till engaged, one of the veriest tyrants when engaged—to what higher could an Egyptian boy aspire?

To become a dragoman means to go in broadcloth and with gold chains when his fellows are half naked; to lounge and twist the moustache when his kinsfolk are toiling under the water-buckets; to be able to extort backsheesh from all the tradesmen to whom he can introduce a master; to do nothing himself and make others work for him; to be able to look to purchase two, three, even four wives when his father contented himself with one; to soar out of the region of native virtues into that of foreign vices; to be superior to all instilled prejudices against spirits and wine—that is the ideal set before young Egypt through contact with the English and the American tourist.

We all liked Mustapha. No one had a bad word to say of him. Some pious individuals rejoiced to see that he had broken with the Koran, as if this were a first step towards taking up with the Bible. A free-thinking professor was glad to find that Mustapha had emancipated himself from some of those shackles which religion places on august, divine humanity, and that by getting drunk he gave pledge that he had risen into a sphere of pure emancipation, which eventuates in ideal perfection.

As I made my studies I engaged Mustapha to carry my easel and canvas, or camp-stool. I was glad to have him as a study, to make him stand by a wall or sit on a pillar that was prostrate, as artistic exigencies required. He was always ready to accompany me. There was an understanding between us that when a drove of tourists came to Luxor he might leave me for the day to pick up what he could then from the natural prey; but I found him not always keen to be off duty to me. Though he could get more from the occasional visitor than from me, he was above the ravenous appetite for backsheesh which consumed his fellows.

He who has much to do with the native Egyptian will have

[10]

discovered that there are in him a fund of kindliness and a treasure of good qualities. He is delighted to be treated with humanity, pleased to be noticed, and ready to repay attention with touching gratitude. He is by no means as rapacious for backsheesh as the passing traveller supposes; he is shrewd to distinguish between man and man; likes this one, and will do anything for him unrewarded, and will do naught for another for any bribe.

The Egyptian is now in a transitional state. If it be quite true that the touch of England is restoring life to his crippled limbs, and the voice of England bidding him rise up and walk, there are occasions on which association with Englishmen is a disadvantage to him. Such an instance is that of poor, good Mustapha.

It was not my place to caution Mustapha against the pernicious influences to which he was subjected, and, to speak plainly, I did not know what line to adopt, on what ground to take my stand, if I did. He was breaking with the old life, and taking up with what was new, retaining of the old only what was bad in it, and acquiring of the new none of its good parts. Civilization—European civilization—is excellent, but cannot be swallowed at a gulp, nor does it wholly suit the oriental digestion.

That which impelled Mustapha still further in his course was the attitude assumed towards him by his own relatives and the natives of his own village. They were strict Moslems, and they regarded him as one on the highway to becoming a renegade. They treated him with mistrust, showed him aversion, and loaded him with reproaches. Mustapha had a high spirit, and he resented rebuke. Let his fellows grumble and objurgate, said he; they would cringe to him when he became a dragoman, with his pockets stuffed with piastres.

There was in our hotel, the second winter, a young fellow of the name of Jameson, a man with plenty of money, superficial good nature, little intellect, very conceited and egotistic, and this fellow was Mustapha's evil genius. It was Jameson's delight to encourage Mustapha in drinking and gambling. Time hung heavy on his hands. He cared nothing for hieroglyphics, scenery bored him, antiquities, art, had no charm for him. Natural history presented to him no attraction, and the only amusement level with his mental faculties was that of hoaxing natives, or breaking down their religious prejudices.

Matters were in this condition as regarded Mustapha, when an incident occurred during my second winter at Luxor that completely altered the tenor of Mustapha's life.

One night a fire broke out in the nearest village. It originated in a mud hovel belonging to a fellah; his wife had spilled some oil on the hearth, and the flames leaping up had caught the low thatch, which immediately burst into a blaze. A wind was blowing from the direction of the Arabian desert, and it carried the flames and ignited the thatch before it on other roofs; the conflagration spread, and the whole village was menaced with destruction. The greatest excitement and alarm prevailed. The inhabitants lost their heads. Men ran about rescuing from their hovels their only treasures—old sardine tins and empty marmalade pots; women wailed, children sobbed; no one made any attempt to stay the fire; and, above all, were heard the screams of the woman whose incaution had caused the mischief, and who was being beaten unmercifully by her husband.

The few English in the hotel came on the scene, and with their instinctive energy and system set to work to organize a corps and subdue the flames. The women and girls who were rescued from the menaced hovels, or plucked out of those already on fire, were in many cases unveiled; and so it came to pass that Mustapha, who, under English direction was ablest and most vigorous in his efforts to stop the conflagration, met his fate in the shape of the daughter of Ibraim the Farrier.

By the light of the flames he saw her, and at once resolved to make that fair girl his wife.

No reasonable obstacle intervened, so thought Mustapha. He had amassed a sufficient sum to entitle him to buy a wife and set up a household of his own. A house consists of four mud walls and a low thatch, and housekeeping in an Egyptian house is as elementary and economical as the domestic architecture. The maintenance of a wife and family is not costly after the first outlay, which consists in indemnifying the father for the expense to which he has been put in rearing a daughter.

The ceremony of courting is also elementary, and the addresses of the suitor are not paid to the bride, but to her father, and not in person by the candidate, but by an intermediary.

Mustapha negotiated with a friend, a fellow hanger-on at the hotel, to open proceedings with the farrier. He was to represent to the worthy man that the suitor entertained the most ardent admiration for the virtues of Ibraim personally, that he was inspired with but one ambition, which was alliance with so distinguished a family as his. He was to assure the father of the damsel that Mustapha undertook to proclaim through Upper and Lower Egypt, in the ears of Egyptians, Arabs, and Europeans, that Ibraim was the most remarkable man that ever existed for solidity of judgment, excellence of parts, uprightness of dealing, nobility of sentiment, strictness in observance of the precepts of the Koran, and that finally Mustapha was anxious to indemnify this same paragon of genius and virtue for his condescension in having cared to breed and clothe and feed for several years a certain girl, his daughter, if Mustapha might have that daughter as his wife. Not that he cared for the daughter in herself, but as a means whereby he might have the honour of entering into alliance with one so distinguished and so esteemed of Allah as Ibraim the Farrier.

To the infinite surprise of the intermediary, and to the no less surprise and mortification of the suitor, Mustapha was refused. He was a bad Moslem. Ibraim would have no alliance with one who had turned his back on the Prophet and drunk bottled beer.

Till this moment Mustapha had not realised how great was the alienation between his fellows and himself—what a barrier he had set up between himself and the men of his own blood. The refusal of his suit struck the young man to the quick. He had known and played with the farrier's daughter in childhood, till she had come of age to veil her face; now that he had seen her in her ripe charms, his heart was deeply stirred and engaged. He entered into himself, and going to the mosque he there made a solemn vow that if he ever touched wine, ale, or spirits again he would cut his throat, and he sent word to Ibraim that he had done so, and begged that he would not dispose of his daughter and finally reject him till he had seen how that he who had turned in thought and manner of life from the Prophet would return with firm resolution to the right way.

2

From this time Mustapha changed his conduct. He was obliging and attentive as before, ready to exert himself to do for me what I wanted, ready also to extort money from the ordinary tourist for doing nothing, to go with me and carry my tools when I went forth painting, and to joke and laugh with Jameson; but, unless he were unavoidably detained, he said his prayers five times daily in the mosque, and no inducement whatever would make him touch anything save sherbet, milk, or water.

Mustapha had no easy time of it. The strict Mohammedans mistrusted this sudden conversion, and believed that he was playing a part. Ibraim gave him no encouragement. His relatives maintained their reserve and stiffness towards him.

His companions, moreover, who were in the transitional stage, and those who had completely shaken off all faith in Allah and trust in the Prophet and respect for the Koran, were incensed at his desertion. He was ridiculed, insulted; he was waylaid and beaten. The young fellows mimicked him, the elder scoffed at him.

Jameson took his change to heart, and laid himself out to bring him out of his pot of scruples.

'Mustapha ain't any sport at all now,' said he. 'I'm hanged if he has another para from me.' He offered him bribes in gold, he united with the others in ridicule, he turned his back on him, and refused to employ him. Nothing availed. Mustapha was respectful, courteous, obliging as before, but he had returned, he said, to the faith and rule of life in which he had been brought up, and he would never again leave it.

'I have sworn,' said he, 'that if I do I will cut my throat.'

I had been, perhaps, negligent in cautioning the young fellow the first winter that I knew him against the harm likely to be done him by taking up with European habits contrary to his law and the feelings and prejudices of his people. Now, however, I had no hesitation in expressing to him the satisfaction I felt at the courageous and determined manner in which he had broken with acquired habits that could do him no good. For one thing, we were now better acquaintances, and I felt that as one who had known him for more than a few months in the winter, I had a good right to speak. And, again, it is always easier or pleasanter to praise than to reprimand.

One day when sketching I cut my pencil with a pruning-knife I happened to have in my pocket; my proper knife of many blades had been left behind by misadventure.

Mustapha noticed the knife and admired it, and asked if it had cost a great sum.

'Not at all,' I answered. 'I did not even buy it. It was given me. I ordered some flower seeds from a seeds-man, and when he sent me the consignment he included this knife in the case as a present. It is not worth more than a shilling in England.'

He turned it about, with looks of admiration.

'It is just the sort that would suit me,' he said. 'I know your other knife with many blades. It is very fine, but it is too small. I do not

[14]

want it to cut pencils. It has other things in it, a hook for taking stones from a horse's hoof, a pair of tweezers for removing hairs. I do not want such, but a knife such as this, with such a curve, is just the thing.'

'Then you shall have it,' said I. 'You are welcome. It was for rough work only that I brought the knife to Egypt with me.'

I finished a painting that winter that gave me real satisfaction. It was of the great court of the temple of Luxor by evening light, with the last red glare of the sun over the distant desert hills, and the eastern sky above of a purple depth. What colours I used! the intensest on my palette, and yet fell short of the effect.

The picture was in the Academy, was well hung, abominably represented in one of the illustrated guides to the galleries, as a blotch, by some sort of photographic process on gelatine; my picture sold, which concerned me most of all; and not only did it sell at a respectable figure, but it also brought me two or three orders for Egyptian pictures. So many English and Americans go up the Nile, and carry away with them pleasant reminiscences of the Land of the Pharaohs, that when in England they are fain to buy pictures which shall remind them of scenes in that land.

I returned to my hotel at Luxor in November, to spend there a third winter. The fellaheen about there saluted me as a friend with an affectionate delight, which I am quite certain was not assumed, as they got nothing out of me save kindly salutations. I had the Egyptian fever on me, which, when once acquired, is not to be shaken off—an enthusiasm for everything Egyptian, the antiquities, the history of the Pharaohs, the very desert, the brown Nile, the desolate hill ranges, the ever-blue sky, the marvellous colorations at rise and set of sun, and last, but not least, the prosperity of the poor peasants.

I am quite certain that the very warmest welcome accorded to me was from Mustapha, and almost the first words he said to me on my meeting him again were: 'I have been very good. I say my prayers. I drink no wine, and Ibraim will give me his daughter in the second Iomada—what you call January.'

'Not before, Mustapha?'

'No, sir; he says I must be tried for one whole year, and he is right.'

'Then soon after Christmas you will be happy!'

'I have got a house and made it ready. Yes. After Christmas there will be one very happy man—one very, very happy man in Egypt, and that will be your humble servant, Mustapha.'

[15]

We were a pleasant party at Luxor, this third winter, not numerous, but for the most part of congenial tastes. For the most part we were keen on hieroglyphics, we admired Queen Hatasou and we hated Rameses II. We could distinguish the artistic work of one dynasty from that of another. We were learned on cartouches, and flourished our knowledge before the tourists dropping in.

One of those staying in the hotel was an Oxford don, very good company, interested in everything, and able to talk well on everything —I mean everything more or less remotely connected with Egypt. Another was a young fellow who had been an attaché at Berlin, but was out of health—nothing organic the matter with his lungs, but they were weak. He was keen on the political situation, and very anti-Gallican, as every man who has been in Egypt naturally is, who is not a Frenchman.

There was also staying in the hotel an American lady, fresh and delightful, whose mind and conversation twinkled like frost crystals in the sun, a woman full of good-humour, of the most generous sympathies, and so droll that she kept us ever amused.

And, alas! Jameson was back again, not entering into any of our pursuits, not understanding our little jokes, not at all content to be there. He grumbled at the food—and, indeed, that might have been better; at the monotony of the life at Luxor, at his London doctor for putting the veto on Cairo because of its drainage, or rather the absence of all drainage. I really think we did our utmost to draw Jameson into our circle, to amuse him, to interest him in something; but one by one we gave him up, and the last to do this was the little American lady.

From the outset he had attacked Mustapha, and endeavoured to persuade him to shake off his 'squeamish nonsense', as Jameson called his resolve. 'I'll tell you what it is, old fellow,' he said, 'life isn't worth living without good liquor, and as for that blessed Prophet of yours, he showed he was a fool when he put a bar on drinks.'

But as Mustapha was not pliable he gave him up. 'He's become just as great a bore as that old Rameses,' said he. 'I'm sick of the whole concern, and I don't think anything of fresh dates, that you fellows make such a fuss about. As for that stupid old Nile—there ain't a fish worth eating comes out of it. And those old Egyptians were arrant humbugs. I haven't seen a lotus since I came here, and they made such a fuss about them too.'

The little American lady was not weary of asking questions relative to English home life, and especially to country-house living and amusements.

'Oh, my dear!' said she, 'I would give my ears to spend a Christmas in the fine old fashion in a good ancient manor-house in the country.'

'There is nothing remarkable in that,' said an English lady.

'Not to you, maybe; but there would be to us. What we read of and make pictures of in our fancies, that is what you live. Your facts are our fairy tales. Look at your hunting.'

'That, if you like, is fun,' threw in Jameson. 'But I don't myself think anything save Luxor can be a bigger bore than country-house life at Christmas time—when all the boys are back from school.'

'With us,' said the little American, 'our sportsmen dress in pink like yours—the whole thing—and canter after a bag of aniseed that is trailed before them.'

'Why do they not import foxes?'

'Because a fox would not keep to the road. Our farmers object pretty freely to trespass; so the hunting must of necessity be done on the highway, and the game is but a bag of aniseed. I would like to see an English meet and a run.'

This subject was thrashed out after having been prolonged unduly for the sake of Jameson.

'Oh, dear me!' said the Yankee lady. 'If but that chef could be persuaded to give us plum-puddings for Christmas, I would try to think I was in England.'

'Plum-pudding is exploded,' said Jameson. 'Only children ask for it now. A good trifle or a tipsy-cake is much more to my taste; but this hanged cook here can give us nothing but his blooming custard pudding and burnt sugar.'

'I do not think it would be wise to let him attempt a plum-pudding,' said the English lady. 'But if we can persuade him to permit me I will mix and make the pudding, and then he cannot go far wrong in the boiling and dishing up.'

'That is the only thing wanting to make me perfectly happy,' said the American. 'I'll confront monsieur. I am sure I can talk him into a good humour, and we shall have our plum-pudding.'

No one has yet been found, I do believe, who could resist that little woman. She carried everything before her. The cook placed himself and all his culinary apparatus at her feet. We took part in the stoning of the raisins, and the washing of the currants, even the chopping of

[17]

the suet; we stirred the pudding, threw in sixpence apiece, and a ring, and then it was tied up in a cloth, and set aside to be boiled. Christmas Day came, and the English chaplain preached us a practical sermon on 'Goodwill towards men'. That was his text, and his sermon was but a swelling out of the words just as rice is swelled to thrice its size by boiling.

We dined. There was an attempt at roast beef—it was more like baked leather. The event of the dinner was to be the bringing in and eating of the plum-pudding.

Surely all would be perfect. We could answer for the materials and the mixing. The English lady could guarantee the boiling. She had seen the plum-pudding 'on the boil', and had given strict injunctions as to the length of time during which it was to boil.

But, alas! the pudding was not right when brought on the table. It was not enveloped in lambent blue flame—it was not crackling in the burning brandy. It was sent in dry, and the brandy arrived separate in a white sauce-boat, hot indeed, and sugared, but not on fire.

There ensued outcries of disappointment. Attempts were made to redress the mistake by setting fire to the brandy in a spoon, but the spoon was cold. The flame would not catch, and finally, with a sigh, we had to take our plum-pudding as served.

'I say, chaplain!' exclaimed Jameson, 'practice is better than precept, is it not?'

'To be sure it is.'

'You gave us a deuced good sermon. It was short, as it ought to be; but I'll go better on it, I'll practise where you preached, and have larks, too!'

Then Jameson started from table with a plate of plum-pudding in one hand and the sauce-boat in the other. 'By Jove!' he said, 'I'll teach these fellows to open their eyes. I'll show them that we know how to feed. We can't turn out scarabs and cartouches in England, that are no good to anyone, but we can produce the finest roast beef in the world, and do a thing or two in puddings.'

And he left the room.

We paid no heed to anything Jameson said or did. We were rather relieved that he was out of the room, and did not concern ourselves about the 'larks' he promised himself, and which we were quite certain would be as insipid as were the quails of the Israelites.

In ten minutes he was back, laughing and red in the face.

'I've had splitting fun,' he said. 'You should have been there.'

'Where, Jameson?'

'Why, outside. There were a lot of old moolahs and other hoky-pokies sitting and contemplating the setting sun and all that sort of thing, and I gave Mustapha the pudding. I told him I wished him to try our great national English dish, on which her Majesty the Queen dines daily. Well, he ate and enjoyed it, by George. Then I said, "Old fellow, it's uncommonly dry, so you must take the sauce to it." He asked if it was only sauce—flour and water. "It's sauce, by Jove," said I, "a little sugar to it; no bar on the sugar, Musty." So I put the boat to his lips and gave him a pull. By George, you should have seen his face! It was just thundering fun. "I've done you at last, old Musty," I said. "It is best cognac." He gave me such a look! He'd have eaten me, I believe—and he walked away. It was just splitting fun. I wish you had been there to see it.'

I went out after dinner, to take my usual stroll along the river-bank, and to watch the evening lights die away on the columns and obelisk. On my return I saw at once that something had happened which had produced commotion among the servants of the hotel. I had reached the salon before I inquired what was the matter.

The boy who was taking the coffee round said: 'Mustapha is dead. He cut his throat at the door of the mosque. He could not help himself. He had broken his vow.'

I looked at Jameson without a word. Indeed, I could not speak; I was choking. The little American lady was trembling, the English lady crying. The gentlemen stood silent in the windows, not speaking a word.

Jameson's colour changed. He was honestly distressed, uneasy, and tried to cover his confusion with bravado and a jest.

4

I could not sleep. My blood was in a boil. I felt that I could not speak to Jameson again. He would have to leave Luxor. That was tacitly understood among us. Coventry was the place to which he would be consigned.

I tried to finish in a little sketch I had made in my notebook when I was in my room, but my hand shook, and I was constrained to lay my pencil aside. Then I took up an Egyptian grammar, but could not fix my mind on study. The hotel was very still. Everyone had gone to bed at an early hour that night, disinclined for conversation. No one was moving. There was a lamp in the passage; it was partly turned down. Jameson's room was next to mine. I heard him stir as he undressed, and talk to himself. Then he was quiet. I wound up my watch, and emptying my pocket, put my purse under the pillow. I was not in the least heavy with sleep. If I did go to bed I should not be able to close my eyes. But then—if I sat up I could do nothing.

I was about leisurely to undress, when I heard a sharp cry, or exclamation of mingled pain and alarm, from the adjoining room. In another moment there was a rap at my door. I opened, and Jameson came in. He was in his nightshirt, and looking agitated and frightened.

'Look here, old fellow,' said he in a shaking voice, 'there is Musty in my room. He has been hiding there, and just as I dropped asleep he ran that knife of yours into my throat.'

'My knife?'

'Yes—that pruning-knife you gave him, you know. Look here—I must have the place sewn up. Do go for a doctor, there's a good chap.'

'Where is the place?'

'Here on my right gill.'

Jameson turned his head to the left, and I raised the lamp. There was no wound of any sort there.

I told him so.

'Oh, yes! I tell you I felt his knife go in.'

'Nonsense, you were dreaming.'

'Dreaming! Not I. I saw Musty as distinctly as I now see you.'

'This is a delusion, Jameson,' I replied. 'The poor fellow is dead.'

'Oh, that's very fine,' said Jameson. 'It is not the first of April, and I don't believe the yarns that you've been spinning. You tried to make believe he was dead, but I know he is not. He has got into my room, and he made a dig at my throat with your pruning-knife.'

'I'll go into your room with you.'

'Do so. But he's gone by this time. Trust him to cut and run.'

I followed Jameson, and looked about. There was no trace of anyone beside himself having been in the room. Moreover, there was no place but the nut-wood wardrobe in the bedroom in which anyone could have secreted himself. I opened this and showed that it was empty.

After a while I pacified Jameson, and induced him to go to bed again, and then I left his room. I did not now attempt to court sleep. I wrote letters with a hand not the steadiest, and did my accounts.

As the hour approached midnight I was again startled by a cry from the adjoining room, and in another moment Jameson was at my door.

'That blooming fellow Musty is in my room still,' said he. 'He has been at my throat again.'

'Nonsense,' I said. 'You are labouring under hallucinations. You locked your door.'

'Oh, by Jove, yes—of course I did; but, hang it, in this hole, neither doors nor windows fit, and the locks are no good, and the bolts nowhere. He got in again somehow, and if I had not started up the moment I felt the knife, he'd have done for me. He would, by George. I wish I had a revolver.'

I went into Jameson's room. Again he insisted on my looking at his throat.

'It's very good of you to say there is no wound,' said he. 'But you won't gull me with words. I felt his knife in my windpipe, and if I had not jumped out of bed—'

'You locked your door. No one could enter. Look in the glass there is not even a scratch. This is pure imagination.'

'I'll tell you what, old fellow, I won't sleep in that room again. Change with me, there's a charitable buffer. If you don't believe in Musty, Musty won't hurt you, maybe—anyhow you can try if he's solid or a phantom. Blow me if the knife felt like a phantom.'

'I do not quite see my way to changing rooms,' I replied; 'but this I will do for you. If you like to go to bed again in your own apartment, I will sit up with you till morning.'

'All right,' answered Jameson. 'And if Musty comes in again, let out at him and do not spare him. Swear that.'

I accompanied Jameson once more to his bedroom. Little as I liked the man, I could not deny him my presence and assistance at this time. It was obvious that his nerves were shaken by what had occurred, and he felt his relation to Mustapha much more than he cared to show. The thought that he had been the cause of the poor fellow's death preyed on his mind, never strong, and now it was upset with imaginary terrors.

I gave up letter writing, and brought my Baedeker's *Upper Egypt* into Jameson's room, one of the best of all guide-books, and one crammed with information. I seated myself near the light, and with my back to the bed, on which the young man had once more flung himself.

[21]

'I say,' said Jameson, raising his head, 'is it too late for a brandy-and-soda?'

'Everyone is in bed.'

'What lazy dogs they are. One never can get anything one wants here.'

'Well, try to go to sleep.'

He tossed from side to side for some time, but after a while, either he was quiet, or I was engrossed in my Baedeker, and I heard nothing till a clock struck twelve. At the last stroke I heard a snort and then a gasp and a cry from the bed. I started up, and looked round. Jameson was slipping out with his feet on to the floor.

'Confound you!' said he angrily, 'you are a fine watch, you are, to let Mustapha steal in on tiptoe whilst you are cartouching and all that sort of rubbish. He was at me again, and if I had not been sharp he'd have cut my throat. I won't go to bed any more!'

'Well, sit up. But I assure you no one has been here.'

'That's fine. How can you tell? You had your back to me, and these devils of fellows steal about like cats. You can't hear them till they are at you.'

It was of no use arguing with Jameson, so I let him have his way.

'I can feel all the three places in my throat where he ran the knife in,' said he. 'And—don't you notice?—I speak with difficulty.'

So we sat up together the rest of the night. He became more reasonable as dawn came on, and inclined to admit that he had been a prey to fancies.

The day passed very much as did others—Jameson was dull and sulky. After déjeuner he sat on at table when the ladies had risen and retired, and the gentlemen had formed in knots at the window, discussing what was to be done in the afternoon.

Suddenly Jameson, whose head had begun to nod, started up with an oath and threw down his chair.

'You fellows!' he said, 'you are all in league against me. You let that Mustapha come in without a word, and try to stick his knife into me.'

'He has not been here.'

'It's a plant. You are combined to bully me and drive me away. You don't like me. You have engaged Mustapha to murder me. This is the fourth time he has tried to cut my throat, and in the *salle à manger*, too, with you all standing round. You ought to be ashamed to call yourselves Englishmen. I'll go to Cairo. I'll complain.'

It really seemed that the feeble brain of Jameson was affected. The

Oxford don undertook to sit up in the room the following night.

The young man was fagged and sleep-weary, but no sooner did his eyes close, and clouds form about his head, than he was brought to wakefulness again by the same fancy or dream. The Oxford don had more trouble with him on the second night than I had on the first, for his lapses into sleep were more frequent, and each such lapse was succeeded by a start and a panic.

The next day he was worse, and we felt that he could no longer be left alone. The third night the attaché sat up to watch him.

Jameson had now sunk into a sullen mood. He would not speak, except to himself, and then only to grumble.

During the night, without being aware of it, the young attaché, who had taken a couple of magazines with him to read, fell asleep. When he went off he did not know. He woke just before dawn, and in a spasm of terror and self-reproach saw that Jameson's chair was empty.

Jameson was not on his bed. He could not be found in the hotel.

At dawn he was found—dead at the door of the mosque, with his throat cut.

THE SINISTER INN

F. S. Smythe

Frank Sydney Smythe (1900–49)
was one of the world's greatest mountaineers
during the 1930s, and also a prolific writer and
photographer. His many books include *The
Kangchenjunga Adventure, Peaks and Valleys,
The Spirit of the Hills, My Alpine Album*, and
Adventures of a Mountaineer. He climbed
extensively in the Swiss Alps (where the
following story is set) and the Himalayas, taking
part in three Everest expeditions. 'The Sinister
Inn' originally appeared in the Extra Christmas
Number of *Chambers's Journal*, 1931, the same
year that Smythe reached the highest point on
Earth ever achieved by man at that time, when
he conquered Mt. Kamet, the first peak
over 25,000 feet to be climbed.

1

It was late in the afternoon when the Doctor and I reached the Col des Papillons. Behind us, the thin thread of our ski-track zigzagged down the long snow slopes we had ascended, and traced a minute wavering line over the bosom of the glacier we had trudged up in the morning. We halted. Above, and to the uttermost horizon, the sky was greying; the jumbled ranges were a livid white, the colour of a shark's belly, in the fading light. Now and again petulant gusts of bitter wind blew in our faces.

'Blizzard coming,' remarked the Doctor tersely. He drew off his heavy gloves, pulled a map from his pocket, unfolded it, and jabbed a finger. 'If we run down this side we get to Les Cressons. It's a goodish way, about twenty-five kilometres; we shall be devilish late. The alternative is to return by the way we have come.'

'But that's just as far,' I objected, 'and through complicated country.'

'We have our tracks to follow.'

'A blizzard would soon cover them up.'

'True; we had better go on, then.' The Doctor replaced the map. 'Ready? Then here's for it!' and springing round on his ski, he shot off down the snow slopes.

I followed. It was a perfect run; the parted snow swished behind the ski, the wind roared in the ears. Within a few minutes, seconds it seemed, we had descended some three thousand feet. Then, unexpectedly, the ground steepened, becoming more broken. Care was necessary. Ere we reached the long valley we must follow to Les Cressons the blizzard was gathering its forces. A mysterious fuzziness was creeping up out of the west, engulfing the peaks one by one. Even as we turned down the valley a snowflake, the first harbinger of the storm, came sailing down. Another followed, and another, and finally countless millions. A gust of wind swept up the valley, driving the snowflakes before it in a hurrying multitude.

The Doctor, who was leading, turned, a grim smile beneath his icicle-fringed moustache. 'A curious way of spending Christmas Eve, Jack!'

Christmas Eve! Yes, of course it was; I had forgotten. When the Doctor and I did our annual cross-country Alpine ski-tour we didn't keep a strict tally of time or dates. Still, Christmas Eve!

The blizzard got steadily worse; its gusts were paralysing. Up to now no thought of danger had occurred, but the growing darkness and the difficulty of finding our way through an utter blankness of whirling snow made us realise how formidable was the task that we had embarked upon. It was numbingly cold, too, and already our clothes and Balaclava helmets were sheeted in ice. We had pictured the warmth and comfort of a hotel at Les Cressons; now, it seemed as though we should be lucky to find a deserted chalet or cow-hut in which to spend a miserable night.

Suddenly the Doctor stopped. 'What's that?' he shouted.

Above the roar of the storm came a faint groan, followed by a momentary silence and another groan. For an instant we listened, and then by common consent turned towards the sound. A few yards, and

an indistinct mass loomed ahead. A chalet? No, an inn, for a suspended sign swung to and fro in the wind with protesting creakings
and groanings. At one end of the building a light showed through a
thin slit in a shuttered window; on the snow before the door were
some irregular tracks, almost obliterated by the drifting snow.

Warmth and shelter! We grinned at each other thankfully, then
slipping our feet out of our ski-bindings, approached the door. It was
locked, but with one ski-stick the Doctor rapped a loud and imperative tattoo. We heard the vibrations echoing within; they died away,
but there was no answering movement.

'Strange,' I said. 'Surely they heard us?'

The Doctor did not reply; instead he beat another vigorous tattoo
on the door, at the same time shouting, 'Open the door! Open the
door!'

Once more there was silence. We looked at each other in
astonishment.

'They must be deaf,' said the Doctor. 'We had better try the
window.'

'One moment,' I said; 'here comes someone.'

We heard the sound of slow footfalls; a key grated in the lock, and
the heavy door swung slowly open for perhaps a foot. A hairy hand,
carrying a smoking oil-lamp, was thrust into the opening; behind the
lamp two piercing dark eyes gleamed from above a tangle of black
beard.

'Who are you? What do you want?' The questions were spat at us in
a vile patois.

'Food, and a night's lodging,' replied the Doctor.

'You cannot have it! You cannot stay here! The inn is not open.
There is no food. It is better that you go to Les Cressons—it is but a
short distance, twelve kilometres.' The Innkeeper spoke with extraordinary vehemence.

'What! In this weather?' exclaimed the Doctor testily. 'Certainly
not! This is an inn, and you must put us up.'

A look as of apprehension, even fear, passed over the Innkeeper's
sullen countenance. He half-turned his head, glancing uneasily behind him; he gazed past us into the blizzard. Then, as though coming
to a decision, his mouth tightened, he shrugged. 'As you say, the
weather is bad. Perhaps it is best for you to stop here. Come, then.'

Opening the door, he ushered us over the threshold into a stone-
flagged passage, where we stood our ski against the wall, removed our

[26]

gloves, and beat the plastered snow and ice from our clothes. Next, and without a word, he motioned us into a room. Though designated *salle à manger* it was but poorly furnished with a long wooden table and half a dozen chairs. A few cheap German lithographs hung from the walls. In one corner stood a tall, green-tiled stove, but it was unlit.

'I will see that my wife lights it,' said the Innkeeper, as he followed our gaze, and setting the lamp on the table, he turned towards the door.

'Meanwhile,' I said, beating my numbed hands together, 'we should like to get warm in the kitchen.'

The Innkeeper swung round abruptly. 'The kitchen! No, no! You cannot come into the kitchen. It is impossible, quite impossible! No one, no tourist, is allowed in the kitchen. But I will see that the fire is lit, that you are soon warm'; and he withdrew from the room.

The Doctor looked at me with a questioning gaze. 'Well, Jack, what do you think of it?'

'We seem to have struck a queer place, Doc,' I replied. 'And, apart from the obvious lack of hospitality and the extraordinary behaviour of that man, this isn't an exactly exhilarating atmosphere.'

'Precisely,' said the Doctor thoughtfully; 'that's how I feel about it. There is certainly a peculiarly depressing atmosphere, and the Innkeeper's behaviour is, to say the least of it, unusual. Why was he so keen for us to go on to Les Cressons? I can't believe, somehow, it was altogether due to there being no grub. And why the blazes wouldn't he let us warm our hands in the kitchen?'

'A surly brute,' said I; 'but it's lucky for us we found this place. Listen to it!'

Outside raged the demons of the storm. A thousand voices yelled and howled. Fierce gusts worried at the shutters, beating them with a sputter of icy particles; at regular intervals came the dismal groaning of the sign-board.

The Doctor's face hardened. 'What possessed him to try and turn us away on a night like this? I doubt whether we should have got to Les Cressons. Damn it, man, it was murder; it was—' he broke off.

There was a shuffling step in the passage; the door opened. A middle-aged woman entered, bearing in her apron a bundle of fire-wood. Without a word she crossed over to the stove and commenced listlessly to lay the wood within it.

'Good evening, madame,' greeted the Doctor cheerily.

'Good evening, monsieur,' replied the woman tonelessly, without turning her head. 'You have travelled far to-day?'

'A long way,' answered the Doctor; 'over the Col des Papillons.'

'The Col des Papillons! Then you have not seen anything?' queried the woman, turning her dark eyes upon us—suspicious eyes that seemed to hold a latent terror in their depths.

The Doctor glanced across at me. 'What should we see, madame, save snow? There were no other ski-runners. It is a lonely pass.' He paused. 'Did you expect us to see anything, or anyone?'

The woman had struck a match and lit the fire as she spoke. Now suddenly she slammed to the door of the stove with a crash, and straightening herself, faced us. She appeared to be stressed by an uncontrollable emotion, for her eyes blazed, her coarse red hands clenched and unclenched, and her breast heaved convulsively. 'See anything,' she echoed, 'see anything! No, no—of course not. Nothing! Nothing! Nothing!' Her voice rose with each word. She passed a shaking hand across her brow. Then, abruptly, she turned and fled from the room.

There was a long silence while we eyed each other in astonishment.

'Hysteria,' murmured the Doctor at length; 'that woman's nerves are almost at breaking-point. I wonder why. It seems to me that there is something very definitely wrong here. By the way, did you notice how alike she is to her husband? Her eyes, for instance, and her nose. Two distinct characteristics.'

'But how—'

'A family resemblance,' continued the Doctor, almost to himself, without noticing my interruption.

'What on earth do you mean by a *family* resemblance between man and wife?'

'I have seen it before,' answered the Doctor, 'up these remote Alpine valleys. It is due to interbreeding, of course. Sometimes a village is little more than one large family.' He pulled his pipe from his pocket and commenced slowly to fill it. 'It's not a healthy sign,' he said, after a while.

'I see what you mean,' I said; 'you think that the woman is a little unbalanced?'

'Possibly,' said the Doctor, 'possibly, but—'

'But what?'

'I don't think so.'

2

In spite of the Innkeeper's statement that no food was available we were provided with an excellent supper. Omelettes and ham were forthcoming, together with a bottle of Château Pontet Carnet. Yet, despite these good things and appeased appetites, a feeling of uneasiness persisted. Perhaps it was due to the woman. All our attempts to promote conversation with her failed miserably. She answered only in monosyllables, and ever there was that same suspicious, furtive look in her eyes. Now and again she glanced uneasily over her shoulder towards the door, and her whole bearing was of one filled with dread. Once, as she was about to place a plate before me, there came the distant bang of a closing door. At the sound she gave a gasp, and the plate, slipping from her fingers, dropped on to the table with a crash and broke into pieces.

'Pardon, monsieur! Pardon!' she muttered, and picking up the pieces with trembling hands, hurried from the room.

The Doctor stared at me beneath raised eye-brows. 'That woman is scared stiff of something or other. I wish I knew of what. Professionally, I don't like to see people in that state; it goes against the grain.' His brow furrowed in thought.

'Perhaps,' I suggested, 'her husband ill-treats her. He's a morose sort of devil.'

'No, no, not that,' said the Doctor decidedly. 'My impression was that he was scared too, almost as much as his wife.'

After supper we sat and smoked our pipes. The room was pleasantly warm now. Outside the blizzard raged. All the furies were abroad that night; sometimes they yelled and screamed, at others whistled and shrilled; now and again they boomed like thunder, seeming to shake the inn to its foundations; and sometimes, too, between the gusts there was a complete and utter silence, followed perhaps by a solitary moan or wail as of some lost soul in torment.

'A man could not live long out there,' remarked the Doctor, indicating the window with the stem of his pipe.

'No, we are lucky to be here,' I answered, 'though I must confess I would rather spend Christmas Eve in more convivial surroundings. You and I, Doc, have spent some queer Christmas Eves together, but none quite like this.'

'True,' agreed the Doctor thoughtfully; 'there certainly is something very strange about this place.' An idea seemed suddenly to strike him. 'Look here, Jack, let's get the Innkeeper in and stand him some wine. It may cheer him up a bit.'

At one side of the door hung a bell-rope. The Doctor rose and pulled it. Somewhere, faintly, we heard a ringing of a bell. An instant or two later there came hurried footsteps in the passage, the door opened, and the Innkeeper burst into the room. 'The bell,' he stammered; 'you rang the bell.' His eyes were wide and fearful, and we gazed at him in amazement.

'And why not?' I demanded. 'Surely it is not unusual!'

But the Innkeeper appeared not to notice the interruption.

'The bell,' he repeated dazedly; 'I had forgotten it, fool that I am! And now he has heard, he will know, he will—'

'Look here,' said the Doctor sternly, springing to his feet and facing the Innkeeper, 'what do you mean by this tomfoolery? My friend and I are beginning to believe that you are mad.'

'Mad, me?' whispered the Innkeeper. 'No! No! No! I am not mad!'

'Well, pull yourself together, then. We merely rang the bell to ask you whether you would care to drink some wine with us. After all, it is Christmas Eve.'

'Christmas Eve,' repeated the Innkeeper slowly. 'Yes, you are right, monsieur. It is Christmas Eve, yes, Christmas Eve.'

'Tell me,' I asked, as I sat facing the Innkeeper over the wine, 'why it is you do not shut this inn up in winter? It cannot pay then?'

The Innkeeper shrugged. 'You are right, monsieur; it does not pay in winter. But then, what would you? This is our home, my wife and I. In summer there are many tourists over the Col des Papillons; then we make money. In winter there are none, yet we continue to stay here. When the weather is good I go to Les Cressons for food. For instance, yesterday I brought up twenty-five kilos of provisions.'

The Doctor leant forward. 'So it was *not* the lack of food that induced you to try and turn us away?'

The Innkeeper shrank back into his seat. He passed a trembling hand agitatedly through his black beard. He struggled to control his agitation. 'You do not understand me, messieurs. I thought perhaps it was best for you to go to Les Cressons. There is a good hotel there, where you would be more comfortable than here; but then, when I saw the blizzard, I knew it would be impossible for you to reach Les Cressons, so *voilà!* You stay here.'

It was an obvious lie, so obvious that we both smiled.

'Well,' I declared, 'you are the first French innkeeper that I have ever met who tried to turn patrons away to another inn.'

[30]

'Be it so, then,' the Innkeeper said indifferently, his face heavy and lowering; 'I do not care.'

There was nothing to be got out of the man, and the Doctor drained his glass. 'Well, I'm for bed, Jack,' he yawned. 'What about you?'

'Same here,' I said. 'It's been a hard day; I can scarcely keep my eyes open.'

'I will see you to your room, messieurs,' said the Innkeeper, rising and lighting a candle on the side-table. 'Come, then; follow me.'

We passed out into the passage. It was bitterly cold there, and the clots of snow that we had shaken from our ski and clothes lay unmelted on the stone flags. A flight of bare wooden stairs led upwards. Each stair was worn and hollowed by the tread of countless feet. The feeble light of the candle lit the massively built roof and walls, whereon green distemper peeled and crumbled. Outside the storm raged with unabated violence, filling the old building with grumblings and rumblings.

We were half-way up, the Innkeeper first, the Doctor second, and I last, when the Innkeeper stopped abruptly. Above me I could see his hand tighten on the banister-rail, tighten until the bloodless knuckles stood out white and sharp. We became aware of a low muttering sound. It burst forth into a sudden snarl, deep, throaty, and terribly menacing. Never in my life have I listened to such a sound. Bestiality, ferocity, hate were concentrated within it. My muscles seemed to contract—an icy shiver passed down my back. In front of me was the rigid figure of the Doctor; he had paused in the act of mounting a step and was listening intently. And then, above the snarling, came the sound of a woman's voice, gentle, soothing, and persuasive. Gradually the snarling died away into silence.

'What's that?' The Doctor's voice was sharp and imperative.

The Innkeeper turned. In the light of the candle his face appeared ashen. Little beads of sweat glistened on his brow. His eyes narrowed until they were two dark slits. 'That is a dog, messieurs, our dog. Ah, but he is a fierce one, that. Always he makes a noise when he hears strangers. We are lonely, my wife and I, so we keep a dog—yes, a fierce dog.'

'A dog!' I exclaimed. 'No dog I ever heard made a noise like that.'

But the Innkeeper paid no heed to my words; he turned and recommenced the ascent. The Doctor and I followed behind.

We reached a broad landing. The light from the solitary candle flickered on dank stone walls.

'This is your room, messieurs,' said the Innkeeper, opening a door.

We found ourselves in a large room with a high, vaulted ceiling, spanned by several wooden beams. Two beds at one end and a wash-hand stand and two or three chairs and tables seemed lost within it. It was one of those rooms that inspire pessimism, gloom, and repulsion.

'Not exactly a Hampstead flatlet,' said the Doctor, his voice echoing drearily around, 'but at least it's airy.'

The Innkeeper lit two candles from the one he held. 'The stove is lit,' he said, 'and you will, I think, find it warm. I trust there is everything that you require.' He paused. There was a strained intentness in his dark eyes—they shifted uneasily from the Doctor to me and back again.

'Well?' said the Doctor.

The Innkeeper seemed to nerve himself. 'You will lock the door! You will keep the windows fastened! And do not, if you value your lives, leave this room!' It was hissed rather than spoken, and between each sentence the Innkeeper drew a sharp breath, as if to impart force to the next.

'What on earth—' I began.

'And that is because of—the dog?' said the Doctor slowly.

A look of relief animated the Innkeeper's face. 'Yes, yes,' he explained eagerly, 'that is it, the dog. He is very fierce, very dangerous, very cunning. Be very careful of him, messieurs; keep the door locked, and the window too.' The Innkeeper had edged towards the door as he spoke. Next moment he had slipped through and closed it behind him.

'Stop!' I shouted. 'Stop!' And made to follow him.

But the Doctor seized me by the arm. 'No good getting excited, Jack,' he remarked quietly.

'What's it mean?'

The Doctor shrugged his shoulders, struck a match, applied it to his pipe; then, taking a long draw, he allowed the smoke to drift upwards in a thin column. 'Let's review the facts. We arrive at this pub in the devil of a blizzard. We are grudged hospitality by a man who is obviously scared out of his wits, and a woman ditto. They are frightened of someone, or something. They are frightened that this someone, or something, may attack us. Surely that is sufficiently obvious? Then, we ourselves hear a peculiarly nasty noise, which the Innkeeper tries to delude us into thinking is the snarl of a dog. It isn't a dog.' The Doctor paused, frowning.

[32]

'Then what—'

'One moment!' The Doctor's frown gave place to a sudden look of excitement. 'The tracks!' he exclaimed. 'You remember those half-snowed-over tracks we saw outside the door?'

'Well?'

'Didn't it strike you that they were rather curious tracks, very irregular, as though someone had been half-walking, half-running?'

'By Jove, yes! Now you mention it I do remember. Then there's someone else here besides the Innkeeper and his wife, someone that the Innkeeper and his wife are frightened of.'

'It certainly seems so,' agreed the Doctor, 'and I don't like it, Jack. That row we heard! There's something wrong. I mean to find out in the morning.' His mouth tightened; there was a light of stern resolve in his eyes.

'Meanwhile,' said I, 'I'm taking the Innkeeper's advice'; and, crossing to the door, I shot the bolt into place and turned the key in the massive lock.

The Doctor walked across to the casement window, and undoing the catch, opened it. The window was protected by shutters; these he opened too. I joined him and we peered outside. The window opened out on to a wooden balcony, along which fierce gusts of wind were sweeping, piling the powdery snow into drifts. Beyond the balcony nothing was to be seen but countless millions of hurrying snowflakes, dimly visible in the light of the candle gleams. We stood gazing for a few moments until a backrush of wind sweeping along the balcony bespattered us with snow.

'Ugh!' shivered the Doctor, as we fastened the shutters of the window; 'what a night!'

We undressed, pulled on the light silk pyjamas which were one of the few luxuries we carried in our rucksacks, and, placing the candle between us, got into bed.

'I don't know about you,' said the Doctor, 'but I feel terribly sleepy. I don't think we need worry, Jack. We're perfectly safe—no one could get in here.'

'No,' I yawned; 'I don't see how they could.'

On looking back upon it afterwards, it seems strange that we should have taken matters with such equanimity; but the long hard day in the open, plus the stern tussle with the blizzard, culminating in a good supper and a not inconsiderable quantity of wine, seemed to produce an almost stupefying effect. Even as I slid in between the sheets the events of the day appeared unreal and fantastic. The howl of the blizzard without seemed to resolve itself into a crooning lullaby. After all, what had the fuss been about? A strange noise—the Innkeeper— locked doors. A multitude of things passed in a procession through my mind, at first in orderly platoons, but gradually degenerating into a confused mass, dragging me along with them. Sleep laid its heavy hand upon me.

3

I dreamt, and my dreams were not pleasant dreams. I was pursued, my steps dogged, by a vague malevolent something. I tried to run, but a freezing horror rooted me to the spot. Behind me, through the abysses of sleep, came a fiendish laugh. I awoke, sweating and trembling in every limb, that dreadful laugh still ringing in my ears. Where was I? Came realization. A dull red glow, the stove. A regular cadence on my right, the Doctor snoring; and outside the shouting and jeering of the storm. Phew! What a nightmare!

But was it nightmare? That laugh! I could not rid my ears of it; and then, even as I lay with wide eyes staring into the darkness, in the comparative silence between two gusts there came a distinct click. A square of dim light became suddenly visible; the shutters had opened, swinging back with a faint creaking. The wind? Had it forced the catch? Was it—

Something dark insinuated itself into that dim square—the outline of an arm and hand, holding something long and pointed.

I leant across and seized the Doctor's shoulder. 'Doc!' I whispered urgently; 'wake up! Wake up!'

'Eh, what—' mumbled the Doctor sleepily.

'Wake up!' I repeated; 'for God's sake. Someone's trying to get in. Look!'

But the Doctor needed no further rousing; he sat up in bed with a jerk.

A shape filled the window. There came a sharp rasping sound. As one man we sprang from our beds.

'Quick, Jack! The matches! Where are they?'

I fumbled on the table, found the box, struck one. The head broke—French matches! I struck another, and applied it to the candle.

There came that same animal-like snarl, full of a dreadful menace, followed immediately by a tearing rip. The window swung open. An arm was thrust inside; with a sudden bound something sprang into the room.

At first we saw little more than an outline of it, but the candle, which had at first burnt low, suddenly flamed up. Something bent, hideous and misshapen like a gorilla, confronted us. It was clad only in a grey shirt, and its legs and feet were bare. One arm, covered with coarse, reddish hair, with a claw-like hand, was stretched out before it. The other hand gripped the hilt of a long dull-coloured knife. And its face! It was the face of neither man nor beast. Its loose lips writhed back from its blackened teeth in a sort of perpetual snarl. Its nose was flat, broad, and ape-like; its tangled reddish hair seemed to grow back from just above a pair of small, evil, black glittering eyes.

For a moment the creature paused, eyeing us; then it commenced a stealthy advance with that deadly-looking knife held in one hand.

Escape? the door, the window? No, there was no time. Long before we could get out of either the creature would be upon us. I glanced round for a weapon. Springing to the washstand, I grasped the water-jug, paused for a fraction of a second to take aim, and hurled its contents into the creature's face. As I did so I saw out of the corner of my eye the Doctor snatch an eiderdown off one of the beds.

Blinded and dazed for a moment by the cold water, the creature paused. A spasm of fierce hate convulsed its face. It seemed to crouch still lower. Then it rushed at me.

I am an old Rugger Blue, and as a full-back learnt the knack of thinking quickly. Hurling the empty jug at the creature's head, I dived for its legs. With a hoarse yell of rage the creature toppled over me and crashed to the floor, its knife driving deep into the wooden boards. With incredible agility it writhed out of my grip; its foul breath was in my nostrils, and its hairy claw-like hand was reaching for my throat, when something soft and enveloping descended on its head and shoulders—the Doctor's eiderdown! Surprised, the creature let go of the knife, leaving it quivering in the boards. I seized it, wrenched it out, and threw it away. A desperate struggle ensued. Though barely five feet in height, the creature was possessed of a demoniacal strength. Its sharp talons tore our thin pyjamas to ribbons and ripped open the eiderdown, until the room was filled with a snowstorm of feathers. It raged, shrieked, and foamed at the mouth, but gradually our strength, the strength of two well-built men both in good training, gained the upper hand. For a while it struggled impotently; then, suddenly, it grew limp.

'Some rope, cord, anything!' panted the Doctor, as he held the creature down. 'A sheet will do.'

I rushed to get one. As I did so our captive came suddenly to life. With convulsive strength it hurled the Doctor and eiderdown from itself, and leapt to its feet. For a second or so it stood with arms raised and great hands opening and shutting, while it seemed to mouth vile imprecations. Then it turned, darted to the window, and was through it in an instant.

I followed, with the Doctor, who had picked himself up from the floor, close behind. We were just in time to see it leap over the balcony and fall with a soft thud into the snow twenty feet beneath. Came another of those maniacal laughs, rising high above the roar of the blizzard. For a few instants we saw a dark form plunging animal-like through the snow. It disappeared into the murk.

We strained forward, gazing and listening intently, and for the last time, faint and far away, we heard its laugh, the epitome of man's damnation in the deeps of hell. Then there was silence.

I felt the Doctor's hand on my arm. 'Shut the window, Jack. I don't think he will come back. God! How cold it is!'

I became aware that we were both shaking like men in the grip of ague, and that our pyjamas were hanging from us in tatters.

'You are not hurt, Jack?'

'Only a few scratches and bruises, I think. Are you?'

'The same,' said the Doctor.

'What was it?'

'It was a man, Jack—a bad case and quite insane. But the Innkeeper will tell us. Where on earth have he and his wife got to?'

'The Innkeeper,' I repeated, 'and his wife! Yes, what's happened to *them*?'

'I don't know,' said the Doctor grimly; 'but we will see when we have got on some clothes.'

With fingers numbed and fumbling we pulled on our clothes, unbolted and unlocked the door, and stepped out on to the landing. Save for the moanings of the storm the old house was ominously quiet.

'Hullo there!' roared the Doctor. His voice echoed and thundered between the stone walls, but there was no reply. 'Hullo there!' he shouted again. 'Where are you?' But again his voice echoed and died unanswered in the recesses of the old building. 'We must search every room, Jack. I don't like it. I'm afraid—'

'Sh! One moment,' I whispered. 'What's that?'

[36]

From somewhere beneath came a dull thudding.

'Come on!' I exclaimed, and holding my candle aloft, I started downstairs, with the Doctor close behind.

It was difficult to locate the sound. Hurrying along the passage, we entered the kitchen, a large cheerless apartment with blackened ceiling, from which were suspended a dozen or more hams. The thudding was louder there. At the far end was a door. Passing through it, we found ourselves in the scullery. The thudding seemed directly beneath us. Again we shouted, and a muffled voice came from under our feet. 'In the corner! in the corner!' it said. We glanced round. In one corner of the stone floor was a square of wood with a ring-bolt in the centre, which was secured by a bolt. The Doctor unshot the bolt and, grasping the ring-bolt, lifted a heavy trap-door.

In the dark opening appeared the face of the Innkeeper, deathly pale. 'You are alive! Thank God, you are alive!' He spoke in a hoarse croak; then, taking his wife, who was behind him, by the hand, he helped her up the steps and through the trap-door.

The woman's face was drawn and haggard; she stared at us wildly, clutched at her husband, and burst into hysterical weeping. 'François! François! My François!' she wailed. 'Where is he? He is dead! Yes, he is dead! I know, you have killed him!'

'If he is dead,' said the Innkeeper dully, 'it is best; it is the will of the good God.'

'Come, come,' said the Doctor compassionately; 'we have not killed him, but he is gone out into the snow.'

'Gone out!' repeated the woman. 'Gone out! Then let us find him, fetch him.'

There was a door; she rushed to it and flung it open. A gust of icy wind charged with snow-flakes whirled through the opening. The Innkeeper sprang after her and dragged her back, while the Doctor and I swung to the door against the fierce blast.

'It is no good, Marie, no good. See the *tourmente*—no one could live in it. It is the will of the good God,' he paused. Suddenly he broke forth passionately, his clenched teeth gleaming in the midst of his black beard, his eyes afire. 'The will of the good God, yes! But His curse has fallen on me and mine'; and, burying his face in his hands, he too broke down and wept like a child.

'You have heard of cretinism, messieurs?' It was an hour or so later, and we were all four seated at the kitchen table.

The Doctor nodded. 'I have made a special study of it. I know, for instance, that it is very prevalent in this district, or was a few years ago, until railways and roads brought new blood among the population.'

'That is so,' agreed the Innkeeper. 'For me, I was born at Les Cressons, born of cretin parents, messieurs.' He halted; there was silence, save for the wail of the blizzard without and the occasional groaning of the signboard from the front of the inn. Even now, on the wings of the storm, I seemed to hear a laugh of madness. The Innkeeper seized the edge of the table and leant forward with burning eyes: 'Of cretin parents, yes—wedded by law, by the Church, the union of idiots. But I—I was sane, though I would to God that I had not been born.'

'Henri! Henri!' exclaimed his wife; 'you must not say that. Have we not been happy, you and I?'

'Happy!' The Innkeeper laughed shrilly. 'Happy, yes—in hell.' He splashed some cognac into a tumbler and gulped it down. It appeared to steady him, and he continued more calmly. 'If my father and mother were vile, they could not make me vile too. They died while I was yet young. I was brought up by my uncle. Marie here is his daughter, my cousin. When I was twenty we were married.'

I looked at his wife, noting once again her dark eyes and thin, bridged nose, so curiously like those of the Innkeeper.

'You will know,' continued the latter, 'that even where there is no cretinism marriage between first cousins is a dangerous thing, but for me, with the blood of cretins already in my veins, it was worse, far worse, for, as you know, cretinism is allied to intermarriage as well as to goitre. In Les Cressons we had no chance. For generations our blood had borne the taint of idiocy and even madness. For generations we had married among ourselves. There were no railways or roads to bring fresh blood to Les Cressons thirty-five years ago, and so you see, messieurs, Marie and I were born without a chance. When I walked through the streets of Les Cressons and saw the misery, the foulness, the hopelessness, I used to wonder whether God Himself had forgotten us. Then I would pray to Him, and implore Him to spare Marie and me the curse of our fathers.'

Once more he lifted the cognac to his lips, but his thin hand shook so he could scarcely control the glass, and some of the cognac, spilling over, ran down into his beard. 'Pardon me, pardon me,' he apologized.

'Don't go on if you would rather not,' said the Doctor.

'Yes, yes, monsieur, I will go on; I will tell you all. Do I not owe you an explanation? Where was I? Ah yes! Well, Marie and I had a little money, and we bought this inn. Thirty-five years ago there were only a few tourists, but we lived and were happy too. And then our son was born. It was such a night as this.' The Innkeeper lowered his voice. 'And it was Christmas Eve too. Surely, I thought, at Christmas of all seasons, the good God will give Marie and me a child free from the taint of our ancestors. The blizzard had lasted for three days, and the doctor did not come. And then, early on Christmas morning, when the blizzard shrieked round the house like the very spirits of the damned, our child was born.' He turned towards his wife and his voice choked. 'When I saw it I could have strangled it, could have torn the life from its body, for it was a cretin.—But you, you!'—and he shot out a finger at his wife—'you loved the child.'

His wife had shrunk back at his outburst; now she drew herself up with a dignity that would have been noble had it not been pathetic. 'I was his mother, Henri,' she said.

But the Innkeeper did not notice the interruption. 'François grew, grew as you saw him, bigger than most of his kind and very strong. This inn was on a route much used formerly by smugglers, who crossed over the frontier into Italy, and these smugglers used frequently to stop here. After all, what would you! They paid me well, and there were few tourists then. Mostly they were good men, rough mountaineers, but kind, gentle, and considerate, especially to our little François. I think they pitied him and us. But there was one, Pierre Devigne, who was not like the others—a great hulking brute of a fellow. *He* used to sneer at us, and taunt us for our child, and worst of all, he would ill-treat François. Cruelly he would beat him and kick him. Ah! He was a devil, was Pierre Devigne. We hated him; but when we tried to rid ourselves of him he threatened to tell all to the gendarmes.

'And so it went on. For many years it went on, until one day Pierre and three others stopped here on their way back from Italy. They had been successful, and as a result they drank much absinthe and became very drunk. I was chopping wood at the back, when I heard the screaming of François. Running round to the front, I found him lying on the ground, where he had been beaten by Pierre. Had the others not dragged Pierre away I believe he would have killed François, for the absinthe had turned him into a fiend incarnate. François did not say much, although he was bruised and bleeding from the cuts of Pierre's heavy stick, but there was a look in his eye that I had never seen before. I knew then that he would kill Pierre if he had the chance.'

The Innkeeper leant forward. He spoke little above a whisper. 'That night Marie and I were awakened by a dreadful yell from the room where Pierre and the other three were sleeping. We rushed in and found François in the grip of the other three, and Pierre on one of the beds in his death agonies. François had stabbed him while he slept. And when I saw François I knew, too, that he was something worse than a cretin, for he was foaming at the mouth, and his eyes were the eyes of a madman.

'They bound him in ropes, and carried him down to the madhouse at Les Cressons, and there he remained for fifteen years. Sometimes we were allowed to visit him, to look at him and greet him through the bars, as though he were some animal. They told us that he was the most dangerous madman they had, and always Marie would weep when she saw him, and pray that he might recover. But I knew that he would not, and that he were better dead. And then, yesterday, soon after it began to snow, he arrived back here. How he had escaped from the madhouse I do not know. The gendarmes, I knew, would be after him, but what could we do but take him in, for I do not think he would have harmed us, and was it not Christmas Eve?'

'Yes, Christmas Eve,' repeated his wife bitterly. 'Surely then a mother may welcome her son?'

'But when I heard your knocks,' went on the Innkeeper, 'I thought it was the gendarmes come to take François back to the madhouse. You will realise how difficult it was for me, for the sight of two strangers would arouse François's worst passions, and I feared for your safety. But when I saw the weather I knew that it was doubtful whether you could get to Les Cressons, so I was bound to accommodate you.

'If only I could conceal your presence from François, it would be all right, but I forgot the bell, and when it rang I could see that he knew that there were others in the house. If I did not tell you the truth it was because Marie made me swear to conceal it. François, she said, was her son, our son, and if the gendarmes came she meant to try and hide him, so that he could at least spend the winter with us away from that terrible madhouse, and I, when I

[40]

thought of the madhouse, agreed to help her.'

'I understand,' said the Doctor, and there was deep sympathy in his voice. 'Would you have acted differently, Jack?' he asked, turning to me.

I shook my head. 'I don't think so.'

There were tears in the Innkeeper's eyes. 'I am glad of that, messieurs,' he said simply.

'You have not told us how you were locked in the cellar,' I said.

'That is simply explained,' replied the Innkeeper. 'When you had gone to bed, Marie and I decided to sit up all night with François. It was the only way. But soon the madness overtook him. I could see the foam gathering round his lips; a red, inhuman glare lighting his eyes. He was like a beast that has once tasted blood and now seeks to taste it again. We tried to calm him, but it was no good. He began to tear the clothes from his body. Then he seized a hunting-knife from a drawer where we had tried to hide it, and threatened to plunge it into us if we did not do his bidding; and I believe he would have done it when I shouted to warn you, had Marie not thrust herself in front of me. It seemed that even in his madness François would not kill his mother. Yes, messieurs, I shouted, for I knew it was you whom François would attack. Ever since he had killed Pierre he imagined every man to be his enemy. But it was evident that you did not hear me, for the kitchen is far from your room.'

'And we were sleeping well,' I said, 'after a hard day and the wine you gave us.'

'And so,' continued the Innkeeper, 'we were forced down into the cellar and the trap-door bolted above us. I think you know the rest, messieurs?'

'Yes,' said the Doctor slowly, 'I think that explains everything.' He rose to his feet and took one of the woman's careworn hands in his. 'I am sorry, more sorry than words can express. Life is sometimes very cruel, very unfair, when we least deserve it. The ways of God are hard to understand.'

There was a long silence, broken only by the sobbing of the woman.

'The wind is dropping,' I said at last; 'and look, the dawn is coming.'

Outside the roar of the wind had subsided to a mutter; a faint light was filtering through the chinks in the shutters.

'Yes, it is Christmas Morning,' said the Innkeeper.

[41]

5

The day was calm as we skied down the long, desolate, upland valley towards Les Cressons. The creaking of our leather ski-bindings spoke of an intense frost, and our ski parted the powdery snow with a gentle swish, raising a light cloud of icy particles, that glittered and flashed like elfin spear-points in the sun. Above, silver peaks wedged a stainless blue sky. Here and there from the highest ridges banners of snow trailed, telling of a wind that yet raged on the heights—the aftermath of the blizzard—whilst a few sun-kissed wisps of mist clung to the knees of the mountains.

Ahead, we espied two tiny figures toiling slowly up the valley. At sight of us they halted and appeared to regard us. Running downwards, we approached them. They were two gendarmes on ski, armed with short rifles slung over their shoulders. They eyed us curiously, inquisitively.

'You are from the inn?' asked the foremost, a tall, broad-shouldered man with keen blue eyes and a heavy dark moustache.

'Yes,' answered the Doctor.

'Then maybe you have seen the madman, François, the son of the Innkeeper? We are come to fetch him back to the madhouse at Les Cressons.'

'Yes, we have seen him, but you will not find him. He is no longer there. Last night he went out into the blizzard. He did not return.' The Doctor paused, and swept one arm round the virgin expanses of snow. 'Somewhere about here he lies. The snow will have covered him.'

'I see, monsieur. Then you are sure that he is dead?'

'Yes,' said the Doctor.

'That is good,' remarked the other gendarme. 'It will save us much trouble.'

In the silence that followed there came from afar the faint melody of church bells.

TARNHELM

Hugh Walpole

Sir Hugh Walpole (1884–1941),
best known for his popular 'Herries' saga,
often introduced elements of horror and the
macabre in his short stories, and novels like
The Old Ladies and *Portrait of a Man with
Red Hair*. 'Tarnhelm', set in Walpole's beloved
Lakeland, is taken from his collection
All Souls' Night (1933).

1

I was, I suppose, at that time a peculiar child, peculiar a little by
nature, but also because I had spent so much of my young life in
the company of people very much older than myself.

After the events that I am now going to relate, some quite indelible
mark was set on me. I became then, and have always been since, one
of those persons, otherwise insignificant, who have decided, without
possibility of change, about certain questions.

Some things, doubted by most of the world, are for these people
true and beyond argument; this certainty of theirs gives them a kind of
stamp, as though they lived so much in their imagination as to have
very little assurance as to what is fact and what fiction. This 'oddness'
of theirs puts them apart. If now, at the age of fifty, I am a man with
very few friends, very much alone, it is because, if you like, my Uncle
Robert died in a strange manner forty years ago and I was a witness of
his death.

I have never until now given any account of the strange proceedings that occurred at Faildyke Hall on the evening of Christmas Eve in the year 1890. The incidents of that evening are still remembered very clearly by one or two people, and a kind of legend of my Uncle Robert's death has been carried on into the younger generation. But no one still alive was a witness of them as I was, and I feel it is time that I set them down upon paper.

I write them down without comment. I extenuate nothing; I disguise nothing. I am not, I hope, in any way a vindictive man, but my brief meeting with my Uncle Robert and the circumstances of his death gave my life, even at that early age, a twist difficult for me very readily to forgive.

As to the so-called supernatural element in my story, everyone must judge for himself about that. We deride or we accept according to our natures. If we are built of a certain solid practical material the probability is that no evidence, however definite, however first-hand, will convince us. If dreams are our daily portion, one dream more or less will scarcely shake our sense of reality.

However, to my story.

My father and mother were in India from my eighth to my thir-teenth years. I did not see them, except on two occasions when they visited England. I was an only child, loved dearly by both my parents, who, however, loved one another yet more. They were an exceedingly sentimental couple of the old-fashioned kind. My father was in the Indian Civil Service, and wrote poetry. He even had his epic, *Tantalus: A Poem in Four Cantos* published at his own expense.

This, added to the fact that my mother had been considered an invalid before he married her, made my parents feel that they bore a very close resemblance to the Brownings, and my father even had a pet name for my mother that sounded curiously like the famous and hideous 'Ba'.

I was a delicate child, was sent to Mr Ferguson's Private Academy at the tender age of eight, and spent my holidays as the rather unwanted guest of various relations.

'Unwanted' because I was, I imagine, a difficult child to understand. I had an old grandmother who lived at Folkestone, two aunts who shared a little house in Kensington, an aunt, uncle and a brood of cousins inhabiting Cheltenham, and two uncles who lived in Cumberland. All these relations, except the two uncles, had their proper share of me and for none of them had I any great affection.

Children were not studied in those days as they are now. I was thin, pale and bespectacled, aching for affection but not knowing at all how to obtain it; outwardly undemonstrative but inwardly emotional and sensitive, playing games, because of my poor sight, very badly, reading a great deal more than was good for me, and telling myself stories all day and part of every night.

All of my relations tired of me, I fancy, in turn, and at last it was decided that my uncles in Cumberland must do their share. These two were my father's brothers, the eldest of a long family of which he was the youngest. My Uncle Robert, I understood, was nearly seventy, my Uncle Constance some five years younger. I remember always thinking that Constance was a funny name for a man.

My Uncle Robert was the owner of Faildyke Hall, a country house between the lake of Wastwater and the little town of Seascale on the sea coast. Uncle Constance had lived with Uncle Robert for many years. It was decided, after some family correspondence, that the Christmas of this year, 1890, should be spent by me at Faildyke Hall.

I was at this time just eleven years old, thin and skinny, with a bulging forehead, large spectacles and a nervous, shy manner. I always set out, I remember, on any new adventures with mingled emotions of terror and anticipation. Maybe *this* time the miracle would occur: I should discover a friend or a fortune, should cover myself with glory in some unexpected way; be at last what I always longed to be, a hero.

I was glad that I was not going to any of my other relations for Christmas, and especially not to my cousins at Cheltenham, who teased and persecuted me and were never free of ear-splitting noises. What I wanted most in life was to be allowed to read in peace. I understood that at Faildyke there was a glorious library.

My aunt saw me into the train. I had been presented by my uncle with one of the most gory of Harrison Ainsworth's romances, *The Lancashire Witches*, and I had five bars of chocolate cream, so that that journey was as blissfully happy as any experience could be to me at that time. I was permitted to read in peace, and I had just then little more to ask of life.

Nevertheless, as the train puffed its way north, this new country began to force itself on my attention. I had never before been in the North of England, and I was not prepared for the sudden sense of space and freshness that I received.

The naked, unsystematic hills, the freshness of the wind on which the birds seemed to be carried with especial glee, the stone walls that ran like grey ribbons about the moors, and, above all, the vast expanse of sky upon whose surface clouds swam, raced, eddied and extended as I had never anywhere witnessed . . .

I sat, lost and absorbed, at my carriage window, and when at last, long after dark had fallen, I heard 'Seascale' called by the porter, I was still staring in a sort of romantic dream. When I stepped out on to the little narrow platform and was greeted by the salt tang of the sea wind my first real introduction to the North Country may be said to have been completed. I am writing now in another part of that same Cumberland country, and beyond my window the line of the fell runs strong and bare against the sky, while below it the Lake lies, a fragment of silver glass at the feet of Skiddaw.

It may be that my sense of the deep mystery of this country had its origin in this same strange story that I am now relating. But again perhaps not, for I believe that that first evening arrival at Seascale worked some change in me, so that since then none of the world's beauties—from the crimson waters of Kashmir to the rough glories of our own Cornish coast—can rival for me the sharp, peaty winds and strong, resilient turf of the Cumberland hills.

That was a magical drive in the pony-trap to Faildyke that evening. It was bitterly cold, but I did not seem to mind it. Everything was magical to me.

From the first I could see the great slow hump of Black Combe jet against the frothy clouds of the winter night, and I could hear the sea breaking and the soft rustle of the bare twigs in the hedgerows.

I made, too, the friend of my life that night, for it was Bob Armstrong who was driving the trap. He has often told me since (for although he is a slow man of few words he likes to repeat the things that seem to him worth while) that I struck him as 'pitifully lost' that evening on the Seascale platform. I looked, I don't doubt, pinched and cold enough. In any case it was a lucky appearance for me, for I won Armstrong's heart there and then, and he, once he gave it, could never bear to take it back again.

He, on his side, seemed to me gigantic that night. He had, I believe, one of the broadest chests in the world: it was a curse to him, he said, because no ready-made shirts would ever suit him.

I sat in close to him because of the cold; he was very warm, and I could feel his heart beating like a steady clock inside his rough coat. It beat for me that night, and it has beaten for me, I'm glad to say, ever since.

In truth, as things turned out, I needed a friend. I was nearly asleep and stiff all over my little body when I was handed down from the trap and at once led into what seemed to me an immense hall crowded with the staring heads of slaughtered animals and smelling of straw.

I was so sadly weary that my uncles, when I met them in a vast billiard-room in which a great fire roared in a stone fireplace like a demon, seemed to me to be double.

In any case, what an odd pair they were! My Uncle Robert was a little man with grey untidy hair and little sharp eyes hooded by two of the bushiest eyebrows known to humanity. He wore (I remember as though it were yesterday) shabby country clothes of a faded green colour, and he had on one finger a ring with a thick red stone.

Another thing that I noticed at once when he kissed me (I detested to be kissed by anybody) was a faint scent that he had, connected at once in my mind with the caraway-seeds that there are in seed-cake. I noticed, too, that his teeth were discoloured and yellow.

My Uncle Constance I liked at once. He was fat, round, friendly and clean. Rather a dandy was Uncle Constance. He wore a flower in his buttonhole and his linen was snowy white in contrast with his brother's.

I noticed one thing, though, at that very first meeting, and that was that before he spoke to me and put his fat arm around my shoulder he seemed to look towards his brother as though for permission. You may say that it was unusual for a boy of my age to notice so much, but in fact I noticed everything at that time. Years and laziness, alas! have slackened my observation.

2

I had a horrible dream that night; it woke me screaming, and brought Bob Armstrong in to quiet me.

My room was large, like all the other rooms that I had seen, and empty, with a great expanse of floor and a stone fireplace like the one in the billiard-room. It was, I afterwards found, next to the servants' quarters. Armstrong's room was next to mine, and Mrs Spender's, the housekeeper's, beyond his.

Armstrong was then, and is yet, a bachelor. He used to tell me that he loved so many women that he never could bring his mind to choose any one of them. And now he has been too long my personal bodyguard and is too lazily used to my ways to change his condition. He is, moreover, seventy years of age.

Well, what I saw in my dream was this. They had lit a fire for me (and it was necessary; the room was of an icy coldness) and I dreamt that I awoke to see the flames rise to a last vigour before they died away. In the brilliance of that illumination I was conscious that something was moving in the room. I heard the movement for some little while before I saw anything.

I sat up, my heart hammering, and then to my horror discerned, slinking against the farther wall, the evillest-looking yellow mongrel of a dog that you can fancy.

I find it difficult, I have always found it difficult, to describe exactly the horror of that yellow dog. It lay partly in its colour, which was vile, partly in its mean and bony body, but for the most part in its evil head—flat, with sharp little eyes and jagged yellow teeth.

As I looked at it, it bared those teeth at me and then began to creep, with an indescribably loathsome action, in the direction of my bed. I was at first stiffened with terror. Then, as it neared the bed, its little eyes fixed upon me and its teeth bared, I screamed again and again.

The next I knew was that Armstrong was sitting on my bed, his strong arm about my trembling little body. All I could say over and over was, 'The Dog! the Dog! the Dog!'

He soothed me as though he had been my mother.

'See, there's no dog there! There's no one but me! There's no one but me!'

I continued to tremble, so he got into bed with me, held me close to him, and it was in his comforting arms that I fell asleep.

3

In the morning I woke to a fresh breeze and a shining sun and the chrysanthemums, orange, crimson and dun, blowing against the grey stone wall beyond the sloping lawns. So I forgot about my dream. I only knew that I loved Bob Armstrong better than anyone else on earth.

Everyone during the next days was very kind to me. I was so deeply excited by this country, so new to me, that at first I could think of nothing else. Bob Armstrong was Cumbrian from the top of his flaxen head to the thick nails under his boots, and, in grunts and mono-syllables, as was his way, he gave me the colour of the ground.

There was romance everywhere: smugglers stealing in and out of

Drigg and Seascale, the ancient Cross in Gosforth churchyard, Ravenglass, with all its seabirds, once a port of splendour.

Muncaster Castle and Broughton and black Wastwater with the grim Screes, Black Combe, upon whose broad back the shadows were always dancing—even the little station at Seascale, naked to the sea-winds, at whose bookstalls I bought a publication entitled the *Weekly Telegraph* that contained, week by week, instalments of the most thrilling story in the world.

Everywhere romance—the cows moving along the sandy lanes, the sea thundering along the Drigg beach, Gable and Scafell pulling their cloud-caps about their heads, the slow voices of the Cumbrian farmers calling their animals, the little tinkling bell of the Gosforth church—everywhere romance and beauty.

Soon, though, as I became better accustomed to the country, the people immediately around me began to occupy my attention, stimu-late my restless curiosity, and especially my two uncles. They were, in fact, queer enough.

Faildyke Hall itself was not queer, only very ugly. It had been built about 1830, I should imagine, a square white building, like a thick-set, rather conceited woman with a very plain face. The rooms were large, the passages innumerable, and everything covered with a very hideous whitewash. Against this whitewash hung old photographs yellowed with age, and faded, bad water-colours. The furniture was strong and ugly.

One romantic feature, though, there was—and that was the little Grey Tower where my Uncle Robert lived. This Tower was at the end of the garden and looked out over a sloping field to the Scafell group beyond Wastwater. It had been built hundreds of years ago as a defence against the Scots. Robert had had his study and bedroom there for many years and it was his domain; no one was allowed to enter it save his old servant Hucking, a bent, wizened, grubby little man who spoke to no one and, so they said in the kitchen, managed to go through life without sleeping. He looked after my Uncle Robert, cleaned his rooms, and was supposed to clean his clothes.

I, being both an inquisitive and romantic-minded boy, was soon as eagerly excited about this Tower as was Bluebeard's wife about the forbidden room. Bob told me that whatever I did I was never to set foot inside.

And then I discovered another thing—that Bob Armstrong hated, feared and was proud of my Uncle Robert. He was proud of him because he was head of the family, and because, so he said, he was the cleverest old man in the world.

'Nothing he can't seemingly do,' said Bob, 'but he don't like you to watch him at it.'

All this only increased my longing to see the inside of the Tower, although I couldn't be said to be fond of my Uncle Robert either.

It would be hard to say that I disliked him during those first days. He was quite kindly to me when he met me, and at meal-times, when I sat with my two uncles at the long table in the big, bare, whitewashed dining-room, he was always anxious to see that I had plenty to eat. But I never liked him; it was perhaps because he wasn't clean. Children are sensitive to those things. Perhaps I didn't like the fusty, seed-cakey smell that he carried about with him.

Then there came the day when he invited me into the Grey Tower and told me about Tarnhelm.

Pale slanting shadows of sunlight fell across the chrysanthemums and the grey stone walls, the long fields and the dusky hills. I was playing by myself by the little stream that ran beyond the rose garden, when Uncle Robert came up behind me in the soundless way he had, and, tweaking me by the ear, asked me whether I would like to come with him inside his Tower. I was, of course, eager enough; but I was frightened too, especially when I saw Hucking's moth-eaten old countenance peering at us from one of the narrow slits that pretended to be windows.

However, in we went, my hand in Uncle Robert's hot dry one. There wasn't, in reality, so very much to see when you were inside —all untidy and musty, with cobwebs over the doorways and old pieces of rusty iron and empty boxes in the corners, and the long table in Uncle Robert's study covered with a thousand things— books with the covers hanging on them, sticky green bottles, a looking-glass, a pair of scales, a globe, a cage with mice in it, a statue of a naked woman, an hour-glass—everything old and stained and dusty.

However, Uncle Robert made me sit down close to him, and told me many interesting stories. Among others the story about Tarnhelm.

Tarnhelm was something that you put over your head, and its magic turned you into any animal that you wished to be. Uncle Robert told me the story of a god called Wotan, and how he teased the dwarf who possessed Tarnhelm by saying that he couldn't turn himself into a mouse or some such animal; and the dwarf, his pride wounded, turned himself into a mouse, which the god easily cap tured and so stole Tarnhelm.

On the table, among all the litter, was a grey skull-cap.

'That's my Tarnhelm,' said Uncle Robert, laughing. 'Like to see me put it on?'

But I was suddenly frightened, terribly frightened. The sight of Uncle Robert made me feel quite ill. The room began to run round and round. The white mice in the cage twittered. It was stuffy in that room, enough to turn any boy sick.

4

That was the moment, I think, when Uncle Robert stretched out his hand towards his grey skull-cap—after that I was never happy again in Faildyke Hall. That action of his, simple and apparently friendly though it was, seemed to open my eyes to a number of things.

We were now within ten days of Christmas. The thought of Christmas had then—and, to tell the truth, still has—a most happy effect on me. There is the beautiful story, the geniality and kindliness, still, in spite of modern pessimists, much happiness and goodwill. Even now I yet enjoy giving presents and receiving them—then it was an ecstasy to me, the look of the parcel, the paper, the string, the exquisite surprise.

Therefore I had been anticipating Christmas eagerly. I had been promised a trip into Whitehaven for present-buying, and there was to be a tree and a dance for the Gosforth villagers. Then after my visit to Uncle Robert's Tower, all my happiness of anticipation vanished. As the days went on and my observation of one thing and another developed, I would, I think, have run away back to my aunts in Kensington, had it not been for Bob Armstrong.

It was, in fact, Armstrong who started me on that voyage of observation that ended so horribly, for when he had heard that Uncle Robert had taken me inside his Tower his anger was fearful. I had never before seen him angry; now his great body shook, and he caught me and held me until I cried out.

He wanted me to promise that I would never go inside there again. What? Not even with Uncle Robert? No, most especially not with Uncle Robert; and then, dropping his voice and looking around him to be sure that there was no one listening, he began to curse Uncle Robert. This amazed me, because loyalty to his masters was one of Bob's great laws. I can see us now, standing on the stable cobbles in the falling white dusk while the horses stamped in their stalls, and the little sharp stars appeared one after another glittering between the driving clouds.

'I'll not stay,' I heard him say to himself. 'I'll be like the rest. I'll not be staying. To bring a child into it . . .'

From that moment he seemed to have me very specially in his charge. Even when I could not see him I felt that his kindly eye was upon me, and this sense of the necessity that I should be guarded made me yet more uneasy and distressed.

The next thing that I observed was that the servants were all fresh, had been there not more than a month or two. Then, only a week before Christmas, the housekeeper departed. Uncle Constance seemed greatly upset at these occurrences; Uncle Robert did not seem in the least affected by them.

I come now to my Uncle Constance. At this distance of time it is strange with what clarity I still can see him—his stoutness, his shining cleanliness, his dandyism, the flower in his buttonhole, his little brilliantly shod feet, his thin, rather feminine voice. He would have been kind to me, I think, had he dared, but something kept him back. And what that something was I soon discovered; it was fear of my Uncle Robert.

It did not take me a day to discover that he was utterly subject to his brother. He said nothing without looking to see how Uncle Robert took it; suggested no plan until he first had assurance from his brother; was terrified beyond anything that I had before witnessed in a human being at any sign of irritation in my uncle.

I discovered after this that Uncle Robert enjoyed greatly to play on his brother's fears. I did not understand enough of their life to realize what were the weapons that Robert used, but that they were sharp and piercing I was neither too young nor too ignorant to perceive.

Such was our situation, then, a week before Christmas. The weather had become very wild, with a great wind. All nature seemed in an uproar. I could fancy when I lay in my bed at night and heard the shouting in my chimney that I could catch the crash of the waves upon the beach, see the black waters of Wastwater cream and curdle under the Screes. I would lie awake and long for Bob Armstrong—the strength of his arm and the warmth of his breast—but I considered myself too grown a boy to make any appeal.

I remember that now almost minute by minute my fears increased. What gave them force and power who can say? I was much alone, I had now a great terror of my uncle, the weather was wild, the rooms of the house large and desolate, the servants mysterious, the walls of the passages lit always with an unnatural glimmer because of their white colour, and although Armstrong had watch over me he was busy in his affairs and could not always be with me.

I grew to fear and dislike my Uncle Robert more and more. Hatred and fear of him seemed to be everywhere and yet he was always soft-voiced and kindly. Then, a few days before Christmas, occurred the event that was to turn my terror into panic.

I had been reading in the library Mrs Radcliffe's *Romance of the Forest*, an old book long forgotten, worthy of revival. The library was a fine room run to seed, bookcases from floor to ceiling, the windows small and dark, holes in the old faded carpet. A lamp burnt at a distant table. One stood on a little shelf at my side.

Something, I know not what, made me look up. What I saw then can even now stamp my heart in its recollection. By the library door, not moving, staring across the room's length at me, was a yellow dog.

I will not attempt to describe all the pitiful fear and mad freezing terror that caught and held me. My main thought, I fancy, was that that other vision on my first night in the place had not been a dream. I was not asleep now; the book in which I had been reading had fallen to the floor, the lamps shed their glow, I could hear the ivy tapping on the pane. No, this was reality.

The dog lifted a long, horrible leg and scratched itself. Then very slowly and silently across the carpet it came towards me.

I could not scream; I could not move; I waited. The animal was even more evil than it had seemed before, with its flat head, its narrow eyes, its yellow fangs. It came steadily in my direction, stopped once to scratch itself again, then was almost at my chair.

It looked at me, bared its fangs, but now as though it grinned at me, then passed on. After it was gone there was a thick foetid scent in the air—the scent of caraway-seed.

5

I think now on looking back that it was remarkable enough that I, a pale, nervous child who trembled at every sound, should have met the situation as I did. I said nothing about the dog to any living soul, not even to Bob Armstrong. I hid my fears—and fears of a beastly and sickening kind they were, too—within my breast. I had the intelligence to perceive—and *how* I caught in the air the awareness of this I can't, at this distance, understand—that I was playing my little part in the climax to something that had been piling up, for many a month, like the clouds over Gable.

Understand that I offer from first to last in this no kind of explanation. There is possibly—and to this day I cannot quite be sure—nothing to explain. My Uncle Robert died simply—but you shall hear.

What was beyond any doubt or question was that it was after my seeing the dog in the library that Uncle Robert changed so strangely in his behaviour to me. That may have been the merest coincidence. I only know that as one grows older one calls things coincidence more and more seldom.

In any case, that same night at dinner Uncle Robert seemed twenty years older. He was bent, shrivelled, would not eat, snarled at anyone who spoke to him and especially avoided even looking at me. It was a painful meal, and it was after it, when Uncle Constance and I were sitting alone in the old yellow-papered drawing-room—a room with two ticking clocks for ever racing one another—that the most extraordinary thing occurred. Uncle Constance and I were playing draughts. The only sounds were the roaring of the wind down the chimney, the hiss and splutter of the fire, the silly ticking of the clocks. Suddenly Uncle Constance put down the piece that he was about to move and began to cry.

To a child it is always a terrible thing to see a grown-up person cry, and even to this day to hear a man cry is very distressing to me. I was moved desperately by poor Uncle Constance, who sat there, his head in his white plump hands, all his stout body shaking. I ran over to him and he clutched me and held me as though he would never let me go. He sobbed incoherent words about protecting me, caring for me . . . seeing that that monster . . .

At the word I remember that I too began to tremble. I asked my uncle what monster, but he could only continue to murmur incoherently about hate and not having the pluck, and if only he had the courage . . .

Then, recovering a little, he began to ask me questions. Where had I been? Had I been into his brother's Tower? Had I seen anything that frightened me? If I did would I at once tell him? And then he muttered that he would never have allowed me to come had he known that it would go as far as this, that it would be better if I went away that night, and that if he were not afraid. . . Then he began to tremble again and to look at the door, and I trembled too. He held me in his arms; then we thought that there was a sound and we listened, our

[54]

heads up, our two hearts hammering. But it was only the clocks ticking and the wind shrieking as though it would tear the house to pieces.

That night, however, when Bob Armstrong came up to bed he found me sheltering there. I whispered to him that I was frightened; I put my arms around his neck and begged him not to send me away; he promised me that I should not leave him and I slept all night in the protection of his strength.

How, though, can I give any true picture of the fear that pursued me now? For I knew from what both Armstrong and Uncle Constance had said that there was real danger, that it was no hysterical fancy of mine or ill-digested dream. It made it worse that Uncle Robert was now no more seen. He was sick; he kept within his Tower, cared for by his old wizened manservant. And so, being nowhere, he was everywhere. I stayed with Armstrong when I could, but a kind of pride prevented me from clinging like a girl to his coat.

A deathly silence seemed to fall about the place. No one laughed or sang, no dog barked, no bird sang. Two days before Christmas an iron frost came to grip the land. The fields were rigid, the sky itself seemed to be frozen grey, and under the olive cloud Scafell and Gable were black.

Christmas Eve came.

On that morning, I remember, I was trying to draw—some childish picture of one of Mrs Radcliffe's scenes—when the double doors unfolded and Uncle Robert stood there. He stood there, bent, shrivelled, his long, grey locks falling over his collar, his bushy eyebrows thrust forward. He wore his old green suit and on his finger gleamed his heavy red ring. I was frightened, of course, but also I was touched with pity. He looked so old, so frail, so small in this large empty house.

I sprang up. 'Uncle Robert,' I asked timidly, 'are you better?'

He bent still lower until he was almost on his hands and feet; then he looked up at me, and his yellow teeth were bared, almost as an animal snarls. Then the doors closed again.

The slow, stealthy, grey afternoon came at last. I walked with Armstrong to Gosforth village on some business that he had. We said no word of any matter at the Hall. I told him, he has reminded me, of how fond I was of him and that I wanted to be with him always, and he answered that perhaps it might be so, little knowing how true that prophecy was to stand. Like all children I had a great capacity for forgetting the atmosphere that I was not at that moment in, and I walked beside Bob along the frozen roads, with some of my fears surrendered.

But not for long. It was dark when I came into the long, yellow drawing-room. I could hear the bells of Gosforth church pealing as I passed from the ante-room.

A moment later there came a shrill, terrified cry: 'Who's that? Who is it?'

It was Uncle Constance, who was standing in front of the yellow silk window curtains, staring at the dusk. I went over to him and he held me close to him.

'Listen!' he whispered. 'What can you hear?'

The double doors through which I had come were half open. At first I could hear nothing but the clocks, the very faint rumble of a cart on the frozen road. There was no wind.

My uncle's fingers gripped my shoulder. 'Listen!' he said again. And now I heard. On the stone passage beyond the drawing-room was the patter of an animal's feet. Uncle Constance and I looked at one another. In that exchanged glance we confessed that our secret was the same. We knew what we should see.

A moment later it was there, standing in the double doorway, crouching a little and staring at us with a hatred that was mad and sick—the hatred of a sick animal crazy with unhappiness, but loathing us more than its own misery.

Slowly it came towards us, and to my reeling fancy all the room seemed to stink of caraway-seed.

'Keep back! Keep away!' my uncle screamed.

I became oddly in my turn the protector.

'It shan't touch you! It shan't touch you, uncle!' I called.

But the animal came on.

It stayed for a moment near a little round table that contained a composition of dead waxen fruit under a glass dome. It stayed here, its nose down, smelling the ground. Then, looking up at us, it came on again.

Oh God!—even now as I write after all these years it is with me again, the flat skull, the cringing body in its evil colour and that loathsome smell. It slobbered a little at its jaw. It bared its fangs.

Then I screamed, hid my face in my uncle's breast and saw that he held, in his trembling hand, a thick, heavy, old-fashioned revolver.

Then he cried out:

[56]

'Go back, Robert. . . Go back!'

The animal came on. He fired. The detonation shook the room. The dog turned and, blood dripping from its throat, crawled across the floor.

By the door it halted, turned and looked at us. Then it disappeared into the other room.

My uncle had flung down his revolver; he was crying, sniffling; he kept stroking my forehead, murmuring words.

At last, clinging to one another, we followed the splotches of blood, across the carpet, beside the door, through the doorway.

Huddled against a chair in the outer sitting-room, one leg twisted under him, was my Uncle Robert, shot through the throat.

On the floor, by his side, was a grey skull-cap.

THE CROWN
DERBY PLATE

Marjorie Bowen

Marjorie Bowen (1885–1952;
pseudonym of Mrs Gabrielle Margaret
Vere Campbell Long) wrote nearly 200 books—
novels, collections, and biographies—under a
variety of pseudonyms. Her best supernatural and
horror stories (or 'twilight tales', as she preferred
to call them) were collected together in *The Last*
Bouquet (1933). She wrote several excellent
Christmas stories, some of which have appeared
in the present series ('The Prescription',
'Marwood's Ghost Story', 'The Chinese Apple'),
and 'The Crown Derby Plate' is among
her finest in the genre.

M artha Pym said that she had never seen a ghost and that she would very much like to do so, 'particularly at Christmas, for you can laugh as you like, that is the correct time to see a ghost.'

'I don't suppose you ever will,' replied her cousin Mabel comfortably, while her cousin Clara shuddered and said that she hoped they would change the subject for she disliked even to think of such things.

The three elderly, cheerful women sat round a big fire, cosy and content after a day of pleasant activities; Martha was the guest of the other two, who owned the handsome, convenient country house; she always came to spend her Christmas with the Wyntons and found the leisurely country life delightful after the bustling round of London, for Martha managed an antique shop of the better sort and worked extremely hard. She was, however, still full of zest for work or pleasure, though sixty years old, and looked backwards and forwards to a succession of delightful days.

The other two, Mabel and Clara, led quieter but none the less agreeable lives; they had more money and fewer interests, but nevertheless enjoyed themselves very well.

'Talking of ghosts,' said Mabel, 'I wonder how that old woman at Hartleys is getting on, for Hartleys, you know, is supposed to be haunted.'

'Yes, I know,' smiled Miss Pym, 'but all the years that we have known of the place we have never heard anything definite, have we?'

'No,' put in Clara; 'but there *is* that persistent rumour that the house is uncanny, and for myself, *nothing* would induce me to live there!'

'It is certainly very lonely and dreary down there on the marshes,' conceded Mabel. 'But as for the ghost—you never hear *what* it is supposed to be even.'

'Who has taken it?' asked Miss Pym, remembering Hartleys as very desolate indeed, and long shut up.

'A Miss Lefain, an eccentric old creature—I think you met her here once, two years ago—'

'I believe that I did, but I don't recall her at all.'

'We have not seen her since, Hartleys is so un-get-at-able and she didn't seem to want visitors. She collects china, Martha, so really you ought to go and see her and talk "shop."'

With the word 'china' some curious associations came into the mind of Martha Pym; she was silent while she strove to put them together, and after a second or two they all fitted together into a very clear picture.

She remembered that thirty years ago—yes, it must be thirty years ago, when, as a young woman, she had put all her capital into the antique business, and had been staying with her cousins (her aunt had then been alive) that she had driven across the marsh to Hartleys, where there was an auction sale; all the details of this she had completely forgotten, but she could recall quite clearly purchasing a set of gorgeous china which was still one of her proud delights, a perfect set of Crown Derby save that one plate was missing.

'How odd,' she remarked, 'that this Miss Lefain should collect china too, for it was at Hartleys that I purchased my dear old Derby service—I've never been able to match that plate—'.

'A plate was missing? I seem to remember,' said Clara. 'Didn't they say that it must be in the house somewhere and that it should be looked for?'

'I believe they did, but of course I never heard any more and that missing plate has annoyed me ever since. Who had Hartleys?'

'An old connoisseur, Sir James Sewell; I believe he was some relation to this Miss Lefain, but I don't know—'

'I wonder if she has found the plate,' mused Miss Pym. 'I expect she has turned out and ransacked the whole place—'

'Why not trot over and ask?' suggested Mabel. 'It's not much use to her, if she has found it, one odd plate.'

'Don't be silly,' said Clara. 'Fancy going over the marshes, this weather, to ask about a plate missed all those years ago. I'm sure Martha wouldn't think of it—'

But Martha did think of it; she was rather fascinated by the idea; how queer and pleasant it would be if, after all these years, nearly a lifetime, she should find the Crown Derby plate, the loss of which had always irked her! And this hope did not seem so altogether fantastical, it was quite likely that old Miss Lefain, poking about in the ancient house, had found the missing piece.

And, of course, if she had, being a fellow-collector, she would be quite willing to part with it to complete the set.

Her cousin endeavoured to dissuade her; Miss Lefain, she declared, was a recluse, an odd creature who might greatly resent such a visit and such a request.

'Well, if she does I can but come away again,' smiled Miss Pym. 'I suppose she can't bite my head off, and I rather like meeting these curious types—we've got a love for old china in common, anyhow.'

'It seems so silly to think of it—after all these years—a plate!'

'A Crown Derby plate,' corrected Miss Pym. 'It is certainly strange that I didn't think of it before, but now that I have got it into my head I can't get it out. Besides,' she added hopefully, 'I might see the ghost.'

So full, however, were the days with pleasant local engagements that Miss Pym had no immediate chance of putting her scheme into practice; but she did not relinquish it, and she asked several different people what they knew about Hartleys and Miss Lefain.

And no one knew anything save that the house was supposed to be haunted and the owner 'cracky'.

'Is there a story?' asked Miss Pym, who associated ghosts with neat tales into which they fitted as exactly as nuts into shells.

But she was always told—'Oh, no, there isn't a story, no one knows anything about the place, don't know how the idea got about; old Sewell was half-crazy, I believe, he was buried in the garden and that gives a house a nasty name—'

'Very unpleasant,' said Martha Pym, undisturbed.

This ghost seemed too elusive for her to track down; she would have to be content if she could recover the Crown Derby plate; for that at least she was determined to make a try and also to satisfy that faint tingling of curiosity roused in her by this talk about Hartleys and the remembrance of that day, so long ago, when she had gone to the auction sale at the lonely old house.

So the first free afternoon, while Mabel and Clara were comfortably taking their afternoon repose, Martha Pym, who was of a more lively habit, got out her little governess cart and dashed away across the Essex flats.

She had taken minute directions with her, but she had soon lost her way.

Under the wintry sky, which looked as grey and hard as metal, the marshes stretched bleakly to the horizon, the olive-brown broken reeds were harsh as scars on the saffron-tinted bogs, where the sluggish waters that rose so high in winter were filmed over with the first stillness of a frost; the air was cold but not keen, everything was damp; the faintest of mists blurred the black outlines of trees that rose stark from the ridges above the stagnant dykes; the flooded fields were haunted by black birds and white birds, gulls and crows whining above the long ditch grass and wintry wastes.

Miss Pym stopped the little horse and surveyed this spectral scene, which had a certain relish about it to one sure to return to a homely village, a cheerful house and good company.

A withered and bleached old man, in colour like the dun landscape, came along the road between the sparse alders.

Miss Pym, buttoning up her coat, asked the way to Hartleys as he passed her; he told her, straight on, and she proceeded, straight indeed across the road that went with undeviating length across the marshes.

'Of course,' thought Miss Pym, 'if you live in a place like this, you are bound to invent ghosts.'

The house sprang up suddenly on a knoll ringed with rotting trees, encompassed by an old brick wall that the perpetual damp had overrun with lichen, blue, green, white colours of decay.

Hartleys, no doubt, there was no other residence of human being in sight in all the wide expanse; besides, she could remember it, surely, after all this time, the sharp rising out of the marsh, the colony of tall trees, but then fields and trees had been green and bright—there had been no water on the flats, it had been summer time.

'She certainly', thought Miss Pym, 'must be crazy to live here. And I rather doubt if I shall get my plate.'

She fastened up the good little horse by the garden gate which stood negligently ajar and entered; the garden itself was so neglected that it was quite surprising to see a trim appearance in the house, curtains at the window and a polish on the brass door knocker, which must have been recently rubbed there, considering the taint in the sea damp which rusted and rotted everything.

It was a square-built, substantial house with 'nothing wrong with it but the situation', Miss Pym decided, though it was not very attractive, being built of that drab plastered stone so popular a hundred years ago, with flat windows and door, while one side was gloomily shaded by a large evergreen tree of the cypress variety which gave a blackish tinge to that portion of the garden.

There was no pretence at flower-beds nor any manner of cultivation in this garden where a few rank weeds and straggling bushes matted together above the dead grass; on the enclosing wall which appeared to have been built high as protection against the ceaseless winds that swung along the flats were the remains of fruit trees; their crucified branches, rotting under the great nails that held them up, looked like the skeletons of those who had died in torment.

Miss Pym took in these noxious details as she knocked firmly at the door; they did not depress her; she merely felt extremely sorry for anyone who could live in such a place.

She noticed, at the far end of the garden, in the corner of the wall, a headstone showing above the sodden colourless grass, and remembered what she had been told about the old antiquary being buried there, in the grounds of Hartleys.

As the knock had no effect she stepped back and looked at the house; it was certainly inhabited—with those neat windows, white curtains and drab blinds all pulled to precisely the same level.

And when she brought her glance back to the door she saw that it had been opened and that someone, considerably obscured by the

[62]

darkness of the passage, was looking at her intently.

'Good afternoon,' said Miss Pym cheerfully. 'I just thought that I would call to see Miss Lefain—it is Miss Lefain, isn't it?'

'It's my house,' was the querulous reply.

Martha Pym had hardly expected to find any servants here, though the old lady must, she thought, work pretty hard to keep the house so clean and tidy as it appeared to be.

'Of course,' she replied. 'May I come in? I'm Martha Pym, staying with the Wyntons, I met you there—'

'Do come in,' was the faint reply. 'I get so few people to visit me, I'm really very lonely.'

'I don't wonder,' thought Miss Pym; but she had resolved to take no notice of any eccentricity on the part of her hostess, and so she entered the house with her usual agreeable candour and courtesy.

The passage was badly lit, but she was able to get a fair idea of Miss Lefain; her first impression was that this poor creature was most dreadfully old, older than any human being had the right to be, why, she felt young in comparison—so faded, feeble and pallid was Miss Lefain.

She was also monstrously fat; her gross, flaccid figure was shapeless and she wore a badly cut, full dress of no colour at all, but stained with earth and damp where Miss Pym supposed she had been doing futile gardening; this gown was doubtless designed to disguise her stoutness, but had been so carelessly pulled about that it only added to it, being rucked and rolled 'all over the place' as Miss Pym put it to herself.

Another ridiculous touch about the appearance of the poor old lady was her short hair; decrepit as she was, and lonely as she lived she had actually had her scanty relics of white hair cropped round her shaking head.

'Dear me, dear me,' she said in her thin treble voice. 'How very kind of you to come. I suppose you prefer the parlour? I generally sit in the garden.'

'The garden? But not in this weather?'

'I get used to the weather. You've no idea how used one gets to the weather.'

'I suppose so,' conceded Miss Pym doubtfully. 'You don't live here quite alone, do you?'

'Quite alone, lately. I had a little company, but she was taken away, I'm sure I don't know where. I haven't been able to find a trace of her anywhere,' replied the old lady peevishly.

'Some wretched companion that couldn't stick it, I suppose,' thought Miss Pym. 'Well, I don't wonder—but someone ought to be here to look after her.'

They went into the parlour, which, the visitor was dismayed to see, was without a fire but otherwise well kept.

And there, on dozens of shelves, was a choice array of china at which Martha Pym's eyes glistened.

'Aha!' cried Miss Lefain. 'I see you've noticed my treasures! Don't you envy me? Don't you wish that you had some of those pieces?'

Martha Pym certainly did and she looked eagerly and greedily round the walls, tables and cabinets while the old woman followed her with little thin squeals of pleasure.

It was a beautiful little collection, most choicely and elegantly arranged, and Martha thought it marvellous that this feeble ancient creature should be able to keep it in such precise order as well as doing her own housework.

'Do you really do everything yourself here and live quite alone?' she asked, and she shivered even in her thick coat and wished that Miss Lefain's energy had risen to a fire, but then probably she lived in the kitchen, as these lonely eccentrics often did.

'There was someone,' answered Miss Lefain cunningly, 'but I had to send her away. I told you she's gone, I can't find her, and I am so glad. Of course,' she added wistfully, 'it leaves me very lonely, but then I couldn't stand her impertinence any longer. She used to say that it was *her* house and her collection of china! Would you believe it? She used to try to chase me away from looking at my own things!'

'How very disagreeable,' said Miss Pym, wondering which of the two women had been crazy. 'But hadn't you better get someone else?'

'Oh no,' was the jealous answer. 'I would rather be alone with my things, I daren't leave the house for fear someone takes them away— there was a dreadful time once when an auction sale was held here—'

'Were you here then?' asked Miss Pym; but indeed she looked old enough to have been anywhere.

'Yes, of course,' Miss Lefain replied rather peevishly, and Miss Pym decided that she must be a relation of old Sir James Sewell. Clara and Mabel had been very foggy about it all. 'I was very busy hiding all the china—but one set they got—a Crown Derby tea service—'

'With one plate missing!' cried Martha Pym. 'I bought it, and do you know, I was wondering if you'd found it—'

'I hid it,' piped Miss Lefain.

[64]

'Oh, you did, did you? Well, that's rather funny behaviour. Why did you hide the stuff away instead of buying it?'

'How could I buy what was mine?'

'Old Sir James left it to you, then?' asked Martha Pym, feeling very muddled.

'*She* bought a lot more,' squeaked Miss Lefain, but Martha Pym tried to keep her to the point.

'If you've got the plate,' she insisted, 'you might let me have it—I'll pay quite handsomely, it would be so pleasant to have it after all these years.'

'Money is no use to me,' said Miss Lefain mournfully. 'Not a bit of use. I can't leave the house or the garden.'

'Well, you have to live, I suppose,' replied Martha Pym cheerfully. 'And, do you know, I'm afraid you are getting rather morbid and dull, living here all alone—you really ought to have a fire—why, it's just on Christmas and very damp.'

'I haven't felt the cold for a long time,' replied the other; she seated herself with a sigh on one of the horsehair chairs and Miss Pym noticed with a start that her feet were covered only by a pair of white stockings; 'one of those nasty health fiends,' thought Miss Pym, 'but she doesn't look too well for all that.'

'So you don't think that you could let me have the plate?' she asked briskly, walking up and down, for the dark, neat, clean parlour was very cold indeed, and she thought that she couldn't stand this much longer; as there seemed no sign of tea or anything pleasant and comfortable she had really better go.

'I might let you have it,' sighed Miss Lefain, 'since you've been so kind as to pay me a visit. After all, one plate isn't much use, is it?'

'Of course not, I wonder you troubled to hide it—'

'I couldn't *bear*,' wailed the other, 'to see the things going out of the house!'

Martha Pym couldn't stop to go into all this; it was quite clear that the old lady was very eccentric indeed and that nothing very much could be done with her; no wonder that she had 'dropped out' of everything and that no one ever saw her or knew anything about her, though Miss Pym felt that some effort ought really to be made to save her from herself.

'Wouldn't you like a run in my little governess cart?' she suggested. 'We might go to tea with the Wyntons on the way back, they'd be delighted to see you, and I really think that you do want taking out of yourself.'

'I was taken out of myself some time ago,' replied Miss Lefain. 'I really was, and I couldn't leave my things—though,' she added with pathetic gratitude, 'it is very, very kind of you—'

'Your things would be quite safe, I'm sure,' said Martha Pym, humouring her. 'Who ever would come up here, this hour of a winter's day?'

'They do, oh, they do! And *she* might come back, prying and nosing and saying that it was all hers, all my beautiful china, hers!'

Miss Lefain squealed in her agitation and rising up ran round the wall fingering with flaccid yellow hands the brilliant glossy pieces on the shelves.

'Well, then, I'm afraid that I must go, they'll be expecting me, and it's quite a long ride; perhaps some other time you'll come and see us?'

'Oh must you go?' quavered Miss Lefain dolefully. 'I do like a little company now and then and I trusted you from the first—the others, when they do come, are always after my things and I have to frighten them away!'

'Frighten them away!' replied Martha Pym. 'However do you do that?'

'It doesn't seem difficult, people are so easily frightened, aren't they?'

Miss Pym suddenly remembered that Hartleys had the reputation of being haunted—perhaps the queer old thing played on that; the lonely house with the grave in the garden was dreary enough around which to create a legend.

'I suppose you've never seen a ghost?' she asked pleasantly. 'I'd rather like to see one, you know—'

'There is no one here but myself,' said Miss Lefain.

'So you've never seen anything? I thought it must be all nonsense. Still, I do think it rather melancholy for you to live here all alone—'

Miss Lefain sighed:

'Yes, it's very lonely. Do stay and talk to me a little longer.' Her whistling voice dropped cunningly. 'And I'll give you the Crown Derby plate!'

'Are you sure you've really got it?' Miss Pym asked.

'I'll show you.'

Fat and waddling as she was, she seemed to move very lightly as she slipped in front of Miss Pym and conducted her from the room, going slowly up the stairs—such a gross odd figure in that clumsy dress with the fringe of white hair hanging on to her shoulders.

The upstairs of the house was as neat as the parlour, everything well in its place; but there was no sign of occupancy; the beds were covered with dust sheets, there were no lamps or fires set ready. 'I suppose,' said Miss Pym to herself, 'she doesn't care to show me where she really lives.'

But as they passed from one room to another, she could not help saying:

'Where do *you* live, Miss Lefain?'

'Mostly in the garden,' said the other.

Miss Pym thought of those horrible health huts that some people indulged in.

'Well, sooner you than I,' she replied cheerfully.

In the most distant room of all, a dark, tiny closet, Miss Lefain opened a deep cupboard and brought out a Crown Derby plate which her guest received with a spasm of joy, for it was actually that missing from her cherished set.

'It's very good of you,' she said in delight. 'Won't you take something for it, or let me do something for you?'

'You might come and see me again,' replied Miss Lefain wistfully.

'Oh yes, of course I should like to come and see you again.'

But now that she had got what she had really come for, the plate, Martha Pym wanted to be gone; it was really very dismal and depressing in the house and she began to notice a fearful smell—the place had been shut up too long, there was something damp rotting somewhere, in this horrid little dark closet no doubt.

'I really must be going,' she said hurriedly.

Miss Lefain turned as if to cling to her, but Martha Pym moved quickly away.

'Dear me,' wailed the old lady. 'Why are you in such haste?'

'There's—a smell,' murmured Miss Pym rather faintly.

She found herself hastening down the stairs, with Miss Lefain complaining behind her.

'How peculiar people are—*she* used to talk of a smell—'

'Well, you must notice it yourself.'

Miss Pym was in the hall; the old woman had not followed her, but stood in the semi-darkness at the head of the stairs, a pale shapeless figure.

Martha Pym hated to be rude and ungrateful but she could not stay another moment; she hurried away and was in her cart in a moment— really—that smell—

'Good-bye!' she called out with false cheerfulness, 'and thank you *so* much!'

There was no answer from the house.

Miss Pym drove on; she was rather upset and took another way than that by which she had come, a way that led past a little house raised above the marsh; she was glad to think that the poor old creature at Hartleys had such near neighbours, and she reined up the horse, dubious as to whether she should call someone and tell them that poor old Miss Lefain really wanted a little looking after, alone in a house like that, and plainly not quite right in her head.

A young woman, attracted by the sound of the governess cart, came to the door of the house and seeing Miss Pym called out, asking if she wanted the keys of the house?

'What house?' asked Miss Pym.

'Hartleys, mum, they don't put a board out, as no one is likely to pass, but it's to be sold. Miss Lefain wants to sell or let it—'

'I've just been up to see her—'

'Oh, no, mum—she's been away a year, abroad somewhere, couldn't stand the place, it's been empty since then, I just run in every day and keep things tidy—'

Loquacious and curious, the young woman had come to the fence; Miss Pym had stopped her horse.

'Miss Lefain is there now,' she said. 'She must have just come back—'

'She wasn't there this morning, mum, 'tisn't likely she'd come, either—fair scared she was, mum, fair chased away, didn't dare move her china. Can't say I've noticed anything myself, but I never stay long—and there's a smell—'

'Yes,' murmured Martha Pym faintly, 'there's a smell. What—what —chased her away?'

The young woman, even in that lonely place, lowered her voice.

'Well, as you aren't thinking of taking the place, she got an idea in her head that old Sir James—well, he couldn't bear to leave Hartleys, mum, he's buried in the garden, and she thought he was after her, chasing round them bits of china—'

'Oh!' cried Miss Pym.

'Some of it used to be his, she found a lot stuffed away, he said they were to be left in Hartleys, but Miss Lefain would have the things sold, I believe—that's years ago—'

'Yes, yes,' said Miss Pym with a sick look. 'You don't know what he was like, do you?'

'No, mum—but I've heard tell he was very stout and very old—I wonder who it was you saw up at Hartleys?'

Miss Pym took a Crown Derby plate from her bag.

'You might take that back when you go,' she whispered. 'I shan't want it, after all—'

Before the astonished young woman could answer Miss Pym had darted off across the marsh; that short hair, that earth-stained robe, the white socks, 'I generally live in the garden—'

Miss Pym drove away, breakneck speed, frantically resolving to mention to no one that she had paid a visit to Hartleys, nor lightly again to bring up the subject of ghosts.

She shook and shuddered in the damp, trying to get out of her clothes and her nostrils—that indescribable smell.

THE STOCKING

Nigel Kneale

Nigel Kneale (b. 1922) will
always be remembered for his three classic
Quatermass television serials which chilled and
thrilled vast audiences in the 1950s. His first
success came in 1949 with his short story
collection *Tomato Cain*, which won the Somerset
Maugham award. Among the memorable tales in
this book are 'Minuke' (poltergeist-infested
house), 'The Pond' (a terrible revenge on a
man who kills frogs), and the unusual
Christmas story reprinted here.

O n the day before Christmas the sun came through the window so low that it lit the highest broken patch on the wall.

It was very cold when Ma came home, and she put an extra cover on his cot; the cover from their bed with the paper stuffing. A corner of paper stuck out with a picture of a lady on it.

She gave him a piece of bread and fat while she made the tea.

'Ma,' he said.

Ma looked hard and said, 'Yes?'

'Will you hang up a stocking for me tonight?'

Ma laughed and said, 'All right.'

'I got a big bag of sweets in it last year,' he said. 'Daddy Christmas is kind, isn't he, Ma?'

Ma laughed again and afterwards he heard her counting the money in her purse.

'Maybe Daddy Christmas'll come and maybe he won't,' she said, 'but Pa'll hang a stocking up for you.'

When Pa had finished his soup in the evening, he brought a chair and fastened an old one of Ma's long stockings to the wooden beam that ran across the room above the cot, a little below the ceiling.

Pa leaned on the cot as he stepped down, and it creaked and swayed. 'That'll never do,' said Pa, and he knocked four nails into the cot to hold it more firmly to the wall; it had no legs.

Plaster crumbled into his eyes as Pa hammered, and Pa leaned into the cot and rubbed away some of the grit with his sleeve. Ma said, 'Turn over, silly creature.'

He pulled himself on to his face until the hammering was over. 'That'll keep it fast,' said Pa, and his mouth twitched at Ma as he jerked his head at the places where the Minkeys lived.

Ma nodded and she said in the little voice he was not meant to hear, 'He doesn't mind the rats.'

Loudly, she said, 'You don't mind the Mickey Mouses, love. You're too big to be afraid of them.'

He smiled at Ma, though the plaster was still hurting his eyes. She meant the Minkeys.

They lived high up and they had fur on their bodies and long tails. And when the dark came and Ma and Pa went to bed, the Minkeys ran about inside the ceiling; sometimes they scratched on the floor below the cot. But when it was light they never came.

'There's plenty of room in that stocking,' said Pa and he laughed.

Ma laughed too, and then she said to Pa, 'Coming now?' and Pa said, 'Yes, the usual?'

Ma counted her money again and smiled. 'We can celebrate tonight.'

'He'll have the house to himself,' said Pa.

'Why aren't there any other people now?' he asked from the cot.

Pa laughed. 'They thought there were too many Mickey Mouses.'

'Oh, it'll be closing time before you come!' Ma shouted.

When they had gone, everything was still, only the candle flickering softly.

He looked up at the stocking, hanging straight from the beam; it might have a bulge in it by morning.

He sang to himself in the cot, faintly, a little song that turned out to be about the Minkeys; their strange ways, their quietness and their scuttling walk.

He listened to the noise of ships on the distant river, and wondered why his legs would not move, although he was five.

He wondered about Christmas, and why it was not in the summer.

He wondered about many things, and shivered and tried to screw himself up.

There was a tiny sound in the ceiling; a faint scraping noise as if somebody very small was shifting their feet. That would be a Minkey.

There came another little sound, and another, and presently a soft slither as if something had jumped on to the beam above. The Minkeys were coming out.

He looked up towards the dark ceiling, and saw the green glimmer of two tiny eyes, and then two more and then others.

The ceiling was full of a rustling and scuttling, as it always was when the house became still.

Minkeys didn't like you to see them.

A loose nail tumbled from above and clattered on the floor.

He saw that the whole wide beam was bulging on each side, and that the bulges were moving and changing; often a long tail twitched and curled.

Everywhere was a scratching and the little squeaky sound of Minkeys' talk, like the talk of the yellow bird that died, only quicker and sharper.

Suddenly it stopped.

He looked upwards again, and the flickering eyes peeped down from the beam. He saw that the long Daddy Christmas stocking was moving, swaying from side to side, and jerking. It seemed to have thickened at the place Pa had tied it to the beam; then it had thickened lower down, and lower.

And there was a Minkey, clinging to the stocking, and slowly dropping. Its eyes twinkled as it swung and its head shot this way and that.

He could smell the dark smell of the Minkey very close.

When the furry body had reached the end of the stocking, it hung curled upside down; and its tail twisted here and there, feeling the folds in the stocking. He started with the quickness of the Minkey's jump. For all at once the stocking was tossing empty, and the Minkey crouched on the foot of the cot, watching him.

But when he looked back at the stocking there were three more Minkeys climbing down, swinging like the first one. Yet there was no noise at all.

[72]

The Minkeys jumped on to the edge of the cot, one by one; and others took their place at the top of the stocking. They climbed down quickly, and many more bodies bobbed along the beam above.

The first Minkey crouched, and jumped into the cot.

He could feel its weight gently pressing the bedclothes down, and at the same time there was a small, cold feeling inside his head. But he was not afraid of furry Minkeys.

He held out his hand gently towards the first one. It did not move. Then suddenly there was a little sharp pain in his finger and he pulled it back.

The Minkey stared at him, with black, round eyes like the end of Ma's hat-pin.

There was a tiny red bead on his finger that was salt when he tasted it.

And everywhere was full of Minkeys and strange with the smell and warmth of them. All the whiskers and eyes and pointed faces moved together. They went 'Now—now—now,' like the bumping of the heart inside his chest.

There was a gentle weight on him.

He looked down. The first Minkey sat on his chest, watching his eyes with its own.

His hands were as log-heavy as his legs.

He saw its mouth open, narrow and sharp and pale; it gave one shrill cry of Minkey talk.

And instantly the whole room turned to hot, leaping fur. Squealing and tearing and chattering and biting.

THE SPIDER

F. McDermott

Major F. McDermott (1896–1975), a Fellow
of the Royal Geographical Society, produced
several educational travel films and was a popular
broadcaster of travel talks on the Schools
Programme in the 1930s. Among his books were
William Penn, *Thomas Gray and Stoke Poges*,
Through Atlantic Clouds, and *The Amazing
Amazon*. 'The Spider' first appeared in the *London
Mystery Magazine*, October 1951, and was adapted
the following year on American television. This
story was based on a dream and set in a
Cornish mill-house which the
author knew well.

Christmas Eve, and Cornwall, of all counties, decided to have
snow. Thick, unhurried snowflakes began to outline the trees
overhanging the little lane in which I found myself. I was
lost. Because the lane would lead to some sort of habitation, I decided
to go down it. Towards its lower end I found a building which had
obviously been a mill-house; the ancient wheel was still in place.
There was a welcome glow of light from one of the windows, so I
pressed a bell at the side of the oak door, which was opened by an old
man.

'You are indeed out of your way,' he said courteously. 'Tonight, of
all nights, you must have a glass of wine before you leave.'

We entered a large stone-flagged room roofed with huge oak beams.
In the open fireplace logs blazed. On the walls and side-tables were

pictures and tapestries and ornaments which were obviously very valuable.

As I stopped before a curved niche in the wall, my host's soft cultured voice remarked: 'That jewelled Buddha is a rare example of the standing figure, as opposed to the more conventional squatting position. From Mandalay . . . poor Mandalay. I wonder what Kipling would have said . . . but we must not get on to politics, must we?'

He then unhooked a tapestry bag from the wall, and handed it to me. 'That was made by the womenfolk of one of the hill tribes—the Kachins. Perhaps you know Burma?'

'Yes,' I answered, recalling leeches, mosquitoes, and Jap machine-gun nests. 'I certainly do know Burma. And this'—reaching out for a curved sword which had been hanging near the bag—'is a Kachin *dah*.'

'Don't touch it!' His voice was so urgent that I hurriedly withdrew my hand.

'Please forgive me!'—he was again urbane—'but, you see, I'm blind, and the only way I can be certain of finding things is if I only touch them.'

'Blind!' I echoed, in astonishment. 'But you had the light on. But, of course, that is for the rest of your household.'

'I live alone. But I always light that lamp in case a wayfarer, such as yourself, or a visitor calls. Please sit down, and I will get you some sherry and a biscuit.'

The sherry was of the first quality, and as I sipped it my host warmed his long thin hands over the leaping flames.

'A pity,' he said suddenly. 'I would have liked you to share my evening meal. But already your relatives and friends will be getting anxious about you?'

I laughed. 'I, too, am a lonely soul. That's why I'm wandering about at Christmas time. I'm often away from my hotel for two or three nights, and the proprietor would only get worried if I didn't eventually turn up to pay his bill.'

'Really!' Again there was a curious shrillness in the old man's voice. 'Then that settles it. You will not only dine, but stay the night. I will show you my treasures.'

With amazing deftness he set the table. Shining tumblers, surmounted by white table napkins, were adroitly placed next to cut-glass wineglasses. There were silver bowls of fruit and nuts. The meal came up to the promise of its setting. The peas, which accompanied the chicken, might well have come from a country garden in June. The sauce, served with the Christmas pudding, had the flavour of old brandy.

When I had helped myself to port I pushed the decanter towards my host.

'The port is on your right-hand side,' I said. 'May I help you?'

'Thank you, no,' he replied. 'You will have noticed I did not join you in the sherry. Wine disagrees with me, and I seldom take it. But that is no reason why I should not provide it for my guests.'

'But surely you don't get many visitors in this isolated spot?' I asked.

'No, not many. But those who do come are sometimes important. For instance, there was the Scandinavian woman . . . but I will tell you of her later. Do try some of these Brazil nuts. They're a fresh consignment, and as good as they can be in this country. Of course, to taste a Brazil as it should be tasted, you must eat it fresh from the tree.'

'You've been in Brazil?'

'I did quite a bit of exploration out there at one time. I don't know if you've ever heard of a native tribe called the Jivaros—they're in Peru, of course, not Brazil. They held me prisoner for five years. They're the people who cut off their enemies' heads and shrink them, you know.'

'Good Lord!' I exclaimed. 'What an experience! Did they torture you?'

'It depends what you mean by torture. They put me to no physical discomfort. But they forced me to take drugs compounded from various vines and trees in the jungle. This is the result of one of them.' He motioned with his hand towards his eyes.

'Did they ever allow you to see any of their head-shrinking business?' I asked. 'Is it really true that the head becomes the size of an orange?'

He nodded. 'Oh yes—sometimes smaller. I have a couple here. If it conforms with your idea of Christmas merriment, perhaps you might care to look at them.'

'I've always wanted to see one,' I exclaimed.

'Good! Then if you've finished your port, come along! As they're upstairs, I shall have to ask you to carry this candle, unless, of course, you have an electric torch.'

I had no torch, so, lighting the candle, I followed him as with assured steps he made his way up an ancient oak staircase.

In the room into which he led me the beams were, if anything, even more massive than downstairs. But here the roof sloped up to a point, vanishing in the dancing shadows cast by the candle.

Again there was the resemblance to a museum, and I recognized rare little ivory Netsuke figures from Japan, beautifully carved ivory and ebony chopsticks from China, and an astonishing and rather terrifying collection of grotesque Indian gods and goddesses.

'Here they are!' said my host, motioning towards one of the corners. A native drum was flanked on one side by a tall mahogany pipe for blowing poison darts and on the other by long arrows, fletched with brilliant-coloured birds' feathers and tipped with sharpened bone. On the taut skin of the drum were two tiny human heads, one much smaller than the other.

With an appearance almost of reverence the old man picked them up.

'Let us sit on the bed while we examine them,' he said. 'They had a party for the school-children up in the village this afternoon, and borrowed all my small bedroom chairs. I shall probably have to worry them for a week before I get them back.'

With a curious tingling at the back of my scalp I accepted from his hand the smaller of the two heads, which was little bigger than a billiard ball, yet had perfect features.

'You know, a lot is said about secret processes and so on,' he said, 'but really the whole thing is quite simple. They have to cut the scalp before they can remove the skull. Then they sew it up again, forming a kind of bag, and fill that tightly with sand. Most of the rest of the business is simply a matter of smoothing the features with very hot stones which causes them to shrink proportionately. That one is a gipsy child, and it took me in all only about three hours to do it.'

'You mean, they actually allowed you to take part in the proceedings?' I asked incredulously.

'Oh, dear me, no! They would have killed me promptly if I'd touched anything connected with that ceremony. Even the pots in which the heads are placed have to be covered with leaves, and must only be seen by the witch doctors. I did that one here.'

I felt my heart miss a beat.

'Here!' I echoed.

'Yes. Luckily I've plenty of sand around and a small quarry actually in my own grounds where there's just the right type of stones. Strange how that child was never missed—or at any rate, no fuss was made about it. That's why I'm sure it was a gipsy. Now this other one, the Scandinavian woman, caused a frightful uproar. I made the mistake of thinking that because she was a foreigner no enquiries would be made.

But she was a famous authoress, and I thought they'd never stop the hullabaloo. Luckily, to avoid publicity, she'd come to Cornwall incognito, without leaving her address, and her supposed disappearance took place in Sussex. Otherwise . . .'

He shrugged, and reaching out took the smaller head back from me.

By now I had quite recovered my self-possession. I was obviously being entertained by a maniac. But he was just a frail old man. Even allowing for the strength said to be possessed by the insane, he was blind, and obviously incapable of doing me harm provided I remained on my guard.

'Of course, they're imperfect,' he went on. 'They really ought to have the lips sewn up. The idea is to prevent the dead person's spirit from cursing the one who is doing the shrinking. But the cord has to be left hanging down, and they would have looked too awful if I'd used ordinary string. So I thought it best to leave them unfinished.'

'Quite!' I murmured, thinking to humour him.

'Still, luck is with me'—his voice was now little more than a whisper—'I've been so much wanting the set. A child . . . a woman . . . and now you come along.'

In spite of my feeling of physical superiority, this confirmation of a suspicion which had been dawning on me made me decide to act forthwith. The old man was undeniably clever, and might strike me down without the least warning. I would go at once and inform the police.

But, as I tried to rise, my legs suddenly refused to act, and I sank back heavily on the bed.

'Just right,' said the old man, who had evidently been waiting for this movement on the bed. 'Six minutes and thirty-five seconds for the legs. In another ten seconds you will be completely stiff, so I advise you to lie down . . . like this.'

Turning, he pressed me back on the bed, and I found I had no power to resist.

'It's one of the most interesting of the Jivaro drugs,' he went on. 'They used to make it from a kind of orchid which they gathered on the tops of very high trees. I got away with quite a lot. It has a pleasant flavour, hasn't it? It was in the port, you know. I've often tried it on myself and timed it. The limbs become completely stiff in whatever position they are, just six minutes and forty-five seconds after the dose has been taken. Mental faculties are not impaired at all. For some reason the recovery time varies. Usually, it's in the region of two hours.

[78]

I've never felt any ill-effects afterwards—rather the contrary.'

He got up and replaced the two small heads carefully on the top of the drum.

Then he came back, and, stroking his chin, looked down on me thoughtfully. 'There's one thing I must apologize for,' he said—and there was genuine regret in his voice. 'To get the best results, I must make the severance while you are still alive. But I can assure you that it will be absolutely painless. The whole body is rendered incapable of feeling by this drug. If it weren't that I need it for my own purposes, I should certainly introduce it to the medical authorities. The Scandinavian woman was not inconvenienced in the least. And now, if you'll excuse me, I'll just go and make some preparations.'

My eyes remained immovably fixed on the old beams, disappearing from view in a mass of cobwebs and dust. With a strange calmness I considered my position. Even if I had been able to talk with the old man—to reason with him—there might have been some hope. But had I been a wax dummy I could not have been less capable of offering any form of resistance, mental or otherwise.

I could see and I could hear. The ticking of a cheap alarm clock on a small table near the bed seemed unnaturally loud and terribly slow. As the minutes passed I longed for something to happen, even the return of the old maniac whose one object in life was now my murder.

I tried to move. Quietly, and still with that mental calmness of desperation, I attempted to alter the position of each of my limbs in turn. It was hopeless. Not even a finger would respond.

Then I saw it . . . one of the biggest spiders I have ever seen in my life; up there on a beam just above me. Now, for some strange reason, from my earliest childhood I have had an utterly inexplicable horror of spiders. And, although I got through the Burma campaign with nothing worse than a mild dose of malaria, just to run into a spider's web in an ordinary English garden . . . just to feel it across my face, has always been sufficient to bring on a severe illness which lasts several days.

As I saw that huge hairy creature making its way round the beam just above my head, a surge of unreasoning terror swept through me. To be decapitated alive had, I suppose, seemed so fantastic, that I cannot say I had felt more than an acute anxiety. But this was different. That loathsome thing might drop on me while I was still unable to move.

Almost as if in answer to my thought, I saw it sway backwards and forwards, apparently hang suspended for a fraction of a second, then fall straight towards my head.

As it alighted on me I emitted what would normally have been a loud scream, but which I heard as a gurgle, and simultaneously *I brushed it off my face.*

I am not well enough versed in psychology to explain what had happened. Presumably the overwhelming primitive horror I had felt had proved sufficiently strong to overcome the effects of the drug. At any rate, in the course of a few seconds full power of movement had returned to me.

Cautiously I made my way down the stairs again. There was no sign of the old man. He must have been engaged in the domestic quarters of the house.

With a great sobbing sigh of relief I stumbled out into the snow. The moon was now shining brilliantly, and from a nearby tree an owl hooted.

The police-sergeant chuckled as he motioned me to the old-fashioned settee, which formed the only sitting accommodation in his parlour-cum-police-station.

'Sorry you've had the journey for nothing, sir,' he said; 'but he's quite harmless. As batty as you make 'em, of course . . . he's even told me that story about the heads . . . me.'

The sergeant patted his ample middle and roared with laughter.

'But—' I began.

The sergeant interrupted me with a wave of his hand.

'It's no good, sir. Don't you worry yourself any more. We took it seriously at one time ourselves. But there never has been a child reported missing in this neighbourhood. As for that Swedish writer woman, don't you remember her body was washed up on one of the Sussex beaches? A bit smashed up, so the report said, but they hadn't any doubts who it was. Besides, there'd have been somebody missing this end too, wouldn't there? And what about the bodies? Where there are heads there are bodies too, you know, sir. And even he couldn't tell us what he'd done with those. No, it's a well-known form of mania, so I've been told. Like to get notoriety and make themselves feel important. Of course, I suppose we could get him put away. But he's a decent enough old boy except for this delusion . . . gives quite a lot to local charities.'

'And the drug?' I asked.

The sergeant winked knowingly.

'It's Christmas time, sir. I don't blame you. I've felt pretty paralytic myself sometimes . . . after a Christmas party.'

And there it ended. Except for the newspaper cutting. I clipped that out of the *Cornish and Devon Sentinel* dated last Friday. It reads:

'Considerable anxiety is now felt for the safety of Mr Manoel Rodriguez, the Portuguese scientist, at present in Cornwall to study rock formations, who left his hotel in Lostwannock on Tuesday afternoon last and has not been heard of since. It was known that he intended to visit inland quarries, but though a number of these have been searched . . .' and so on.

I can't help wondering what that police-sergeant is doing about it. You see, Lostwannock was where I had that strange experience.

THE VISITING
STAR

Robert Aickman

Robert Aickman (1914–81) wrote
some of the most highly praised 'strange' tales
of the century, and these are now considered by
many admirers to be the most literate and
important body of work in the horror genre since
Poe. 'We are all potential victims of the powers
Aickman so skilfully conjures and commands',
wrote Robert Bloch. Aickman's first editions are
eagerly sought collectors items. 'The Visiting Star'
is taken from *Powers of Darkness* (1966).

T he first time that Colvin, who had never been a frequent theatre-goer, ever heard of the great actress Arabella Rokeby was when he was walking past the Hippodrome one night and Malnik, the Manager of the Tabard Players, invited him into his office.

Had Colvin not been awarded a grant, remarkably insufficient for present prices, upon which to compose, collate, and generally scratch together a book upon the once thriving British industries of lead and plumbago mining, he would probably never have set eyes upon this bleak town. Tea was over (today it had been pilchard salad and chips); and Colvin had set out from the Emancipation Hotel, where he boarded, upon his regular evening walk. In fifteen or twenty minutes he would be beyond the gas-lights, the granite setts, the nimbus of the pits. (Lead and plumbago mining had long been replaced by coal as the town's main industry.) There had been no one else for tea and Mrs Royd had made it clear that the trouble he was causing had not passed unnoticed.

Outside it was blowing as well as raining, so that Palmerston Street was almost deserted. The Hippodrome (called, when built, the Grand Opera House) stood at the corner of Palmerston Street and Aberdeen Place. Vast, ornate, the product of an unfulfilled aspiration that the town would increase in size and devotion to the Muses, it had been for years unused and forgotten. About it like rags, when Colvin first beheld it, had hung scraps of posters: 'Harem Nights. Gay! Bright! ! Alluring ! ! !' But a few weeks ago the Hippodrome had reopened to admit the Tabard Players ('In Association with the Arts Council'); and, it was hoped, their audiences. The Tabard Players offered soberer joys: a new and respectable play each week, usually a light comedy or West End crook drama; but, on one occasion, *Everyman*. Malnik, their Manager, a youngish bald man, was an authority on the British Drama of the Nineteenth Century, upon which he had written an immense book, bursting with carefully verified detail. Colvin had met him one night in the Saloon Bar of the Emancipation Hotel; and, though neither knew anything of the other's subject, they had exchanged cultural life-belts in the ocean of apathy and incomprehensible interests which surrounded them. Malnik was lodging with the sad-faced Rector, who let rooms.

Tonight, having seen the curtain up on Act I, Malnik had come outside for a breath of the wind. There was something he wanted to impart; and, as he regarded the drizzling and indifferent town, Colvin obligingly came into sight. In a moment, he was inside Malnik's roomy but crumbling office.

'Look,' said Malnik.

He shuffled a heap of papers on his desk and handed Colvin a photograph. It was yellow, and torn at the edges. The subject was a wild-eyed young man with much dark curly hair and a blobby face. He was wearing a high stiff collar, and a bow like Chopin's.

'John Nethers,' said Malnik. Then, when no light of rapture flashed from Colvin's face, he said 'Author of *Cornelia*.'

'Sorry,' said Colvin, shaking his head.

'John Nethers was the son of a chemist in this town. Some books say a miner, but that's wrong. A chemist. He killed himself at twenty-two. But before that I've traced that he'd written at least six plays.

[83]

Cornelia, which is the best of them, is one of the great plays of the nineteenth century.'

'Why did he kill himself?'

'It's in his eyes. You can see it. *Cornelia* was produced in London with Arabella Rokeby. But never here. Never in the author's own town. I've been into the whole thing closely. Now we're going to do *Cornelia* for Christmas.'

'Won't you lose money?' asked Colvin.

'We're losing money all the time, old man. Of course we are. We may as well do something we shall be remembered by.'

Colvin nodded. He was beginning to see that Malnik's life was a single-minded struggle for the British Drama of the Nineteenth Century and all that went with it.

'Besides I'm going to do *As You Like It* also. As a fill-up.' Malnik stooped and spoke close to Colvin's ear as he sat in a bursting leather armchair, the size of a Judge's seat. 'You see, Arabella Rokeby's *coming*'.

'But how long is it since —'

'Better not be too specific about that. They say it doesn't matter with Arabella Rokeby. She can get away with it. Probably in fact she can't. Not altogether. But all the same, think of it. Arabella Rokeby in *Cornelia*. In *my* theatre.'

Colvin thought of it.

'Have you ever seen her?'

'No, I haven't. Of course she doesn't play regularly nowadays. Only special engagements. But in this business one has to take a chance sometimes. And golly what a chance!'

'And she's willing to come? I mean at Christmas,' Colvin added, not wishing to seem rude.

Malnik did seem slightly unsure. 'I have a contract,' he said. Then he added: 'She'll love it when she gets here. After all: *Cornelia*! And she must know that the nineteenth-century theatre is my subject.' He had seemed to be reassuring himself, but now he was glowing.

'But *As You Like It*'? said Colvin, who had played Touchstone at his preparatory school. 'Surely she can't manage Rosalind?'

'It was her great part. Happily you can play Rosalind at any age. Wish I could get old Ludlow to play Jaques. But he won't.' Ludlow was the company's veteran.

'Why not?'

'He played with Rokeby in the old days. I believe he's afraid she'll see he isn't the Grand Old Man he should be. He's a good chap, but proud. Of course he may have other reasons. You never know with Ludlow.'

The curtain was down on Act I.

Colvin took his leave and resumed his walk.

Shortly thereafter Colvin read about the Nethers Gala in the local evening paper ('this forgotten poet', as the writer helpfully phrased it), and found confirmation that Miss Rokeby was indeed to grace it ('the former London star'). In the same issue of the paper appeared an editorial to the effect that wide-spread disappointment would be caused by the news that the Hippodrome would not be offering a pantomime at Christmas in accordance with the custom of the town and district.

'She can't 'ardly stop 'ere, Mr Colvin,' said Mrs Royd, when Colvin, thinking to provide forewarning, showed her the news, as she lent a hand behind the saloon bar. 'This isn't the Cumberland. She'd get across the staff.'

'I believe she's quite elderly,' said Colvin soothingly.

'If she's elderly, she'll want special attention, and that's often just as bad.'

'After all, where she goes is mainly a problem for her, and perhaps Mr Malnik.'

'Well, there's nowhere else in town for her to stop, is there?' retorted Mrs Royd with fire. 'Not nowadays. She'll just 'ave to make do. We did for theatricals in the old days. Midgets once. Whole troupe of 'em.'

'I'm sure you'll make her very comfortable.'

'Can't see what she wants to come at all for, really. Not at Christmas.'

'Miss Rokeby needs no *reason* for her actions. What she does is sufficient in itself. You'll understand that, dear lady, when you meet her.' The speaker was a very small man, apparently of advanced years, white-haired, and with a brown sharp face, like a Levantine. The bar was full, and Colvin had not previously noticed him, although he was conspicuous enough, as he wore an overcoat with a fur collar and a scarf with a large black pin in the centre. 'I wonder if *I* could beg a room for a few nights,' he went on. 'I assure you I'm no trouble at all.'

'There's only Number Twelve A. It's not very comfortable,' replied Mrs Royd sharply.

'Of course you must leave room for Miss Rokeby.'

'Nine's for her. Though I haven't had a word from her.'

'I think she'll need two rooms. She has a companion.'

'I can clear out Greta's old room upstairs. If she's a friend of yours, you might ask her to let me know when she's coming.'

'Not a friend,' said the old man, smiling. 'But I follow her career.'

Mrs Royd brought a big red book from under the bar.

'What name, please?'

'Mr Superbus,' said the little old man. He had yellow, expressionless eyes.

'Will you register?'

Mr Superbus produced a gold pen, long and fat. His writing was so curvilinear that it seemed purely decorative, like a design for ornamental ironwork. Colvin noticed that he paused slightly at the 'Permanent Address' column, and then simply wrote (although it was difficult to be sure) what appeared to be 'North Africa'.

'Will you come this way?' said Mrs Royd, staring suspiciously at the newcomer's scrollwork in the visitor's book. Then, even more suspiciously, she added: 'What about luggage?'

Mr Superbus nodded gravely. 'I placed two bags outside.'

'Let's hope they're still there. They're rough in this town, you know.'

'I'm sure they're still there,' said Mr Superbus.

As he spoke the door opened suddenly and a customer almost fell into the bar. 'Sorry, Mrs Royd,' he said with a mildness which in the circumstances belied Mrs Royd's words. 'There's something on the step.'

'My fault, I'm afraid,' said Mr Superbus. 'I wonder—have you a porter?'

'The porter works evenings at the Hippodrome nowadays. Scene-shifting and that.'

'Perhaps I could help?' said Colvin.

On the step outside were what appeared to be two very large suitcases. When he tried to lift one of them, he understood what Mr Superbus had meant. It was remarkably heavy. He held back the bar door, letting in a cloud of cold air. 'Give me a hand, someone,' he said.

The customer who had almost fallen volunteered, and a short procession, led by Mrs Royd, set off along the little dark passage to Number Twelve A. Colvin was disconcerted when he realized that

Twelve A was the room at the end of the passage, which had no number on its door and had never, he thought, been occupied since his arrival; the room, in fact, next to his.

'Better leave these on the floor,' said Colvin, dismissing the rickety luggage-stand.

'Thank you,' said Mr Superbus, transferring a coin to the man who had almost fallen. He did it like a conjuror unpalming something.

'I'll send Greta to make up the bed,' said Mrs Royd. 'Tea's at six.'

'At six?' said Mr Superbus, gently raising an eyebrow. 'Tea?' Then, when Mrs Royd and the man had gone, he clutched Colvin very hard on the upper part of his left arm. 'Tell me,' enquired Mr Superbus, 'are you in love with Miss Rokeby? I overheard you defending her against the impertinence of our hostess.'

Colvin considered for a moment.

'Why not admit it?' said Mr Superbus, gently raising the other eyebrow. He was still clutching Colvin's arm much too hard.

'I've never set eyes on Miss Rokeby.'

Mr Superbus let go. 'Young people nowadays have no imagination,' he said with a whinny, like a wild goat.

Colvin was not surprised when Mr Superbus did not appear for tea (pressed beef and chips that evening).

After tea Colvin, instead of going for a walk, wrote to his mother. But there was little to tell her, so that at the end of the letter he mentioned the arrival of Mr Superbus. 'There's a sort of sweet blossomy smell about him like a meadow,' he ended. 'I think he must use scent.'

When the letter was finished, Colvin started trying to construct tables of output from the lead and plumbago mines a century ago. The partitions between the bedrooms were thin, and he began to wonder about Mr Superbus's nocturnal habits.

He wondered from time to time until the time came for sleep; and wondered a bit also as he dressed the next morning and went to the bathroom to shave. For during the whole of this time no sound whatever had been heard from Number Twelve A, despite the thinness of the plywood partition; a circumstance which Colvin already thought curious when, during breakfast, he overheard Greta talking to Mrs Royd in the kitchen. 'I'm ever so sorry, Mrs Royd. I forgot about it with the crowd in the bar.' To which Mrs Royd simply replied: 'I wonder what 'e done about it. 'E could 'ardly do without sheets or blankets, and this December. Why didn't 'e *ask*?' And when Greta said, 'I suppose nothing ain't happened to him?' Colvin put down his porridge spoon and unobtrusively joined the party which went out to find out.

Mrs Royd knocked several times upon the door of Number Twelve A, but there was no answer. When they opened the door, the bed was bare as Colvin had seen it the evening before, and there was no sign at all of Mr Superbus except that his two big cases lay on the floor, one beside the other.

'What's he want to leave the window open like that for?' enquired Mrs Royd. She shut it with a crash. 'Someone will fall over those cases in the middle of the floor.'

Colvin bent down to slide the heavy cases under the bed. But the pair of them now moved at a touch.

Colvin picked one case up and shook it slightly. It emitted a muffled flapping sound, like a bat in a box. Colvin nearly spoke, but stopped himself, and stowed the cases, end on, under the unmade bed in silence.

'Make up the room, Greta,' said Mrs Royd. 'It's no use just standing about.' Colvin gathered that it was not altogether unknown for visitors to the Emancipation Hotel to be missing from their rooms all night.

But there was a further little mystery. Later that day in the bar, Colvin was accosted by the man who had helped to carry Mr Superbus's luggage.

'Look at that.' He displayed, rather furtively, something which lay in his hand.

It was a sovereign.

'He gave it me last night.'

'Can I see it?' It had been struck in Queen Victoria's reign, but gleamed like new.

'What d'you make of that?' asked the man.

'Not much,' replied Colvin, returning the pretty piece. 'But now I come to think of it, *you* can make about forty-five shillings.'

When this incident took place, Colvin was on his way to spend three or four nights in another town where lead and plumbago mining had formerly been carried on, and where he needed to consult an invaluable collection of old records which had been presented to the Public Library at the time the principal mining company went bankrupt.

On his return, he walked up the hill from the station through a thick mist, laden with coal dust and sticky smoke, and apparently in no way diminished by a bitter little wind, which chilled while hardly troubling to blow. There had been snow, and little archipelagos of slush remained on the pavements, through which the immense boots of the miners crashed noisily. The male population wore heavy mufflers and were unusually silent. Many of the women wore shawls over their heads in the manner of their grandmothers.

Mrs Royd was not in the bar, and Colvin hurried through it to his old room, where he put on a thick sweater before descending to tea. The only company consisted in two commercial travellers, sitting at the same table and eating through a heap of bread and margarine but saying nothing. Colvin wondered what had happened to Mr Superbus.

Greta entered as usual with a pot of strong tea and a plate of bread and margarine.

'Good evening, Mr Colvin. Enjoy your trip?'

'Yes, thank you, Greta. What's for tea?'

'Haddock and chips.' She drew a deep breath. 'Miss Rokeby's come . . . I don't think she'll care for haddock and chips do you, Mr Colvin?' Colvin looked up in surprise. He saw that Greta was trembling. Then he noticed that she was wearing a thin black dress, instead of her customary casual attire.

Colvin smiled up at her. 'I think you'd better put on something warm. It's getting colder every minute.'

But at that moment the door opened and Miss Rokeby entered.

Greta stood quite still, shivering all over, and simply staring at her. Everything about Greta made it clear that this was Miss Rokeby. Otherwise the situation was of a kind which brought to Colvin's mind the cliché about there being some mistake.

The woman who had come in was very small and slight. She had a triangular gazelle-like face, with very large dark eyes, and a mouth which went right across the lower tip of the triangle, making of her chin another, smaller triangle. She was dressed entirely in black, with a high-necked black silk sweater, and wore long black earrings. Her short dark hair was dressed like that of a faun; and her thin white hands hung straight by her side in a posture resembling some Indian statuettes which Colvin recalled but could not place.

Greta walked towards her, and drew back a chair. She placed Miss Rokeby with her back to Colvin.

'Thank you. What can I eat?' Colvin was undecided whether Miss

Rokeby's voice was high or low: it was like a bell beneath the ocean.

Greta was blushing. She stood, not looking at Miss Rokeby, but at the other side of the room, shivering and reddening. Then tears began to pour down her cheeks in a cataract. She dragged at a chair, made an unintelligible sound, and ran into the kitchen.

Miss Rokeby half turned in her seat, and stared after Greta. Colvin thought she looked quite as upset as Greta. Certainly she was very white. She might almost have been eighteen . . .

'Please don't mind. It's nerves, I think.' Colvin realized that his own voice was far from steady, and that he was beginning to blush also, he hoped only slightly.

Miss Rokeby had risen to her feet and was holding on to the back of her chair.

'I didn't say anything which could frighten her.'

It was necessary to come to the point, Colvin thought.

'Greta thinks the menu unworthy of the distinguished company.'

'What?' She turned and looked at Colvin. Then she smiled. 'Is that it?' She sat down again. 'What is it? Fish and chips?'

'Haddock. Yes.' Colvin smiled back, now full of confidence.

'Well. There it is.' Miss Rokeby made the prospect of haddock sound charming and gay. One of the commercial travellers offered to pour the other a fourth cup of tea. The odd little crisis was over.

But when Greta returned, her face seemed set and a trifle hostile. She had put on an ugly custard-coloured cardigan.

'It's haddock and chips.'

Miss Rokeby merely inclined her head, still smiling charmingly.

Before Colvin had finished, Miss Rokeby, with whom further conversation had been made difficult by the fact that she had been seated with her back to him, and by the torpid watchfulness of the commercial travellers, rose, bade him, 'Good evening', and left.

Colvin had not meant to go out again that evening, but curiosity continued to rise in him, and in the end he decided to clear his thoughts by a short walk, taking in the Hippodrome. Outside it had become even colder; the fog was thicker, the streets emptier.

Colvin found that the entrance to the Hippodrome had been transformed. From frieze to floor, the walls were covered with large photographs. The photographs were not framed, but merely mounted on big sheets of pasteboard. They seemed to be all the same size. Colvin saw at once that they were all portraits of Miss Rokeby.

The entrance hall was filled with fog, but the lighting within had been greatly reinforced since Colvin's last visit. Tonight the effect was mistily dazzling. Colvin began to examine the photographs. They depicted Miss Rokeby in the widest variety of costumes and make-up, although in no case was the name given of the play or character. In some Colvin could not see how he recognized her at all. In all she was alone. The number of the photographs, their uniformity of presentation, the bright swimming lights, the emptiness of the place (for the Box Office had shut) combined to make Colvin feel that he was dreaming. He put his hands before his eyes, inflamed by the glare and the fog. When he looked again, it was as if all the Miss Rokebys had been so placed that their gaze converged upon the spot where he stood. He closed his eyes tightly and began to feel his way to the door and the dimness of the street outside. Then there was a flutter of applause behind him; the evening's audience began to straggle out, grumbling at the weather; and Malnik was saying 'Hullo, old man. Nice to see you.'

Colvin gesticulated uncertainly. 'Did she bring them all with her?'

'Not a bit of it, old man. Millie found them when she opened up.'

'Where did she find them?'

'Just lying on the floor. In two whacking great parcels. Rokeby's agent, I suppose, though she appeared not to have one. Blest if I know, really. I myself could hardly shift one of the parcels, let alone two.'

Colvin felt rather frightened for a moment; but he only said: 'How do you like her?'

'Tell you when she arrives.'

'She's arrived.'

Malnik stared.

'Come back with me and see for yourself.'

Malnik seized Colvin's elbow. 'What's she look like?'

'Might be any age.'

All the time Malnik was bidding good night to patrons, trying to appease their indignation at being brought out on such a night.

Suddenly the lights went, leaving only a pilot. It illumined a photograph of Miss Rokeby holding a skull.

'Let's go,' said Malnik. 'Lock up, Frank, will you?'

'You'll need a coat,' said Colvin.

'Lend me your coat, Frank.'

*

[91]

On the short cold walk to the Emancipation Hotel, Malnik said little. Colvin supposed that he was planning the encounter before him. Colvin did ask him whether he had ever heard of a Mr Superbus, but he hadn't.

Mrs Royd was, it seemed, in a thoroughly bad temper. To Colvin it appeared that she had been drinking; and that she was one whom drink soured rather than mellowed. 'I've got no one to send,' she snapped. 'You can go up yourself, if you like. Mr Colvin knows the way.' There was a roaring fire in the bar, which after the cold outside seemed very overheated.

Outside Number Nine, Colvin paused before knocking. Immediately he was glad he had done so, because inside were voices speaking very softly. All the evening he had been remembering Mr Superbus's reference to a 'companion'.

In dumb-show he tried to convey the situation to Malnik, who peered at his efforts with a professional's dismissal of the amateur. Then Malnik produced a pocket-book, wrote in it, and tore out the page, which he thrust under Miss Rokeby's door. Having done this, he prepared to return with Colvin to the bar, and await a reply. Before they had taken three steps, however, the door was open, and Miss Rokeby was inviting them in.

To Colvin she said, 'We've met already', though without enquiring his name.

Colvin felt gratified; and at least equally pleased when he saw that the fourth person in the room was a tall, frail-looking girl with long fair hair drawn back into a tight bun. It was not the sort of companion he had surmised.

'This is Myrrha. We're never apart.'

Myrrha smiled slightly, said nothing, and sat down again. Colvin thought she looked positively wasted. Doubtless by reason of the cold, she wore heavy tweeds, which went oddly with her air of fragility.

'How well do you know the play?' asked Malnik at the earliest possible moment.

'Well enough not to play in it.' Colvin saw Malnik turn grey. 'Since you've got me here, I'll play Rosalind. The rest was lies. Do you know,' she went on, addressing Colvin, 'that this man tried to trick me? You're not in the theatre, are you?'

Colvin, feeling embarrassed, smiled and shook his head.

'*Cornelia* is a masterpiece,' said Malnik furiously. 'Nethers was a genius.'

[92]

Miss Rokeby simply said 'Was' very softly, and seated herself on the arms of Myrrha's armchair, the only one in the room. It was set before the old-fashioned gas-fire.

'It's announced. Everyone's waiting for it. People are coming from London. They're even coming from Cambridge.' Myrrha turned away her head from Malnik's wrath.

'I was told—Another English Classic. Not an out-pouring by little Jack Nethers. I won't do it.'

'*As You Like It* is only a fill-up. What more is it ever? *Cornelia* is the whole point of the Gala. Nethers was *born* in this town. Don't you understand?'

Malnik was so much in earnest that Colvin felt sorry for him. But even Colvin doubted whether Malnik's was the best way to deal with Miss Rokeby.

'Please play for me. Please.'

'Rosalind only.' Miss Rokeby was swinging her legs. They were young and lovely. There was more than one thing about this interview which Colvin did not care for.

'We'll talk it over in my office tomorrow.' Colvin identified this as a customary admission of defeat.

'This is a horrid place, isn't it?' said Miss Rokeby conversationally to Colvin.

'I'm used to it,' said Colvin, smiling. 'Mrs Royd has her softer side.'

'She's put poor Myrrha in a cupboard.'

Colvin remembered about Greta's old room upstairs.

'Perhaps she'd like to change rooms with me? I've been away and haven't even unpacked. It would be easy.'

'How kind you are! To that silly little girl! To me! And now to Myrrha! May I see?'

'Of course.'

Colvin took her into the passage. It seemed obvious that Myrrha would come also, but she did not. Apparently she left it to Miss Rokeby to dispose of her. Malnik sulked behind also.

Colvin opened the door of his room and switched on the light. Lying on his bed and looking very foolish was his copy of Bull's *Graphite and Its Uses*. He glanced round for Miss Rokeby. Then for the second time that evening, he felt frightened.

Miss Rokeby was standing in the ill-lit passage, just outside his doorway. It was unpleasantly apparent that she was terrified. Formerly pale, she was now quite white. Her hands were clenched, and she was

[93]

breathing unnaturally deeply. Her big eyes were half shut, and to Colvin it seemed that it was something she *smelt* which was frightening her. This impression was so strong that he sniffed the chilly air himself once or twice, unavailingly. Then he stepped forward, and his arms were around Miss Rokeby, who was palpably about to faint. Immediately Miss Rokeby was in his arms, such emotion swept through him as he had never before known. For what seemed a long moment, he was lost in the wonder of it. Then he was recalled by something which frightened him more than anything else, though for less reason. There was a sharp sound from Number Twelve A. Mr Superbus must have returned.

Colvin supported Miss Rokeby back to Number Nine. Upon catching sight of her, Myrrha gave a small but jarring cry, and helped her on to the bed.

'It's my heart,' said Miss Rokeby. 'My absurd heart.'

Malnik now looked more black than grey. 'Shall we send for a doctor?' he enquired, hardly troubling to mask the sarcasm.

Miss Rokeby shook her head once. It was the sibling gesture to her nod.

'Please don't trouble about moving,' she said to Colvin.

Colvin, full of confusion, looked at Myrrha, who was being resourceful with smelling-salts.

'Good night,' said Miss Rokeby, softly but firmly. And as Colvin followed Malnik out of the room, she touched his hand.

Colvin passed the night almost without sleep, which was another new experience for him. A conflict of feelings about Miss Rokeby, all of them strong, was one reason for insomnia: another was the sequence of sounds from Number Twelve A. Mr Superbus seemed to spend the night in moving things about and talking to himself. At first it sounded as if he were rearranging all the furniture in his room. Then there was a period, which seemed to Colvin timeless, during which the only noise was of low and unintelligible mutterings, by no means continuous, but broken by periods of silence and then resumed as before just as Colvin was beginning to hope that all was over. Colvin wondered whether Mr Superbus was saying his prayers. Ultimately the banging about recommenced. Presumably Mr Superbus was still dissatisfied with the arrangement of the furniture; or perhaps was returning it to its original dispositions. Then Colvin heard the sash-window thrown sharply open. He remembered the sound from the occasion when Mrs Royd had sharply shut it. After that silence continued. In the end Colvin turned on the light and looked at his watch. It had stopped.

At breakfast, Colvin asked when Mr Superbus was expected down. 'He doesn't come down,' replied Greta. 'They say he has all his meals out.'

Colvin understood that rehearsals began that day, but Malnik had always demurred at outsiders being present. Now, moreover, he felt that Colvin had seen him at an unfavourable moment, so that his cordiality was much abated. The next two weeks, in fact, were to Colvin heavy with anti-climax. He saw Miss Rokeby only at the evening meal, which, however, she was undeniably in process of converting from tea to dinner, by expending charm, will-power, and cash. Colvin participated in this improvement, as did even such few of the endless commercial travellers as wished to do so; and from time to time Miss Rokeby exchanged a few pleasant, generalities with him, though she did not ask him to sit at her table, nor did he, being a shy man, dare to invite her. Myrrha never appeared at all; and when on one occasion Colvin referred to her interrogatively, Miss Rokeby simply said, 'She pines, poor lamb,' and plainly wished to say nothing more. Colvin remembered Myrrha's wasted appearance, and concluded that she must be an invalid. He wondered if he should again offer to change rooms. After that single disturbed night, he had heard no more of Mr Superbus. But from Mrs Royd he had gathered that Mr Superbus had settled for several weeks in advance. Indeed, for the first time in years the Emancipation Hotel was doing good business.

It continued as cold as ever during all the time Miss Rokeby remained in the town, with repeated little snow storms every time the streets began to clear. The miners would stamp as they entered the bar until they seemed likely to go through to the cellar beneath; and all the commercial travellers caught colds. The two local papers, morning and evening, continued their efforts to set people against Malnik's now diminished Gala. When *Cornelia* was no longer offered, the two editors pointed out (erroneously, Colvin felt) that even now it was not too late for a pantomime: but Malnik seemed to have succeeded in persuading Miss Rokeby to reinforce *As You Like It* with a piece entitled *A Scrap of Paper* which Colvin had never heard of, but which an elderly local citizen whom the papers always consulted upon matters theatrical described as 'very old-fashioned'. Malnik caused further comment by proposing to open on Christmas Eve, when the unfailing tradition had been Boxing Night.

The final week of rehearsal was marred by an exceedingly distressing incident. It happened on the Tuesday. Coming in that morning from a cold visit to the Technical Institute Library, Colvin found in the stuffy little saloon bar a number of the Tabard Players. The Players usually patronized an establishment nearer to the Hippodrome; and the fact that the present occasion was out of the ordinary was emphasized by the demeanour of the group, who were clustered together and talking in low, serious voices. Colvin knew none of the players at all well, but the group looked so distraught that, partly from curiosity and partly from compassion, he ventured to enquire of one of them, a middle-aged actor named Shillitoe to whom Malnik had introduced him, what was the matter. After a short silence, the group seemed collectively to decide upon accepting Colvin among them, and all began to enlighten him in short strained bursts of over-eloquence. Some of the references were not wholly clear to Colvin, but the substance of the story was simple.

Colvin gathered that when the Tabard Players took possession of the Hippodrome, Malnik had been warned that the 'grid' above the stage was undependable, and that scenery should not be 'flown' from it. This restriction had caused grumbling, but had been complied with until, during a rehearsal of A Scrap of Paper, the producer had rebelled and asked Malnik for authority to use the grid. Malnik had agreed; and two stage-hands began gingerly to pull on some of the dusty lines which disappeared into the almost complete darkness far above. Before long one of them had cried out that there was 'something up there already'. At these words, Colvin was told, everyone in the theatre fell silent. The stage-hand went on paying out line, but the stage was so ample and the grid so high that an appreciable time passed before the object came slowly into view.

The narrators stopped, and there was a silence which Colvin felt must have been like the silence in the theatre. Then Shillitoe resumed: 'It was poor old Ludlow's body. He'd hanged himself right up under the grid. Eighty feet above the floor of the stage. Some time ago, too. He wasn't in the Christmas plays, you know. Or in this week's play. We all thought he'd gone home.'

Colvin learnt that the producer had fainted right away; and, upon tactful enquiry, that Miss Rokeby had fortunately not been called for that particular rehearsal.

On the first two Sundays after her arrival, Miss Rokeby had been no more in evidence than on any other day; but on the morning of the third Sunday Colvin was taking one of his resolute lonely walks across the windy fells which surrounded the town when he saw her walking ahead of him through the snow. The snow lay only an inch or two deep upon the hillside ledge along which the path ran; and Colvin had been wondering for some time about the small footsteps which preceded him. It was the first time he had seen Miss Rokeby outside the Emancipation Hotel, but he had no doubt that it was she he saw, and his heart turned over at the sight. He hesitated; then walked faster, and soon had overtaken her. As he drew near, she stopped, turned, and faced him. Then, when she saw who it was, she seemed unsurprised. She wore a fur coat with a collar which reached almost to the tip of her nose; a fur hat; and elegant boots which laced to the knee.

'I'm glad to have a companion,' she said gravely, sending Colvin's thought to her other odd companion. 'I suppose you know all these paths well?'

'I come up here often to look for lead-workings. I'm writing a dull book on lead and plumbago mining.'

'I don't see any mines up here.' She looked around with an air of grave bewilderment.

'Lead mines aren't like coal mines. They're simply passages in hillsides.'

'What do you do when you find them?'

'I mark them on a large-scale map. Sometimes I go down them.'

'Don't the miners object?'

'There are no miners.'

A shadow crossed her face.

'I mean, not any longer. We don't mine lead any more.'

'Don't we? Why not?'

'That's a complicated story.'

She nodded. 'Will you take me down a mine?'

'I don't think you'd like it. The passages are usually both narrow and low. One of the reasons why the industry's come to an end is that people would no longer work in them. Besides, now the mines are disused, they're often dangerous.'

She laughed. It was the first time he had ever heard her do so. 'Come on.' She took hold of his arm. 'Or aren't there any mines on this particular hillside?' She looked as concerned as a child.

'There's one about a hundred feet above our heads. But there's nothing to see. Only darkness.'

'Only *darkness*,' cried Miss Rokeby. She implied that no reasonable person could want more. 'But you don't go down all these passages only to see darkness?'

'I take a flashlight.'

'Have you got it now?'

'Yes.' Colvin never went to the fells without it.

'Then that will look after *you*. Where's the mine? Conduct me.'

They began to scramble together up the steep snow-covered slope. Colvin knew all the workings round here; and soon they were in the entry.

'You see,' said Colvin. 'There's not even room to stand, and a fat person couldn't get in at all. You'll ruin your coat.'

'I'm not a fat person.' There was a small excited patch in each of her cheeks. 'But you'd better go first.'

Colvin knew that this particular working consisted simply in a long passage, following the vein of lead. He had been to the end of it more than once. He turned on his flashlight. 'I assure you, there's nothing to see,' he said. And in he went.

Colvin perceived that Miss Rokeby seemed indeed to pass along the adit without even stooping or damaging her fur hat. She insisted on going as far as possible, although near the end Colvin made a quite strenuous effort to persuade her to let them return.

'What's that?' enquired Miss Rokeby when they had none the less reached the extremity of the passage.

'It's a big fault in the limestone. A sort of cave. The miners chucked their débris down it.'

'Is it deep?'

'Some of these faults are supposed to be bottomless.'

She took the light from his hand, and, squatting down on the brink of the hole, flashed it round the depths below.

'Careful,' cried Colvin. 'You're on loose shale. It could easily slip.' He tried to drag her back. The only result was that she dropped the flashlight, which went tumbling down the great hole like a meteor, until after many seconds they heard a faint crash. They were in complete darkness.

'I'm sorry,' said Miss Rokeby's voice. 'But you did push me.'

Trying not to fall down the hole, Colvin began to grope his way back. Suddenly he had thought of Malnik, and the irresponsibility of the proceedings upon which he was engaged appalled him. He begged Miss Rokeby to go slowly, test every step, and mind her head; but her unconcern seemed complete. Colvin tripped and toiled along for an endless period of time, with Miss Rokeby always close behind him, calm, sure of foot, and unflagging. As far into the earth as this, it was both warm and stuffy. Colvin began to fear that bad air might overcome them, forced as they were to creep so laboriously and interminably. He broke out in heavy perspiration.

Suddenly he knew that he would have to stop. He could not even pretend that it was out of consideration for Miss Rokeby. He subsided upon the floor of the passage and she seated herself near him, oblivious of her costly clothes. The blackness was still complete.

'Don't feel unworthy,' said Miss Rokeby softly. 'And don't feel frightened. There's no need. We shall get out.'

Curiously enough, the more she said, the worse Colvin felt. The strange antecedents to this misadventure were with him; and, even more so, Miss Rokeby's whole fantastic background. He had to force his spine against the stone wall of the passage if he were not to give way to panic utterly and leap up screaming. Normal speech was impossible.

'Is it me you are frightened of?' asked Miss Rokeby, with dreadful percipience.

Colvin was less than ever able to speak.

'Would you like to know more about me?'

Colvin was shaking his head in the dark.

'If you'll promise not to tell anyone else.'

But, in fact, she was like a child, unable to contain her secret.

'I'm sure you won't tell anyone else . . . It's my helper. He's the queer one. Not me.'

Now that the truth was spoken Colvin felt a little better. 'Yes,' he said in a low, shaken voice, 'I know.'

'Oh, you know . . . I don't see him or—' she paused—'or encounter him, often for years at a time. Years.'

'But you encountered him the other night?'

He could feel her shudder. 'Yes . . . You've seen him?'

'Very briefly . . . How did you . . . encounter him first?'

'It was years ago. Have you any idea how many years?'

'I think so.'

Then she said something which Colvin never really understood; not even later, in his dreams of her. 'You know I'm not here at all, really.

Myrrha's me. That's why she's called Myrrha. That's how I act.'

'How?' said Colvin. There was little else to say.

'My helper took my own personality out of me. Like taking a nerve out of a tooth. Myrrha's my personality.'

'Do you mean your soul?' asked Colvin.

'Artists don't have souls,' said Miss Rokeby. 'Personality's the word . . . I'm anybody's personality. Or everybody's. And when I lost my personality, I stopped growing older. Of course I have to look after Myrrha, because if anything happened to Myrrha—well, you do see,' she continued.

'But Myrrha looks as young as you do.'

'That's what she *looks*.'

Colvin remembered Myrrha's wasted face.

'But how can you live without a personality? Besides,' added Colvin, 'you seem to me to have a very strong personality.'

'I have a mask for every occasion.'

It was only the utter blackness, Colvin felt, which made this impossible conversation possible.

'What do you do in exchange? I suppose you must repay your helper in some way?'

'I suppose I must . . . I've never found out what way it is.'

'What else does your helper do for you?'

'He smooths my path. Rids me of people who want to hurt me. He rid me of little Jack Nethers. Jack was mad, you know. You can see it even in his photograph.'

'Did he rid you of this wretched man Ludlow?'

'I don't know. You see, I can't remember Ludlow. I think he often rids me of people that I don't know want to hurt me.'

Colvin considered.

'Can you be rid of him?'

'I've never really tried.'

'Don't you *want* to be rid of him?'

'I don't know. He frightens me terribly whenever I come near him, but otherwise . . . I don't know . . . But for him I should never have been down a lead mine.'

'How many people know all this?' asked Colvin after a pause.

'Not many. I only told you because I wanted you to stop being frightened.'

As she spoke the passage was filled with a strange sound. Then they were illumined with icy December sunshine. Colvin perceived that they were almost at the entry to the working, and supposed that the portal must have been temporarily blocked by a miniature avalanche of melting snow. Even now there was, in fact, only a comparatively small hole, through which they would have to scramble.

'I told you we'd get out,' said Miss Rokeby. 'Other people haven't believed a word I said. But now *you'll* believe me.'

Not the least strange thing was the matter-of-fact manner in which, all the way back, Miss Rokeby questioned Colvin about his researches into lead and plumbago mining, with occasionally, on the perimeter of their talk, flattering enquiries about himself; although equally strange, Colvin considered, was the matter-of-fact manner in which he answered her. Before they were back in the town he was wondering how much of what she had said in the darkness of the mine had been meant only figuratively; and after that he wondered whether Miss Rokeby had not used the circumstances to initiate an imaginative and ingenious boutade. After all, he reflected, she was an actress. Colvin's hypothesis was, if anything, confirmed when at their parting she held his hand for a moment and said: 'Remember! *No one.*'

But he resolved to question Mrs Royd in a business-like way about Mr Superbus. An opportunity arose when he encountered her after luncheon (at which Miss Rokeby had not made an appearance), reading *The People* before the fire in the saloon bar. The bar had just closed, and it was, Mrs Royd explained, the only warm spot in the house. In fact it was, as usual, hot as a kiln.

'Couldn't say, I'm sure,' replied Mrs Royd to Colvin's firm enquiry, and implying that it was neither her business nor his. 'Anyway, 'e's gone. Went last Tuesday. Didn't you notice, with 'im sleeping next to you?'

After the death of poor Ludlow (the almost inevitable verdict was suicide while of unsound mind), it was as if the papers felt embarrassed about continuing to carp at Malnik's plans; and by the opening night the editors seemed ready to extend the Christmas spirit even to Shakespeare. Colvin had planned to spend Christmas with his mother; but when he learned that Malnik's first night was to be on Christmas Eve, had been unable to resist deferring his departure until after it, despite the perils of a long and intricate railway journey on Christmas Day. With Miss Rokeby, however, he now felt entirely unsure of himself.

On Christmas Eve the town seemed full of merriment. Colvin was surprised at the frankness of the general rejoicing. The shops, as is usual in industrial districts, had long been off-setting the general drabness with drifts of Christmas cards and whirlpools of tinsel. Now every home seemed to be decorated and all the shops to be proclaiming bonus distributions and bumper share-outs. Even the queues, which were a prominent feature of these celebrations, looked more sanguine, Colvin noticed, when he stood in one of them for about half an hour in order to send Miss Rokeby some flowers, as he felt the occasion demanded. By the time he set out for the Hippodrome, the more domestically-minded citizens were everywhere quietly toiling at preparations for the morrow's revels; but a wilder minority, rebellious or homeless, were inaugurating such a carouse at the Emancipation Hotel as really to startle the comparatively retiring Colvin. He suspected that some of the bibbers must be Irish.

Sleet was slowly descending as Colvin stepped out of the sweltering bar in order to walk to the Hippodrome. A spot of it sailed gently into the back of his neck, chilling him in a moment. But notwithstanding the weather, notwithstanding the claims of the season and the former attitude of the Press, there was a crowd outside the Hippodrome such as Colvin had never previously seen there. To his great surprise, some of the audience were in evening dress; many of them had expensive cars, and one party, it appeared, had come in a closed carriage with two flashing black horses. There was such a concourse at the doors that Colvin had to stand a long time in the slowly falling sleet before he was able to join the throng which forced its way, like icing on to a cake, between the countless glittering photographs of beautiful Miss Rokeby. The average age of the audience, Colvin observed, seemed very advanced, and especially of that section of it which was in evening dress. Elderly white-haired men with large noses and carnations in their buttonholes spoke in elegant Edwardian voices to the witch-like ladies on their arms, most of whom wore hot-house gardenias.

Inside, however, the huge and golden Hippodrome looked as it was intended to look when it was still named the Grand Opera House. From his gangway seat in the stalls Colvin looked backwards and upwards at the gilded satyrs and bacchantes who wantoned on the dress-circle balustrade; and at the venerable and orchidaceous figures who peered above them. The small orchestra was frenziedly playing selections from *L'Étoile du Nord*. In the gallery distant figures, unable

[102]

to find seats, were standing watchfully. Even the many boxes, little used and dusty, were filling up. Colvin could only speculate how this gratifying assembly had been collected. But then he was on his feet for the National Anthem, and the faded crimson and gold curtain, made deceivingly splendid by the footlights, was about to rise.

The play began, and then: 'Dear Celia, I show more mirth than I am mistress of, and would you yet I were merrier? Unless you could teach me to forget a banished father, you must not learn me how to remember any extraordinary pleasure.'

Colvin realized that in his heart he had expected Miss Rokeby to be good, to be moving, to be lovely; but the revelation he now had was something he could never have expected because he could never have imagined it; and before the conclusion of Rosalind's first scene in boy's attire in the Forest, he was wholly and terribly bewitched.

No one coughed, no one rustled, no one moved. To Colvin, it seemed as if Miss Rokeby's magic had strangely enchanted the normally journeyman Tabard Players into miracles of judgment. Plainly her spell was on the audience also; so that when the lights came up for the interval, Colvin found that his eyes were streaming, and felt not chagrin, but pride.

The interval was an uproar. Even the bells of fire-engines pounding through the wintry night outside could hardly be heard above the din. People spoke freely to unknown neighbours, groping to express forgotten emotions. 'What a prelude to Christmas!' everyone said. Malnik was proved right in one thing.

During the second half, Colvin, failing of interest in Sir Oliver Martext's scene, let his eyes wander round the auditorium. He noticed that the nearest dress-circle box, previously unoccupied, appeared to be unoccupied no longer. A hand, which, being only just above him, he could see was gnarled and hirsute, was tightly gripping the box's red velvet curtain. Later in the scene between Silvius and Phebe (Miss Rokeby having come and gone meanwhile), the hand was still there, and still gripping tightly; as it was (after Rosalind's big scene with Orlando) during the Forester's song. At the beginning of Act V, there was a rush of feet down the gangway, and someone was crouching by Colvin's seat. It was Greta. 'Mr Colvin! There's been a fire. Miss Rokeby's friend jumped out of the window. She's terribly hurt. Will you tell Miss Rokeby?'

'The play's nearly over,' said Colvin. 'Wait for me at the back.' Greta withdrew, whimpering.

After Rosalind's Epilogue the tumult was millennial. Miss Rokeby, in Rosalind's white dress, stood for many seconds not bowing but quite still and unsmiling, with her hands by her sides as Colvin had first seen her. Then as the curtain rose and revealed the rest of the company, she began slowly to walk backwards upstage. Door-keepers and even stage-hands, spruced up for the purpose, began to bring armfuls upon armfuls of flowers, until there was a heap, a mountain of them in the centre of the stage, so high that it concealed Miss Rokeby's figure from the audience. Suddenly a bouquet flew through the air from the dress-circle box. It landed at the very front of the heap. It was a hideous dusty laurel wreath, adorned with an immense and somewhat tasteless purple bow. The audience were yelling for Miss Rokeby like Dionysians; and the company, flagging from unaccustomed emotional expenditure, and plainly much scared, were looking for her; but in the end the stage-manager had to lower the Safety Curtain and give orders that the house be cleared.

Back at the Emancipation Hotel, Colvin, although he had little title, asked to see the body.

'You wouldn't ever recognize her,' said Mrs Royd. Colvin did not pursue the matter.

The snow, falling ever more thickly, had now hearsed the town in silence.

'She didn't 'ave to do it,' wailed on Mrs Royd. 'The brigade had the flames under control. And tomorrow Christmas Day!'

CHRISTMAS EVE

Ronald Chetwynd-Hayes

Ronald Chetwynd-Hayes (b. 1919)
is one of Britain's most successful and prolific
writers of horror stories, with paperback sales
alone in excess of one million copies. Among his
more recent titles are *Tales of Darkness*, *The
House of Dracula*, *Dracula's Children*, and *The
Curse of the Snake God*. 'Christmas Eve' is taken
from one of his earlier collections, published only
in paperback, *The Night Ghouls* (1975).

Andrew Nesbitt was a wanderer.

Had he been less endowed with this world's goods he would doubtlessly have been a tramp; one of those unfortunates who trudge with bowed heads along never-ending roads and live like stray cats on charitable scraps, thrown to them by a contemptuous society. But Andrew could afford to wander in comfort.

His usual procedure was to buy a railway ticket for some far-off destination, then alight at any station that looked interesting. But of course it rarely was. Most towns look alike; the majority of hotels offer the same service—or lack of it—and all houses are impregnable fortresses, if one has no right of entry. But the urge to keep moving, to see the sky from a different window, was a disease for which he could find no cure—nor did he want to.

It was Christmas Eve when he arrived at Mansville, a little town some twenty miles from the south coast. The shops were bright with plastic goodwill; a large Christmas tree stood in the hotel foyer and the receptionist said: 'The compliments of the season, sir.'

Andrew felt a warm glow of subdued excitement as he unpacked his bag. He still enjoyed Christmas, for although time had expelled him from the land of childhood, he still sought ways and means of recapturing its memories. Christmas was a time of bright lights and roaring log fires, paper-chains and Tiny Tim saying: 'God bless us, one and all.'

He was unlikely to find much of this in The Royal George Hotel, but the spirit of Christmas must surely walk down its corridors or sit enthroned in the large dining-room, while he ate turkey and tinned plum pudding. That he need have no doubt on that score, was demonstrated by a large card pinned on the door. It said in bright, tinsel-edged letters: THE MANAGEMENT WISHES A HAPPY CHRISTMAS AND A PROSPEROUS NEW YEAR TO ALL ITS PATRONS. Fortified by this desire for his well-being, Andrew went down to the restaurant and smiled at a waiter. He responded with a weak grin.

'Good evening, sir. What will it be?'

Andrew, in his present, uplifted mood, would have preferred a less mundane greeting, but he took the proffered menu and ordered roast beef, potatoes and brussels sprouts, with chocolate pudding to follow. Then he sat back and studied his surroundings.

Roughly two-thirds of the tables were occupied; mostly by family groups and parties that had come together for the festive season. But here and there was a solitary being like himself, trying to find colour in a glass of water. But he had no desire for companionship; it was enough to sit and watch; to hear voices, to dine among many but eat alone.

Andrew was mid-way through his roast beef when the girl entered the dining-room and made her way towards an empty table. He watched her with interest, because she was young and pretty, if somewhat pale. She sat down and after slipping out of the fur coat, which she allowed to drape over the chairback, jerked her head so that the rich, auburn hair flew back like a dark, red-tinted wing. Andrew waited until she had taken up the menu before lowering his eyes. She was only another face in the crowd; one more tiny spark of memory that would begin to die as soon as he had left the restaurant. But—and his eyes came slowly up again to study the pale face—would he forget? Her beauty was like a white flame; he experienced a stirring of, not so much desire, as a longing to possess. This was followed by a rising irritation. What right had she to come here and spoil his Christmas Eve? For that, he realized, was exactly what she had done. No matter how much he tried, his eyes would keep wandering back to that pale, flawless face, watching the long-fingered hands while they played with knife and fork. She made eating into an act of poetry—chewing with closed mouth, so that the movement of her jaw muscles was scarcely perceptible.

Then she looked up and for three seconds their eyes met. It seemed to Andrew's inflamed imagination that there was a flicker of recognition. Then she lowered her head and he was left in a limbo of pain.

Andrew went back to toying with his own meal, mentally listing a number of unpalatable truths. 'You are forty-five,' he told himself, 'ugly, balding and probably impotent. Suppose the impossible were to happen and she offered herself to you—what would you do with her?'

The answer was simple, of course. Nothing. But his madness lay beyond the realms of reason. He wanted to touch, look and own. Then he looked up and a great surge of relief made him want to laugh out aloud. She was gone. A half-empty plate and an abandoned knife and fork were the only evidence that she had ever existed. Andrew Nesbitt was like a man who has walked to the gallows, then at the last minute, been reprieved.

'Thank God,' he muttered. 'I am still free.'

The evening had surrendered its grey body into the dark arms of night, when Andrew Nesbitt made his way towards the church.

He was not a religious man—his faith had died long ago—but the midnight service on Christmas Eve still held for him the magic of childhood. The stained-glass windows, the subdued lights, the swelling organ music, the singing voices—again he would be truly alone in a crowd; a member of a congregation, yet not of it.

People sat in groups, occasionally exchanging low whispers as though somewhere—probably behind the candle-lit altar—there was a sleeping deity who must not be wakened. Andrew slid into an empty pew and allowed the warm, burnt-candle atmosphere to close in around him. The ghosts of the long dead must surely haunt old churches. The world outside might be an alien, frightening place, but here was a pocket of time, where only those memories which were comforting, need be preserved. He was playing with this fantasy when the organ began its melodious music and the choir filed out of the vestry. He did not join in the responses, but he did sing those carols which he knew; the prayers he ignored, merely bowing his head and lapsing into thought.

A sound disturbed him. It was low, not more than a choking sigh, but at once his attention was alerted and he jerked his head round in sudden alarm. The girl from the restaurant was sitting on the far end of the pew and she appeared to be crying. Anger and a fierce joy made his heart beat faster; they were followed almost at once by a sense of frustration. Sad or happy she could do no more than disturb his peace of mind. The isolation which cut him off from the rest of his fellow creatures, would not—could not—exclude her. He watched the slight trembling of her shoulders and was relieved that the mane of auburn hair hid her face. When they rose to sing the next carol, he was only too aware that she was not singing, and suddenly the urge to look sideways could not be resisted.

His eyes came round, then froze into a shocked stare. She was watching him. The beautiful, tear-filled eyes looked straight into his and they seemed to flash an appeal—a plea for help that frightened and confused him. Then she abruptly turned and left the pew, pausing once to look back at him over her shoulder, and walked quickly towards the main door.

The remainder of the service was a period of exquisite torture. He should have followed her out. Now he would never know why, and live the rest of his life under the shadow of a giant question mark.

The congregation filed out of church and dispersed, leaving Andrew to walk his lonely way across the square. It was when he reached the narrow dark passage leading to the main street, that the girl came out from the shadows and said: 'Please, help me.'

At that moment he knew his life would never be the same again. Up till then the world had been populated by two kinds of people—him and them. Now someone had broken the barrier. He said: 'What can I do?'

She came close to him and the beautiful grey eyes searched his face. 'You must know.'

For an awful moment he wondered if she was a prostitute who had the originality to procure her clients from a church, and a sick joke flashed across his brain, 'Lust after righteousness'. He dismissed the thought as ridiculous. There was a terrible fear in those eyes, he could almost taste the terror.

'Sorry, I don't understand.'

'But—you're one of us.'

He shook his head in bewilderment.

'I still don't understand . . .'

She repeated the statement with more emphasis.

'You are one of us. Please—you must help me.'

She gripped his arm and began to pull him into the passage.

'You know . . . Come quickly . . .'

He was led—pulled like a half-reluctant mule—along the passage and out into a narrow street. Presently the girl began to speak.

'I only went out for an hour. He seemed all right and I had to get away for a while. I've had to watch him for three weeks—you know how it is. Then when I got back . . .'

She began to cry again and Andrew, not knowing the cause of her grief, could only pat her hand and make sympathetic noises. Presently she was able to continue.

'I never expected to see you in church. I only went there in desperation—you know. The vibrations are sometimes pretty strong in those places. Then I recognized you from the hotel dining-room. Did you get my message?'

'Message?' he repeated the word dully.

She gave him a quick glance. 'You're a non-receptive, aren't you? Must be, or you would have followed me out. But I knew I couldn't be mistaken—I picked up your mental image. You are one of the few. What's your name?'

Andrew had not parted with his Christian name for over twenty years and now it seemed he was committing some kind of sacrilege. 'Nesbitt—Andrew—Andrew Nesbitt.'

'I am Janet Gurney. Have you got a cocoon-knife on you?'

'Knife!'

'No, I don't suppose you have. Non-receps never seem to carry anything useful. How you manage in an emergency, I don't know. Never mind, I've sharpened up some carvers at home. Can you walk a bit faster?'

Andrew obediently lengthened his stride until they were walking a little too fast for comfort. But the girl did not appear in the least distressed and continued to talk in a normal tone.

'He looked awful when I got back from the restaurant—all blown up and surface-hardening had taken place. You know what I mean. But he was still able to speak—there were no air-bubbles in the windpipe —and he said: "Try to find one of us, you'll never be able to handle this on your own." It was then I thought of you. Wasn't I lucky I found you in that church?'

He said, 'Yes,' not knowing what else to say, and uncomfortably aware that they were moving swiftly through streets that looked neither respectable nor healthy. At last she stopped at a door to the right of a dilapidated bookshop, and, fumbling in her coat pocket, produced a Yale key.

'It's only two flights up,' she said as they trudged up a dimly lit staircase. 'The change-over hit him on the first landing. I had an awful job getting him up to our rooms. Thanks be to All-Power, no one saw him.'

The second landing was an evil place with a single green painted door, lit by a twenty-five watt bulb. Janet Gurney opened the door and hurried into the room beyond. Andrew followed and watched the girl as she slipped out of her coat, allowing it to fall to the floor.

'Go into the bedroom,' she nodded towards another door, 'and I will put some water on to boil. See what you think of him. We have about three hours before he strangles.'

She went into what was presumably the kitchen and left Andrew staring at the closed bedroom door. Questions reared up like venomous snakes and demanded answers. Every instinct ordered him to leave that awful room and run back to the world he understood. But he knew he was at the mercy of the demon with a blank face. Curiosity. He must know what lay behind the bedroom door, even if that knowledge meant madness.

The door, with its cracked paint and dented brass handle, seemed to deny that it would hide anything that could shock or horrify. It might be disgusting, possibly, even revolting. Andrew could imagine a room with faded wallpaper, a bed with soiled sheets and curtains that hung in tattered drapes. But not something that required a knife before it strangled. He closed his eyes, opened them, took a deep breath, then opened the door and went in.

The room did justice to his imagination. The pink wallpaper was faded, the green curtains were dusty and moth-eaten and the sheets, which were flung back over the end of the bed, were most certainly soiled. Like a reluctant snail, he crept towards the bed and whatever lay naked upon it.

He tried not to believe the evidence of his dilated eyes. His paralysed brain was numb with horror. What was it? He remembered, with that curious memory reflex that sometimes operates in moments of stress, an advertisement for car tyres that depicted a grotesque rubber man. The thing on the bed could well have been a duplicate. The skin—if indeed the dark grey, flaccid substance could be so called—was ridged in deep, rounded folds from bulging head to bloated foot. The eyes and mouth were buried in six-inch deep pits; the fingers and toes merely ridged stumps. The continuous, obscene movement sent Andrew screaming to the door. Every ridge pulsated, and at regular intervals rippled; a weird twittering sound came from the deeply buried mouth-hole.

The girl came in with three large knives clasped in one hand and two rubber aprons slung over one arm. She laid the knives down on an old-fashioned wash-stand, then handed him an apron.

'Put this on,' she ordered. 'As you know, this is a messy job.'

He shrank back, pointing a shaking hand at the bed.

'In the name of sanity—what is it?'

For a moment the smooth flawless face assumed an expression of dawning surprise, then it changed to one of alarm.

'Don't tell me—Oh, God, don't tell me—you haven't matured.'

He shook his head slowly, not wanting to understand.

'I don't know what you're talking about.'

Her look of horrified despair was that of a bewildered child. Her choking whisper said: 'A nurseling. I had to find a nurseling . . .'

Terror became diluted with pity; and pity turned into a warm flood of tenderness, so that Andrew wanted to take her slim body into his arms and promise to do anything she asked. Anything at all. His fear and repugnance retreated and he said: 'I don't understand. I don't think I want to, but if I can help . . .'

She seized his words as though they were lifelines and clasped his hands in a surprisingly firm grip.

'You will help? You'll do anything I ask? You promise?'

There was only a slight hesitation, then he nodded. 'Tell me what I must do.'

'First, I'll fetch hot water. We must soak the outer pelt—soften it, you understand, otherwise it will blunt the knives. Put the apron on.'

When she had left the room, he put the apron on, examining the ridged horror with something like interest now. It was at least human-shaped. There was no neck worth mentioning, nor any trace of arm or leg joints, but—Andrew tried to ignore an ominous heave in his stomach—a few short black hairs stood up from the ridged skull. He tried to think logically. It was as though the skin had risen up and left all but the longest strands of hair behind. Also, when he peered down into the eyepits, he could see a little fringe of black lashes sprouting round tiny pools of blue.

The girl came back carrying a bowl of steaming water and a pile of towels slung over her left shoulder. She put the bowl down, then proceeded to soak a towel, which she handed to Andrew.

'Lay it across his chest, then push it well down so the water gets into the ridges.'

Andrew did what he was told. When he pressed the thing billowed out on both sides and the arms assumed the proportions of giant sausages. The girl handed him another towel.

'Knead,' she instructed. 'Don't be afraid to put the pressure on. He won't burst.'

As Andrew obeyed, the head inflated and became a monstrous, humped bulge; the eye and mouth holes disappeared and the twittering sound merged into a shrill whistle.

'Harder,' the girl ordered with something like impatience. 'We must soften the outer casing, otherwise you won't get through.'

With perspiration pouring down his face, Andrew kneaded, punched, pressed and heaved, while the thing under his hands bulged, squirmed, rippled, expanded and deflated. He felt like a baker trying to make a mis-shapen loaf.

'I think that will do,' she said after a while. 'Give me the towels, I'll put them back in the bowl, just in case. Do you want a rest before cutting?'

Andrew wiped his brow. 'If I have time to think, I'll never start. Let's get on with it.'

'Right.' She picked up the largest knife. 'Now, listen carefully. I'll sit on his legs and that will make your job a little easier, because then his chest will blow up and stretch the skin. You must make the first cut just under his throat, then slit downwards. I should stand back as far as you can—otherwise you'll get soaked. Have you got all that?'

Andrew tried to nod but gurgled instead.

Without further words, the girl lowered herself down on to the legs and instantly the chest assumed the proportions of an embryo mountain.

'Now,' she shouted, 'stick the knife in.'

Andrew placed the knife point just under the ridged chin and pressed down. The skin bulged on either side, one quarter of the knife disappeared, but the razor-sharp point refused to penetrate.

'Press harder,' the girl ordered. 'Use all your weight.'

Andrew did his best. He even jumped and pressed down at the same time, but the tough skin would not give and at length he sank down on a chair.

'It's no use, I can't get through.' He mopped his streaming brow and tried to regain his breath. 'It's like trying to cut through granite.'

Janet wriggled as though to make herself more comfortable on the grotesque legs, then wiped away a solitary tear.

'Won't you try again? Once you've got through, the rest shouldn't be too difficult.'

It is in the depths of despair that the best ideas are found. Andrew sat up.

'Have you got a hammer?'

She frowned. 'Yes, I think so. Why?'

'Fetch it.'

She brought him a hammer, a heavy affair with a gleaming head. He examined it with some satisfaction.

'Should do the trick. Right, back on his legs.'

The young mountain was reformed, the head grew big and Andrew replaced the knife-point where the throat should have been. Then holding the knife steady, he brought the hammer down on to its handle. The effect was instantaneous. Twin fountains shot up from either side of the knife-blade and generously sprayed Andrew's apron. The girl cried out for joy.

'You are clever,' she said. 'Now slit downwards.'

It took him five minutes to enlarge the hole, and another half an hour before he had a sizeable incision. By now, what appeared to be water was flowing out in a continuous stream and splashing down on to the floor. The girl handed him a bread-knife.

'You can saw the rest of the way down. Then we can slip the skin over his head and the job will be finished.'

Gradually the skin parted and as it did so, the rest of the hideous cocoon was covered in a network of criss-crossing wrinkles, so that it resembled a length of crumpled leather.

'I'll take over now,' the girl said quietly.

Andrew watched with horrified fascination as she plunged her hands into the slit and stretched it to its fullest extent. He had a glimpse of a wet, pink body, then she said: 'Catch hold of the loose head-skin,' and together they eased the cocoon (what else could it be?) over a head, pulled it down and down, until it finally parted company from a pair of feet with a nasty squelching sound. The girl held up the ridged, crumpled skin.

[113]

'When it's washed,' she said thoughtfully, 'it will make up nicely into a dress for wearing round the house.'

But Andrew Nesbitt was looking at the figure on the bed. A young man with a mop of black, curling hair, finely formed features and the body of a god. But he was wet and pink. Slimy wet and pink. The girl must have noticed his look of horror, for she laughed softly.

'He won't always be like that, silly. When I've washed him and given him his first feed, he'll be beautiful. Simply beautiful.'

'Then he . . .'

Janet's eyes were bright and her voice was husky with loving pride. 'Has just been reborn. We all have to go through this stage, sooner or later.' She looked at Andrew with a certain, proprietary affection. 'It will happen to you one day.'

'Are you sure . . .?' he began, but she smilingly interrupted him.

'Absolutely certain. But don't worry, when the time comes, we will know. After all, one good turn deserves another. Now . . .' She began to usher him towards the door. 'You must go.'

'But . . .' the apron was off and he was being eased into his overcoat, '. . . won't I ever see you again?'

'Of course.' The main door was open and the awful landing was waiting. 'When you need us, we'll be there. But tomorrow is moving day. We can never stay long in one place—can we?'

'No, I suppose not.' He was out on the landing, the door was slowly closing. Her beautiful face smiled, her grey eyes glittered, and her soft voice mocked.

'Thank you for everything. And—oh, yes—a merry Christmas.'

The door shut. Time snapped back into place.

The desk-receptionist looked up as a white-faced Andrew staggered in through the swing-doors. He grinned.

'Been celebrating Christmas, sir?'

Andrew grunted.

'Never mind, sir. It only comes once a year.'

Andrew did not bother to answer, but staggered towards the lift.

Upstairs, he went into the bedroom and quickly stripped. Then, naked, he walked over to the wardrobe mirror and examined his body with lively interest. His legs were thin and hairy, his belly sagged, his shoulders bowed, and there were pronounced pouches under his eyes. He looked tired, old and ugly. Aloud, he asked the all-important question.

'What the bloody hell am I?'

THE NIGHT
BEFORE
CHRISTMAS

Robert Bloch

Robert Bloch (b. 1917) is one of
America's best-known writers of horror stories, a
worthy successor to Edgar Allan Poe and H. P.
Lovecraft. Since 1935 he has written hundreds of
short stories, including many classics celebrated
for their macabre twists and 'shock' endings. He
adapted some of these for the movies *Torture
Garden*, *Asylum*, *The House that Dripped Blood*,
and *The Skull* (all starring Peter Cushing).
Among his novels are *Night-World*, *American
Gothic*, and the immortal *Psycho*, filmed by Alfred
Hitchcock. 'The Night Before Christmas' is
taken from Bloch's American collection
Midnight Pleasures (1987).

I don't know how it ends.

Maybe it ended when I heard the shot from behind the closed
door to the living room—or when I ran out and found him lying
there.

Perhaps the ending came after the police arrived; after the inter-
rogation and explanation and all that lurid publicity in the media.

Possibly the real end was my own breakdown and eventual recovery
—if indeed I ever fully recovered.

It could be, of course, that something like this never truly ends as long as memory remains. And I remember it all, from the very beginning.

Everything started on an autumn afternoon with Dirk Otjens, at his gallery on La Cienega. We met at the door just as he returned from lunch. Otjens was late; very probably he'd been with one of his wealthy customers and such people seem to favour late luncheons.

'Brandon!' he said. 'Where've you been? I tried to get hold of you all morning.'

'Sorry—an appointment—'

Dirk shook his head impatiently. 'You ought to get yourself an answering service.'

No sense telling him I couldn't afford one, or that my appointment had been with the unemployment office. Dirk may have known poverty himself at one time, but that was many expensive luncheons ago, and now he moved in a different milieu. The notion of a starving artist turned him off, and letting him picture me in that role was—like hiring an answering service—something I could not now afford. It had been a break for me to be taken on as one of his clients, even though nothing had happened so far.

Or had it?

'You've made a sale?' I tried to sound casual, but my heart was pounding.

'No. But I think I've got you a commission. Ever hear of Carlos Santiago?'

'Can't say that I have.'

'Customer of mine. In here all the time. He saw that oil you did—you know, the one hanging in the upstairs gallery—and he wants a portrait.'

'What's he like?'

Dirk shrugged. 'Foreigner. Heavy accent.' He spoke with all of the disdain of a naturalized American citizen. 'Some kind of shipping magnate, I gather. But the money's there.'

'How much?'

'I quoted him twenty-five hundred. Not top dollar, but it's a start.'

Indeed it was. Even allowing for his cut, I'd still clear enough to keep me going. The roadblock had been broken, and somewhere up ahead was the enchanted realm where everybody has an answering service to take messages while they're out enjoying expensive lunches of their own. Still—

'I don't know,' I said. 'Maybe he's not a good subject for me. A

Spanish shipping tycoon doesn't sound like my line of work. You know I'm not one of those artsy-craftsy temperamental types, but there has to be a certain chemistry between artist and sitter or it just doesn't come off.'

From Dirk's scowl I could see that what I was saying didn't come off either, but it had to be stated. I am, after all, an artist. I spent nine years learning my craft here and abroad—nine long hard years of self-sacrifice and self-discovery which I didn't intend to toss away the first time somebody waved a dollar bill in my direction. If that's all I cared about, I might as well go into mass production, turning out thirty-five-dollar clowns by the gross to sell in open-air shows on supermarket lots. On the other hand—

'I'd have to see him first,' I said.

'And so you shall.' Dirk nodded. 'You've got a three o'clock appointment at his place.'

'Office?'

'No, the house. Up in Trousdale. Here, I wrote down the address for you. Now get going, and good luck.'

I remember driving along Coldwater, then making a right turn on to one of those streets leading into the Trousdale Estates. I remember it very well, because the road ahead climbed steeply along the hillside and I kept wondering if the car would make the grade. The old heap had an inferiority complex and I could imagine how it felt, wheezing its way past the semicircular driveways clogged with shiny new Cadillacs, Lancias, Alfa Romeos, and the inevitable Rolls. This was a neighbourhood in which the Mercedes was the household's second car. I didn't much care for it myself, but Dirk was right: the money was here.

And so was Carlos Santiago.

The car in his driveway was a Ferrari. I parked behind it, hoping no one was watching from the picture window of the sprawling two-storey pseudo palazzo towering above the cypress-lined drive. The house was new and the trees were still small, but who was I to pass judgment? The money was here.

I rang the bell. Chimes susurrated softly from behind the heavy door; it opened, and a dark-haired, uniformed maid confronted me. 'Yes, please?'

'Arnold Brandon. I have an appointment with Mr Santiago.'

She nodded. 'This way. The *señor* waits for you.'

I moved from warm afternoon sunlight into the air-conditioned chill of the shadowy hall, following the maid to the arched doorway of the living room at our left.

The room, with its high ceiling and recessed fireplace, was larger than I'd expected. And so was my host.

Carlos Santiago called himself a Spaniard; as I later learned, he'd been born in Argentina and undoubtedly there was *indio* blood in his veins. But he reminded me of a native of Crete.

The Minotaur.

Not literally, of course. Here was no hybrid, no man's body topped by the head of a bull. The greying curly hair fell over a forehead unadorned by horns, but the heavily lidded eyes, flaring nostrils, and neckless merging of huge head and barrel chest somehow suggested a mingling of the taurine and the human. As an artist, I saw in Santiago the image of the man-bull, the bull-man, the incarnation of macho.

And I hated him at first sight.

The truth is, I've always feared such men; the big, burly, arrogant men who swagger and bluster and brawl their way through life. I do not trust their kind, for they have always been the enemies of art, the book burners, smashers of statues, contemptuous of all creation which does not spurt from their own loins. I fear them even more when they don the mask of cordiality for their own purposes.

And Carlos Santiago was cordial.

He seated me in a huge leather chair, poured drinks, inquired after my welfare, complimented the sample of my work he'd seen at the gallery. But the fear remained, and so did the image of the Minotaur. *Welcome to my labyrinth.*

I must admit the labyrinth was elaborately and expensively designed and tastefully furnished. All of which only emphasized the discordant note in the decor—the display above the fireplace mantel. The rusty, broad-bladed weapon affixed to the wall and flanked by grainy, poorly framed photographs seemed as out of place in this room as the hulking presence of my host.

He noted my stare, and his chuckle was a bovine rumble.

'I know what you are thinking, *amigo*. The oh-so-proper interior decorator was shocked when I insisted on placing those objects in such a setting. But I am a man of sentiment, and I am not ashamed.

'The machete—once it was all I possessed, except for the rags on my back. With it I sweated in the fields for three long years as a common labourer. At the end I still wore the same rags and it was still my only

[118]

possession. But with the money I had saved I made my first investment —a few tiny shares in a condemned oil tanker, making its last voyage. The success of its final venture proved the beginning of my own. I spare you details; the story is in those photographs. These are the ships I came to acquire over the years, the Santiago fleet. Many of them are old and rusty now, like the machete—like myself, for that matter. But we belong together.'

Santiago poured another drink. 'But I bore you, Mr Brandon. Let us speak now of the portrait.'

I knew what was coming. He would tell me what and how to paint, and insist that I include his ships in the background; perhaps he intended to be shown holding the machete in his hand.

He was entitled to his pride, but I had mine. God knows I needed the money, but I wasn't going to paint the Minotaur in any setting. No sense avoiding the issue; I'd have to take the bull by the horns—

'Louise!'

Santiago turned and rose, smiling as she entered. I stared at the girl—tall, slim, tawny-haired, with flawless features dominated by hazel eyes. The room was radiant with her presence.

'Allow me to present my wife.'

Both of us must have spoken, acknowledging the introduction, but I can't recall what we said. All I remember is that my mouth was dry, my words meaningless. It was Santiago's words that were important.

'You will paint her portrait,' he said.

That was the beginning.

Sittings were arranged for in the den just beyond the living room; north light made afternoon sessions ideal. Three times a week I came—first to sketch, then to fill in the background. Reversing the usual procedure, I reserved work on the actual portraiture until all of the other elements were resolved and completed. I wanted her flesh tones to subtly reflect the coloration of setting and costume. Only then would I concentrate on pose and expression, capturing the essence. But how to capture the sound of the soft voice, the elusive scent of perfume, the unconscious grace of movement, the totality of her sensual impact?

I must concede that Santiago, to his credit, proved cooperative. He never intruded upon the sittings, nor inquired as to their progress. I'd stipulated that neither he nor my subject inspect the work before completion; the canvas was covered during my absence. He did not disturb me with questions, and after the second week he flew off to the Middle East on business, loading tankers for a voyage.

While he poured oil across troubled waters, Louise and I were alone.

We were, of course, on a first-name basis now. And during our sessions we talked. *She* talked, rather; I concentrated on my work. But in order to raise portraiture beyond mere representationalism the artist must come to know his subject, and so I encouraged such conversation in order to listen and learn.

Inevitably, under such circumstances, a certain confidential relationship evolves. The exchange, if tape-recorded, might very well be mistaken for words spoken in psychiatric therapy or uttered within the confines of the confessional booth.

But what Louise said was not recorded. And while I was an artist, exulting in the realization that I was working to the fullest extent of my powers, I was neither psychiatrist nor priest. I listened but did not judge.

What I heard was ordinary enough. She was not María Cayetano, Duchess of Alba, any more than I was Francisco José de Goya y Lucientes.

I'd already guessed something of her background, and my surmise proved correct. Hers was the usual story of the unusually attractive girl from a poor family. Cinderella at the high school prom, graduating at the stroke of midnight to find herself right back in the kitchen. Then the frantic effort to escape: runner-up in a beauty contest, failed fashion model, actress ambitions discouraged by the cattle calls where she found herself to be merely one of a dozen duplicates. Of course there were many who volunteered their help as agents, business managers or outright pimps; all of them expected servicing for their services. To her credit, Louise was too street-smart to comply. She still had hopes of finding her Prince. Instead, she met the Minotaur.

One night she was escorted to an affair where she could meet 'important people'. One of them proved to be Carlos Santiago, and before the evening ended he'd made his intentions clear.

Louise had the sense to reject the obvious, and when he attempted to force the issue she raked his face with her nails. Apparently the impression she made was more than merely physical, and next day the flowers began to arrive. Once he had progressed to earrings and bracelets, the ring was not far behind.

So Cinderella married the Minotaur, only to find life in the labyrinth not to her liking. The bull, it seemed, did a great deal of bellowing, but in truth he was merely a steer.

All this, and a great deal more, gradually came out during our sessions together. And led, of course, to the expected conclusion.

I put horns on the bull.

Justification? These things aren't a question of morality. In any case, Louise had no scruples. She'd sold herself to the highest bidder and it proved a bad bargain; I neither condemned nor condoned her. Cinderella had wanted out of the kitchen and took the obvious steps to escape. She lacked the intellectual equipment to find another route, and in our society—despite the earnest disclaimers of women's lib—Beauty usually ends up with the Beast. Sometimes it's a young Beast with nothing to offer but a state of perpetual rut; more often it's an ageing Beast who provides status and security in return for occasional coupling. But even that had been denied Louise; her Beast was an old bull whose pawings and snortings she could no longer endure. Meeting me had intensified natural need; it was lust at first sight.

As for me, I soon realized that behind the flawless façade of face and form there was only a vain and greedy child. She'd created Cinderella out of costume and coiffure and cosmetics; I'd perpetuated the pretence in pigment. It was not Cinderella who writhed and panted in my arms. But knowing this, knowing the truth, didn't help me. I loved the scullery maid.

Time was short, and we didn't waste it in idle declarations or decisions about the future. Afternoons prolonged into evenings and we welcomed each night, celebrating its concealing presence.

Harsh daylight followed quickly enough. It was on 18th December, just a week before Christmas, that Carlos Santiago returned. And on the following afternoon Louise and I met for a final sitting in the sunlit den.

She watched very quietly as I applied last-minute touches to the portrait: a few highlights in the burnished halo of hair, a softening of feral fire in the emerald-flecked hazel eyes.

'Almost done?' she murmured.

'Almost.'

'Then it's over.' Her pose remained rigid but her voice trembled.

I glanced quickly toward the doorway, my voice softening to a guarded whisper.

'Does he know?'

'Of course not.'

'The maid—'

'You always left after a sitting. She never suspected that you came back after she was gone for the night.'

'Then we're safe.'

'Is that all you have to say?' Her voice began to rise and I gestured quickly.

'Please—lower your head just a trifle—there, that's it—'

I put down my brush and stepped back. Louise glanced up at me.

'Can I look now?'

'Yes.'

She rose, moved to stand beside me. For a long moment she stared without speaking, her eyes troubled.

'What's the matter?' I said. 'Don't you like it?'

'Oh, yes—it's wonderful—'

'Then why so sad?'

'Because it's finished.'

'All things come to an end,' I said.

'Must they?' she murmured. 'Must they?'

'Mr Brandon is right.'

Carlos Santiago stood in the doorway, nodding. 'It has been finished for some time now,' he said.

I blinked. 'How do you know?'

'It is the business of every man to know what goes on in his own house.'

'You mean you looked at the portrait?' Louise frowned. 'But you gave Mr Brandon your word—'

'My apologies.' Santiago smiled at me. 'I could not rest until I satisfied myself as to just what you were doing.'

I forced myself to return his smile. 'You are satisfied now?'

'Quite.' He glanced at the portrait. 'A magnificent achievement. You seem to have captured my wife in her happiest mood. I wish it were within my power to bring such a smile to her face.'

Was there mockery in his voice, or just the echo of my own guilt?

'The portrait can't be touched for several weeks now,' I said. 'The paint must dry. Then I'll varnish it and we can select the proper frame.'

'Of course,' said Santiago. 'But first things first.' He produced a cheque from his pocket and handed it to me. 'Here you are. Paid in full.'

[122]

'That's very thoughtful of you—'

'You will find me a thoughtful man.' He turned as the maid entered, carrying a tray which held a brandy decanter and globular glasses.

She set it down and withdrew. Santiago poured three drinks. 'As you see, I anticipated this moment.' He extended glasses to Louise and myself, then raised his own. 'A toast to you, Mr Brandon. I appreciate your great talent, and your even greater wisdom.'

'Wisdom?' Louise gave him a puzzled glance.

'Exactly.' He nodded. 'I have no schooling in art, but I do know that a project such as this can be dangerous.'

'I don't understand.'

'There is always the temptation to go on, to overdo. But Mr Brandon knows when to stop. He has demonstrated, shall we say, the artistic conscience. Let us drink to his decision.'

Santiago sipped his brandy. Louise took a token swallow and I followed suit. Again I wondered how much he knew.

'You do not know just what this moment means to me,' he said. 'To stand here in this house, with this portrait of the one I love—it is the dream of a poor boy come true.'

'But you weren't always poor,' Louise said. 'You told me yourself that your father was a wealthy man.'

'So he was.' Santiago paused to drink again. 'I passed my childhood in luxury; I lacked for nothing until my father died. But then my older brother inherited the *estancia* and I left home to make my own way in the world. Perhaps it is just as well, for there is much in the past which does not bear looking into. But I have heard stories.' He smiled at me. 'There is one in particular which may interest you,' he said.

'Several years after I left, my brother's wife died in childbirth. Naturally he married again, but no one anticipated his choice. A nobody, a girl without breeding or background, but one imagines her youth and beauty enticed him.'

Did his sidelong glance at Louise hold a meaning or was that just *my* imagination? Now his eyes were fixed on me again.

'Unlike his first wife, his new bride did not conceive, and it troubled him. To make certain he was not at fault, during this period he fathered several children by various serving maids at the *estancia*. But my brother did not reproach his wife for her defects; instead he summoned a physician. His examination was inconclusive, but during its course he made another discovery: my brother's wife had the symptoms of an obscure eye condition, a malady which might someday bring blindness.

'The physician advised immediate surgery, but she was afraid the operation itself could blind her. So great was this fear that she made my brother swear a solemn oath upon the Blessed Virgin that, no matter what happened, no one would be allowed to touch her eyes.'

'Poor woman!' Louise repressed a shudder. 'What happened?'

'Naturally, after learning of her condition, my brother abstained from the further exercise of his conjugal rights. According to the physician it was still possible she might conceive, and if so perhaps her malady might be transmitted to the child. Since my brother had no wish to bring suffering into the world he turned elsewhere for his pleasures. Never once did he complain of the inconvenience she caused him in this regard. His was the patience of a saint. One would expect her to be grateful for his thoughtfulness, but it is the nature of women to lack true understanding.'

Santiago took another swallow of his drink. 'To his horror, my brother discovered that his wife had taken a lover. A young boy who worked as a gardener at the *estancia*. The betrayal took place while he was away; he now spent much time in Buenos Aires, where he had business affairs and the consolation of a sympathetic and understanding mistress.

'When the scandal was reported to him he at first refused to believe, but within weeks the evidence was unmistakable. His wife was pregnant.'

'He divorced her?' Louise murmured.

Santiago shrugged. 'Impossible. My brother was a religious man. But there was a need to deal with the gossip, the sly winks, the laughter behind his back. His reputation, his very honour, was at stake.'

I took advantage of his pause to jump in. 'Let me finish the story for you,' I said. 'Knowing his wife's fear of blindness, he insisted on the operation and bribed the surgeon to destroy her eyesight.'

Santiago shook his head. 'You forget: he had sworn to the *pobrecita* that her eyes would not be touched.'

'What did he do?' Louise said.

'He sewed up her eyelids.' Santiago nodded. 'Never once did he touch the eyes themselves. He sewed her eyelids shut with catgut and banished her to a guesthouse with a servingwoman to attend her every need.'

'Horrible!' Louise whispered.

'I am sure she suffered,' Santiago said. 'But mercifully, not for long. One night a fire broke out in the bedroom of the guesthouse while the servingwoman was away. No one knows how it started; perhaps my brother's wife knocked over a candle. Unfortunately the door was locked and the servingwoman had the only key. A great tragedy.'

I couldn't look at Louise, but I had to face him. 'And her lover?' I asked.

'He ran for his life, into the jungle. It was there that my brother tracked him down with the dogs and administered a suitable punishment.'

'What sort of punishment would that be?'

Santiago raised his glass. 'The young man was stripped and tied to a tree. His genitals were smeared with wild honey. You have heard of the fire ants, *amigo*? They swarmed in this area—and they will devour anything which bears even the scent of honey.'

Louise made a strangled sound in her throat, then turned and ran from the room.

Santiago gulped the rest of his drink. 'It would seem I have upset her,' he said. 'This was not my intention—'

'Just what was your intention?' I met the bull-man's gaze. 'Your story doesn't upset me. This is not the jungle. And you are not your brother.'

Santiago smiled. 'I have no brother,' he said.

I drove through dusk. Lights winked on along Hollywood Boulevard from the Christmas decorations festooning lamp-posts and arching overhead. Glare and glow could not completely conceal the shabbiness of sleazy storefronts or blot out the shadows moving past them. Twilight beckoned those shadows from their hiding places; no holiday halted the perpetual parade of pimps and pushers, chicken hawks and hookers, winos and heads. Christmas was coming, but the blaring of tape-deck carols held little promise for such as these, and none for me.

Stonewalling it with Santiago had settled nothing. The truth was that I'd made a little token gesture of defiance, then run off to let Louise face the music.

It hadn't been a pretty tune he'd played for the two of us, and now that she was alone with him he'd be free to orchestrate his fury. Was he really suspicious? How much did he actually know? And what would he do?

For a moment I was prompted to turn and go back. But what then?

[125]

Would I hold Santiago at bay with a tyre iron while Louise packed her things? Suppose she didn't want to leave with me? Did I really love her enough to force the issue?

I kept to my course but the questions pursued me as I headed home.

The phone was ringing as I entered the apartment. My hand wasn't steady as I lifted the receiver and my voice wasn't steady either.

'Yes?'

'Darling, I've been trying to reach you—'

'What's the matter?'

'Nothing's the matter. He's gone.'

'Gone?'

'Please—I'll tell you all about it when I see you. But hurry—'

I hurried.

And after I parked my car in the empty driveway, after we'd clung to one another in the darkened hall, after we settled on the sofa before the fireplace, Louise dropped her bombshell.

'I'm getting a divorce,' she said.

'Divorce—?'

'When you left he came to my room. He said he wanted to apologize for upsetting me, but that wasn't the real reason. What he really wanted to do was tell me how he'd scared you off with that story he'd made up.'

'And you believed him?'

'Of course not, darling! I told him he was a liar. I told him you had nothing to be afraid of, and he had no right to humiliate me. I said I was fed up listening to his sick raving, and I was moving out. That wiped the grin off his face in a hurry. You should have seen him; he looked like he'd been hit with a club!'

I didn't say anything, because I hadn't seen him. But I was seeing Louise now. Not the ethereal Cinderella of the portrait, and not the scullery maid; this was another woman entirely: hot-eyed, harsh-voiced, implacable in her fury.

Santiago must have seen as much, and more. He blustered, he protested, but in the end he pleaded. And when he tried to embrace her, things came full circle again. Once more she raked his face with her nails, but this time in final farewell. And it was he who left, stunned and shaken, without even stopping to pack a bag.

'He actually agreed to a divorce?' I said.

Louise shrugged. 'Oh, he told me he was going to fight it, but that's just talk. I warned him that if he tried to stop me in court I'd let it all

[126]

hang out—the jealousy, the drinking, everything. I'd even testify about how he couldn't get it up.' She laughed. 'Don't worry, I know Carlos. That's one kind of publicity he'd do anything to avoid.'

'Where is he now?'

'I don't know and I don't care.' The hot eyes blazed, the harsh voice sounded huskily in my ear. 'You're here,' she whispered.

And as her mouth met mine, I felt the fury.

I left before the maid arrived in the morning, just as I'd always done, even though Louise wanted me to stay.

'Don't you understand?' I said. 'If you want an uncontested divorce, you can't afford to have me here.'

Dirk Otjens recommended an attorney named Bernie Prager; she went to him and he agreed. He warned Louise not to be seen privately or in public with another man unless there was a third party present.

Louise reported to me by phone. 'I don't think I can stand it, darling—not seeing you—'

'Do you still have the maid?'

'Josefina? She comes in every day, as usual.'

'Then so can I. As long as she's there we have no problem. I'll just show up to put a few more finishing touches on the portrait in the afternoons.'

'And in the evenings—'

'That's when we can blow the whole deal,' I said. 'Santiago has probably hired somebody to check on you.'

'No way.'

'How can you be sure?'

'Prager's nobody's fool. He's used to handling messy divorce cases and he knows it's money in his pocket if he gets a good settlement.' Louise laughed. 'Turns out he's got private investigators on his own payroll. So Carlos is the one being tailed.'

'Where is your husband?'

'He moved into the Sepulveda Athletic Club last night, went to his office today—business as usual.'

'Suppose he hired a private eye by phone?'

'The office lines and the one in his room are already bugged. I told you Prager's nobody's fool.'

'Sounds like an expensive operation.'

'Who cares? Darling, don't you understand? Carlos has money

coming out of his ears. And we're going to squeeze out more. When this is over, I'll be set for life. We'll both be set for life.' She laughed again.

I didn't share her amusement. Granted, Carlos Santiago wasn't exactly Mr Nice. Maybe he deserved to be cuckolded, deserved to lose Louise. But was she really justified in taking him for a bundle under false pretences?

And was I any better if I stood still for it? I thought about what would happen after the divorce settlement was made. No more painting, no more hassling for commissions. I could see myself with Louise, sharing the sweet life, the big house, big cars, travel, leisure, luxuries. And yet, as I sketched a mental portrait of my future, my artist's eye noted a shadow. The shadow of one of those pimps prowling Hollywood Boulevard.

It wasn't a pretty picture.

But when I arrived in the afternoon sunshine of Louise's living room, the shadow vanished in the glow of her gaiety.

'Wonderful news, darling!' she greeted me. 'Carlos is gone.'

'You already told me—'

She shook her head. 'I mean really gone,' she said. 'Prager's people just came through with a report. He phoned in for reservations on the noon flight to New Orleans. One of his tankers is arriving there and he's going to supervise unloading operations. He won't be back until after the holidays.'

'Are you absolutely sure?'

'Prager sent a man to LAX. He saw Carlos take off. And all his calls are being referred to the company office in New Orleans.'

She hugged me. 'Isn't it marvellous? Now we can spend Christmas together.' Her eyes and voice softened. 'That's what I've missed the most. A real old-fashioned Christmas, with a tree and everything.'

'But didn't you and Carlos—'

Louise shook her head. 'Something always came up at the last minute—like this New Orleans trip. If we hadn't split, I'd be on that plane with him right now.

'Did you ever celebrate Christmas in Kuwait? That's where we were last year, eating lamb curry with some greasy port official. Carlos promised, no more holiday business trips, this year we'd stay home and have a regular Christmas together. You see how he kept his word.'

'Be reasonable,' I said. 'Under the circumstances what do you expect?'

'Even if this hadn't happened, it wouldn't change anything.' Once again her eyes smouldered and her voice harshened. 'He'd still go and drag me with him, just to show off in front of his business friends. "Look what I've got—hot stuff, isn't she? See how I dress her, cover her with fancy jewellery?" Oh yes, nothing's too good for Carlos Santiago; he always buys the best!'

Suddenly the hot eyes brimmed and the strident voice dissolved into a soft sobbing.

I held her very close. 'Come on,' I said. 'Fix your face and get your things.'

'Where are we going?'

'Shopping. For ornaments—and the biggest damned Christmas tree in town.'

If you've ever gone Christmas shopping with a child, perhaps you can understand what the next few days were like. We picked up our ornaments in the big stores along Wilshire; like Hollywood Boulevard, this street too was alive with holiday decorations and the sound of Yuletide carols. But there was nothing tawdry behind the tinsel, nothing mechanical about the music, no shadows to blur the sparkle in Louise's eyes. To her this make-believe was reality; each day she became a kid again, eager and expectant.

Nights found her eager and expectant too, but no longer a child. The contrast was exciting, and each mood held its special treasures.

All but one.

It came upon her late in the afternoon of the twenty-third, when the tree arrived. The delivery man set it up on a stand in the den and after he left we gazed at it together in the gathering twilight.

All at once she was shivering in my arms.

'What's the matter?' I murmured.

'I don't know. Something's wrong; it feels like there's someone watching us.'

'Of course.' I gestured towards the easel in the corner. 'It's your portrait.'

'No, not that.' She glanced up at me. 'Darling, I'm scared. Suppose Carlos comes back?'

'I phoned Prager an hour ago. He has transcripts of all your husband's calls up until noon today. Carlos phoned his secretary from New Orleans and said he'll be there through the twenty-seventh.'

'Suppose he comes back without notifying the office?'

'If he does he'll be spotted; Prager's keeping the airport staked out, just in case.' I kissed her. 'Now stop worrying. There's no sense being paranoid—'

'Paranoid.' I could feel her shivering again. 'Carlos is the one who's paranoid. Remember that horrible story he told us—'

'But it was only a story. He has no brother.'

'I think it's true. *He* did those things.'

'That's what he wanted us to think. It was a bluff, and it didn't work. And we're not going to let him spoil our holiday.'

'All right.' Louise nodded, brightening. 'When do we decorate the tree?'

'Christmas Eve,' I said. 'Tomorrow night.'

It was late the following morning when I left—almost noon—and already Josefina was getting ready to depart. She had some last-minute shopping to do, she said, for her family.

And so did I.

'When will you be back?' Louise asked.

'A few hours.'

'Take me with you.'

'I can't; it's a surprise.'

'Promise you'll hurry then, darling.' Her eyes were radiant. 'I can't wait to trim the tree.'

'I'll make it as soon as possible.'

But 'soon' is a relative term and—when applied to parking and shopping on the day before Christmas—an unrealistic one.

I knew exactly what I was looking for, but it was close to closing time in the little custom jewellery place where I finally found it.

I'd never bought an engagement ring before and didn't know if Louise would approve of my choice. The stone was a marquise cut but it looked tiny and insignificant in comparison with the diamonds Santiago had given her. Still, people are always saying it's the sentiment that counts. I hoped she'd feel that way.

When I stepped out on to the street again it was already ablaze with lights and the sky above had dimmed from dusk to darkness. On the way to my car I found a phone booth and put in a call to Prager's office.

There was no answer.

I might have anticipated his office would be closed: if there'd been a party, it was over now. Perhaps I could reach him at home after I got back to the house. On the other hand, why bother? If there'd been

[130]

anything to report he'd have phoned Louise immediately.

The real problem right now was fighting my way back to the parking lot, jockeying the car out into the street, and then enduring the start-stop torture of the traffic.

Celestial choirs sounded from the speaker system overhead.

'Silent night, holy night,
All is calm, all is bright—'

The honking of horns shattered silence with an unholy din; none of my fellow drivers were calm and I doubted if they were bright.

But eventually I battled my way on to Beverly Drive, crawling toward Coldwater Canyon. Here traffic was once again bumper-to-bumper; the hands of my watch inched to seven-thirty. I should have called Louise from that phone booth while I was at it and told her not to worry. Too late now; no public phones in this residential area. Besides, I'd be home soon.

Home.

As I edged into the turnoff which led up through the hillside, the word echoed strangely. This was my home now, or soon would be. *Our* home, that is. Our home, our cars, our money, Louise's and mine—

Nothing is yours. It's his home, his money, his wife. You're a thief. Stealing his honour, his very life—

I shook my head. *Crazy. That's the way Santiago would talk. He's the crazy one.*

I thought about the expression on the bull-man's face as he'd told me the story of his brother's betrayal and revenge. Was he really talking about himself? If so, he had to be insane.

And even if it was just a fantasy, its twisted logic only emphasized a madman's cunning. Swearing not to blind a woman by touching her eyes, and then sewing her eyelids shut—a mind capable of such invention was capable of anything.

Suddenly my foot was flooring the gas pedal; the car leaped forward, careening around the rising curves. I wrenched at the wheel with hands streaked by sweat, hurtling up the hillside past the big homes with their outdoor decorations and the tree lights winking from the windows.

There were no lights at all in the house at the crest of the hill—but when I saw the Ferrari parked in the driveway, I knew.

I jammed to a stop behind it and ran to the front door. Louise had given me a duplicate house key and I twisted it in the lock with a shaking hand.

The door swung open on darkness. I moved down the hall toward the archway at my left.

'Louise!' I called. 'Louise—where are you?'

Silence.

Or almost silence.

As I entered the living room I heard the sound of heavy breathing coming from the direction of the big chair near the fireplace.

My hand moved to the light switch.

'Don't turn it on.'

The voice was slurred, but I recognized it.

'Santiago—what are you doing here?'

'Waiting for you, *amigo*.'

'But I thought—'

'That I was gone? So did Louise.' A chuckle rasped through the darkness.

I took a step forward, and now I could smell the reek of liquor as the slurred whisper sounded again.

'You see, I know about the bugging of the phones and the surveillance. So when I returned this morning I took a different route, with a connecting flight from Denver. No one at the airport would be watching arrivals from that city. I meant to surprise Louise—but it was she who surprised me.'

'When did you get here?' I said.

'After the maid had left. Our privacy was not interrupted.'

'What did Louise tell you?'

'The truth, *amigo*. I had suspected, of course, but I could not be sure until she admitted it. No matter, for our differences are resolved.'

'Where is Louise? Tell me—'

'Of course. I will be frank with you, as she was with me. She told me everything—how much she loved you, what you planned to do together, even her foolish wish to decorate the tree in the den. Her pleading would have melted a heart of stone, *amigo*. I found it impossible to resist.'

'If you've harmed her—'

'I granted her wish. She is in the den now.' Santiago chuckled again, his voice trailing off into a spasm of coughing.

But I was already groping my way to the door of the den, flinging it open.

[132]

The light from the tree bulbs was dim, barely enough for me to avoid stumbling over the machete on the floor. Quickly I looked up at the easel in the corner, half expecting to see the painting slashed. But Louise's portrait was untouched.

I forced myself to gaze down at the floor again, dreading what I might see, then breathed a sigh of relief. There was nothing on the floor but the machete.

Stooping, I picked it up, and now I noticed the stains on the rusty blade—the red stains slowly oozing in tiny droplets to the floor.

For a moment I fancied I could actually hear them fall, then realized they were too minute and too few to account for the steady dripping sound that came from—

It was then that Santiago must have shot himself in the other room, but it was not the sudden sound which prompted my scream.

I stared at the Christmas tree, at the twinkling lights twining gaily across its huge boughs, and at the oddly shaped ornaments draped and affixed to its spiky branches. Stared, and screamed, because the madman had told the truth.

Louise was decorating the Christmas tree.

THE GREATER ARCANA

Ron Weighell

Ron Weighell (b. 1950) is among
Britain's most gifted short story writers,
and his fine tales 'The Case of the Fiery
Messengers' and 'Carven of Onyx' were highlights
of earlier O'Mara anthologies *Mystery for
Christmas* and *Tales of Witchcraft* respectively.
This new story reflects his interest in the
writings of M. R. James, Arthur Machen, and
the western magical tradition.

'"Against the feast of Christmas",' quoted Dr Northwoode with relish, '"every man's house, also their parish churches, were decked with holme, ivy, bayes, and whatsoever the season afforded to be green".'

'It would appear that you have taken that injunction literally,' laughed Professor Dodds. And indeed Northwoode's cosy college rooms, once the dwelling place of a great aesthete and art critic, were decorated with garlands, wreath, and Christmas tree. He had invited a few academic colleagues for a little festive cheer and the talk had come round to old traditions of Christmas.

'That passage you just quoted,' added Dodds, 'isn't there something about a Christmas tree attacked by evil spirits?'

'Yes, that's right. Stow adds that at Candlemas "a standard of tree", as he puts it, "nailed full of holme and ivie for disport of Christmas"—

lovely phrase that, isn't it—was torn up by a malignant spirit in the form of a great storm.'

'By holme,' interjected someone, 'I take him to mean holly.'

Northwoode nodded. 'Then as now a favourite evergreen at this season, though yew and rosemary were also used to deck the halls; even—and this is interesting in view of its present-day associations—even cypress!'

'Let us not forget mistletoe,' added a romantic soul, wistfully.

'But never in churches,' responded Daniels, 'never mistletoe, because of its pagan associations.'

'And yet', rejoined Northwoode, lighting his pipe, 'I seem to remember that at York there was a time when mistletoe was actually carried in solemn procession into the cathedral on Christmas Eve and laid on the high altar! And as long as it lay there, universal pardon and liberty were offered at the four gates of the city.'

'How extraordinary,' said Campbell; 'why should that be, I wonder?'

'Well, for nearly a hundred years York was the capital of the Scandinavian Kingdom founded by Halfdan. To the Scandinavians, mistletoe was sacred. In any case it is a strange survival.'

This led to a discussion as to whether parents would so readily encourage their children to leave offerings for Santa if they realized how like the God Woden he was. The romantic soul raised the question of the kissing bunch, prompting reminiscences of its remembered pleasures. Then the talk got round to ghosts, and a few old college tales were told. Northwoode's particular interest in such matters was well known, so it was perhaps inevitable that he should be pressed to contribute an account from his experience. He sat for a moment watching the smoke from his pipe, then began his story:

It's funny that you should ask that this evening [said Northwoode] because an experience I once had in a college not far from here came back to mind earlier today, as I was out walking. It happened at just this time of year, and I'm afraid that I was, in a way, the cause of all the trouble. It happened this way. I had been invited to a Christmas gathering not unlike this one in the rooms of a good friend of mine, and had left at the same time as a young fellow called Hillyer, who lodged in the city and was engaged in postgraduate research. He was a pleasant enough chap, if a little earnest for my taste; he had no sense of humour. Our way took us down a narrow flight of stone steps into the college cloister, and there we paused to look at a quite remarkable sight.

[135]

The cloisters of our great colleges harbour many examples of the grotesque and antique, and not all of them are human. For over four hundred years, stone-masons have indulged their wildest flights of fancy, producing a clutch of monsters to rival the medieval cathedrals of Europe; we were looking upon the strangest of them. It is a sight familiar to you all, I am sure. Picture it as it was on that night. On three sides of the cloister, upon twenty-two tall pedestals overgrown with ivy and beset by ancient wistaria, stood an assortment of creatures that would have staggered the imagination of a Poe or a Lovecraft. Those in human form were odd enough but the rest were so weird, so suggestive in their incongruous complexity of an arcane and cryptic symbolism that they had become known as the Greater Arcana. In the light of day they can appear quaint, haunting, even a little disturbing. Sensitive souls have been known to ask for a change of rooms rather than live with such forms perpetually crouched outside their windows. By night—and particularly on that bitter December night—with the cloisters in deep shadow, the contorted arms of the wistaria all ghostly with rime, and moonglow glittering diamond hard and diamond cold about their hoar-frosted heads—they were the embodiment of authentic nightmare.

Hillyer was one of those people who suffer short-lived enthusiasms. He would work feverishly on some subject for a few months, then drop it overnight for some new fad. The subject of his research had already changed three times to my knowledge, and now I was alarmed to find that it had taken on yet another form. He spoke ten to the dozen about the Arcana, and how they would furnish the perfect subject for his thesis. I had grown tired of criticizing his gadfly mind, for I had begun to sound like Mr Badger addressing Toad, so I tried to go along with him, pointing out that the symbolism of the Arcana might enable him to encompass every aspect of sixteenth-century philosophy and art into his work. To my dismay, he replied that his approach was to be somewhat less orthodox. He had decided to explore the links between the statues and the fantasy novelist E. R. Bellman, who had written a booklet about them, and in one of whose rooms Hillyer now lived. Much as I admired Bellman's novels on the level of entertainment, I could not see members of the Research Degrees Committee accepting them as a suitable subject for a thesis. Hillyer was adamant, however, claiming that he had discovered something new about Bellman's links with the Arcana that was little less than sensational.

We were still discussing the matter heatedly when we came to the parting of the ways at Devil's Den.

If you think as I do that this sinister alley is aptly named at the best of times, you should have seen it that night, with a crystalline vapour of cold wreathing under the lamps in the oppressive space between its high walls. I joked about it, saying that I was glad to be going the other way, but Hillyer did not seem amused. I reminded him that we were to take part in carol singing for charity around the streets on the next Wednesday, and with that we parted. The matter went completely out of my mind. It seems, however, that Hillyer gave the matter much thought and decided to take some photographs of the Greater Arcana as aids to his research, and possibly as illustrations to the final text.

During the night the first snow of the year fell on the city. Hillyer awoke to a morning of slush on the roads and intermittent sleet on the grey air; but so great was his enthusiasm that he wrapped up well, took up his photographic equipment and set off early to take some preliminary studies. At that hour the cloisters were deserted, the snow on the grass still unmelted. Quite unconsciously he began to photograph the most grotesque of the monsters, had completed studies of three and was setting up his tripod before a fourth, when he became aware of a plump priest in cloak and wide-brimmed hat, observing him from the cloister. Hillyer thought the figure not unlike the silhouette of Father Brown on the spine of a book he had once owned. The priest approached, and Hillyer's heart sank. He had pursued the hobby of photography long enough to anticipate some such inane comment as 'taking pictures, are you?' so he was surprised when the old priest—if priest he was—called to him in a high-pitched, cultivated voice.

'That is not wise, sir, not wise at all.'

'I am sorry,' Hillyer replied. 'I don't understand—'

'Photographing Ripley's Arcana. I would not advise it.'

'Oh really, and whyever not?'

'Because, sir, they are the glyphographs of a pernicious alchemy.'

The ponderous solemnity with which these last words were spoken only served to amuse Hillyer the more, but he concealed his mirth with a show of sincere interest.

'You called them Ripley's Arcana. Who was Ripley?'

'Their creator, a disciple of Adam Grimswade.'

'Wasn't he an architect?'

'He was much more than that, young man. Have you never heard the tale of Ripley's disappearance? One night a clergyman was walking down a lane not far from here when he saw a dark figure dragging someone out of a window. Thinking they were engaged in a drunken revel he went to remonstrate with them, but as he drew near he made out the face of the cloaked figure and fled. He never revealed what he had seen, except to say that it was so loathsome as to be utterly unhuman. The house was one in which Ripley conducted his Black Masses, and after that night he was never seen again. Oh, and the window through which Ripley had been pulled was found to have a solid grille over it; a grille on which flapped a few rags of cloth. The lane was thereafter known as Devil's Den. Yes, Ripley was Grimswade's disciple in more than architecture. If you would know more, read his books, sir, read his books!'

With that the priest raised his head and shouted 'Faustus!' at the top of his voice. Hillyer thought he was dealing with a madman, but when the priest added 'Heel boy, heel!' a large black dog padded up and followed him out of the cloister.

This encounter was very suggestive, for it added a little to Hillyer's information about the link between Bellman and the Arcana. Hillyer's discovery, apparently, was the existence of a second work by Bellman, dealing with the Arcana in a far more esoteric fashion. Now he felt that he could guess why one of the windows in his—that is to say Bellman's—rooms was bricked up. Clearly Bellman had heard the tale of Ripley and believed in it sufficiently to safeguard himself against a similar occurrence. Now Hillyer was really excited for the question came to mind why Bellman should fear the same fate unless he was involved in the same activities? Already the thesis was losing its appeal, for the possibility of a sensational 'bestseller' beckoned.

Of course, I was not to know any of this. I had been doing a little research of my own at the Otterline. To tell the truth, I was hoping that I might encourage Hillyer to see an idea through for once and not throw his opportunities away as I thought he might. It did seem to me that the Arcana might furnish a serious subject after all. True, Stukely dismissed them as grotesques with no meaning, but I did find a Latin manuscript in which one Dr William Reeks had concluded that they symbolized the virtues and vices of the academic life. Certain of the human figures were identified as schoolmaster, lawyer, physician and so on, professions then thought suitable for students. Of the monstrous figures, he seemed less sure, identifying one as a hippopotamus carrying its young on its back, representing he said, a good tutor

[138]

protecting youth. Others he saw as representations of gluttony, drunkenness, fraud and other vices. Whether these were supposed to be characteristics to be avoided, or the traits by which one could identify students, was not made clear. I had my own opinions about Reeks's interpretations, but I could see at least the starting point for some research that would merit serious academic consideration, and that was what Hillyer needed.

The day was so bitterly cold, and the afternoon so far advanced towards ice-misted twilight, that I could have been excused for making the short journey straight home. Instead, I visited the cloister to look once more at the Arcana while the interpretations I had just read were still in my mind.

The glow of the setting sun lay trapped under the rolling cloud cover, casting a faintly ruddy sheen on the snow of the garth, cradling the grotesque carvings in, as it were, a hollow of angry light. Here and there a lamp in a window outlined a wing, a beak, a sinuous neck. It was hard to tell where the coiling wistaria ended and the reptilian limbs and snouts began. As I have intimated, I had not been particularly convinced by the good Dr Reeks's interpretations. Now I dismissed them utterly. The lawyer for instance, supposedly in conference with a client; why were they clinging together in a way that suggested wrestling, or even the intimacy of lovers? That hippopotamus looked more to me like a giraffe with the head of the Loch Ness Monster and the creature on its back looked not so much like its offspring as a feeding parasite. I had at that moment some intimation of a darker side to the Arcana, but I dismissed it.

I did not see Hillyer until the Wednesday of the carol singing. Fresh flurries of seasonal snow were on the air, and the dozen or so carollers, muffled to the ears and carrying lanterns, made a picturesque sight. The temperature was dropping by the minute. I seem to remember that 'In the Bleak Midwinter' was sung with particular depth of feeling. Carolling has always been one of the high spots of the season for me but on that occasion I felt troubled. During the Coventry carol I thought I could catch a low, discordant drone that distorted the tune, pulling it out of shape, as it were. The image came to my mind of a dark current dragging on weeds. Occasionally, it seemed, a single low-toned bell tolled funereally in the distance. As no one else seemed put out, I supposed that I was suffering a kind of tinnitus. I glanced around the gathering. The lamplit faces with frosty breath billowing on the air, and the swirling snowflakes made a perfect picture, but something was not quite right. Some moments passed before I realized what it was. There was a figure I could not place always at the edge of the lamplight. Once I thought I had been mistaken and that it was only Mead, muffled up with the brim of his hat pulled down. I felt strangely relieved. A moment later, Mead made his presence felt with a fine baritone on the other side of the group. So who was the dark figure half-obscured by shadow and swirling snow flakes? Ridiculously, I even found myself trying to count off our number, to eliminate known faces. But some distraction always prevented me from getting beyond thirteen. Sometimes I lost sight of the figure but it always turned up again, never in sufficient light to be identifiable, and, I now realized, always close to Hillyer. I could not shake the conviction that the stranger was somehow connected with the discordant sounds.

However, everyone else seemed to be pleased with the night's proceedings, and certainly the weight of the collecting cups suggested a sizeable sum for charity. As we exchanged our goodbyes and seasonal wishes, I took the opportunity to approach Hillyer. The person who had hung around him was nowhere to be seen. I noticed Hillyer looked tired and pale and I asked him if he was unwell. He assured me that he was all right, but his manner was a little subdued. He produced a sheet of paper and asked 'Would you do something for me, Doctor? See what you can make of this. It is a puzzling thing. I do not know what it can mean.'

[At this point Northwoode broke the narrative to reach into his pocket, and passed around a sheet of crumpled paper.]

It seems that on developing his first batch of photographs, Hillyer had made an interesting discovery. The pedestals on which the figures

[140]

stood were not plain as they appeared to the naked eye, but were covered with these strange letters. A few could have been dismissed as stress fractures in the stone, but some occurred too often in exactly the same form to be natural shapes. Here he felt was something that would undoubtedly interest me. So he had copied one of the inscriptions, taking great care to reproduce the exact shapes of the letters. In fact, he had concentrated so hard upon his work that he had given himself a headache.

Before we parted, I commented that I did not think much of his friend's singing voice, suggesting that he should learn to distinguish between descant and discord. Hillyer did not reply but looked quizzical.

I must give his own account of what happened next. He returned to his lodgings, which were situated in a street of once magnificent eighteenth-century houses, which were now divided into small flats and bedsitting rooms, presided over by formidable landladies. The guardian of Hillyer's dwelling was a woman named Fowler, but he secretly referred to her as Mrs Watt, for she had a way with her tenants' letters that gave an entirely new meaning to the phrase 'the age of steam'.

As he entered he saw Mrs Fowler halfway up the stairs, polishing the handrail with a disgusting rag; only her tenants would have known just how disgusting it was. Until that day it had been wrapped around the soil pipe of the lavatory. On seeing him, she tucked the rag under her arm and came down the steps to meet him.

'Just seen your guests off have you, Mr Hillyer? Not before time. I don't mind parties and such like at this time of year but there is no need for quite so much noise.'

Hillyer struggled to make sense of this. 'Party? Noise? What do you—'

But she was already gone. Hillyer stamped up the stairs, inwardly reciting all the piercing retorts he might have uttered, had she given him time to think of them. On entering his rooms, the thought came to him that she would do well to refrain from criticizing her tenants until she had done something about the drains. The smell from his kitchenette was particularly bad that night. The bricked-up window made it a poorly ventilated room, but a fine darkroom when he developed his films. The equipment for this purpose cluttered the worktops. Fearing a blocked waste pipe, he sniffed the sink, but the source was not there. It was stronger over by the table where he developed his films. The smell hung on the air around the scattered pile of photographs and notes on the pedestal markings. There was upon them a slimy dew, as though—it was a particularly horrible thought—as though something had been looking at them.

Then Hillyer noted something else amiss in the kitchenette. A small oil painting of a grim old man whom Hillyer liked to believe was Ripley had fallen off the wall. The space where it had hung was scratched as though long nails had clawed at the wallpaper. On closer examination, the wall behind proved not to be composed of plaster or brick, but stone. Hillyer picked away at the paper a little. There could be no mistake, the window had been filled in with stone blocks. So Bellman had been more frightened than even Hillyer had supposed. One of the joints between the blocks must have crumbled for there was a gap. Hillyer picked away at the paper a little more. The block was actually loose and was easily pulled free. In the space behind was a stack of old books and a document case tied with ribbon.

The books were battered and stained but had once been finely bound. Their titles, stamped in gold, included the *Steganographia* of Trithemius, the *Astrology Theologised* of Weigelus, the *Dictionnaire Infernal* of De Plancy and a small volume entitled *The Book of the Laws of Pluto*. Each volume had a Ripley bookplate, with the motto *Flectare si requeo superos, Acheronta movebo* (If I cannot bend the Gods, I will let Hell loose). The document case contained letters from Ebenezer Sibley, Joseph Curwen and John Asgarth. To Hillyer's great pleasure, there was also a page of notes signed by Bellman who had clearly intended to write a book on the matter. The Asgarth letter was particularly fascinating.

'As to yr mode of summoning, I could not commend to you the Aklo letters for they are very potent, but little understood, and theyre effects moste volatile. If ye are set on forming gaytes, to open upon the tunnels of Saksaksalim let me commend to yr attention The Theban Letters by whiche if used aright yr purpose should be well served. Yet I think The Book of the Laws of Pluto is not generally understood with regard to those parts that deal with monstrous generations not created by nature. As to a propitious time for this enterprise, might I commend to you the feast of the Xtians. Having myself undertaken the Black Pilgrimage, I know well the virtue of a new rite turnd to old ends.'

At the time I knew nothing of all of this. I had settled down to examine the cryptic letters in confident expectation that half an hour's work would solve the mystery. As you know, I am addicted to codes and ciphers of all kinds, and love puzzles.

To be short, it proved trickier than I had supposed. I could have spent days in vain toil, but luckily I was not working completely in the dark. The letters were of a familiar type; I was sure that I was dealing with a magical alphabet. Even so, I knew that the whole subject of invented languages for magical purposes is a bottomless pit in which the researcher can easily be lost. I ploughed through many an old book, checking Hillyer's page against The Characters of Celestial Writing, the writing called Passing the River, the text called Malachim, all to no avail. I was almost ready to give up for the day when I found The Mysterious Characters of letters delivered by Honorious call'd The Theban Alphabet.

There could be no doubt that the letters were those of the inscription. In a few moments I had my translation:

COME FORTH
EFFRIGIS
LORD OF
SAKSAKSALIM

That was enough for me. The trend of things had grown sufficiently disturbing for me to go at once to Hillyer's flat with the intention of warning him that he should leave the subject of the Arcana well alone. His was not the kind of mind that could tamper with the occult with impunity.

The front door was opened by his landlady, whose appearance and manner confirmed everything that Hillyer had said about her. Even now I am not entirely sure that she was not wearing that unspeakable rag as a scarf. Hillyer it seemed was not at home. I wish now that I had gone looking for him in the most likely place, but I thought that the next day would be soon enough, and went home.

In fact, Hillyer had taken a copy of the text and returned to the cloister. Even as I was making my way home, he was crouching in the twilight gloom before the pedestal examining the surface of the stone. He peered closely at the letters he had copied, then at the pedestal, but he could make out nothing. The light was not good. He had been foolish to come at that time. The letters on the paper blurred as he strained to see them. Strangely, this seemed to help him, for when he looked back at the stone he could make out letters faintly outlined in the reddish light of some window nearby. But when he looked, all the windows in the square were dark. What was causing the faint glow? When he looked back at the pedestal, the letters were clearer than ever, and seemed to be glowing with their own red light. Hillyer describes it looking as if the letters were cut in the wall of a furnace, showing the glow within. Without taking his eyes from it, Hillyer backed away from the pedestal. There seemed to be smoke rising from the statue, and the air became filled with a dry crackling as of flame. That was the last thing Hillyer saw, because after that he ran.

When I visited Hillyer the next day, I found him in a sorry state. It seemed that the episode had not ended in the cloister. On his way home, he had glimpsed a figure in the icy fog halfway down Devil's Den, and had taken the long way home rather than confront it. He said this was because he did not feel up to a lecture from the old priest, but something in the way he said it led me to believe that the figure had not looked as much like that benevolent gentleman as he pretended. Even more disturbing was the dream that had followed that night, in which he clung to a high place in freezing winds, hacking with a strange flint blade at a pillar of ice. The shards glittered in the moonlight as they flew, revealing dark movement and a dry rustling, like black fire within the column of ice.

Hillyer wanted no more of Ripley's magic, and when I had examined the hidden books and letters, I was hardly more enthusiastic. However, if Asgarth's comment about the festival of the 'Xtians' being a propitious time for Ripley's purposes had carried weight, I feared there would be worse to come, with only forty-eight hours to Christmas Day. A particularly rough Beast was slouching its way towards Bethlehem to be born.

It was pointless asking Hillyer to assist me in his present state. In any case, I felt that it was my responsibility. I had done nothing to discourage his interest in the Arcana, and had latched on to what was happening far too slowly. I decided that I had to put things right myself.

As some of you know, I collect magical impedimenta, and I have made some study of rituals. My plan was to take a ceremonial dagger, perform a banishing ritual and place an amulet in the cloister where it might help stave off the manifestations attendant upon the opening of the gate. Since it would require a certain amount of privacy, I had to wait until it was late enough to preclude the possibility of onlookers.

Snow was swirling thickly around the cloisters as I arrived a little before midnight. There was a full moon, giving enough visibility for my purpose. The snow had already begun to lie, softening the lines of the wistaria, distorting the Arcana into malformed mounds of icy whiteness. The dance of the descending flakes was somehow mesmeric in the cold moonlight, as though the garth and the cloisters were rising upwards slowly through rippling veils of whiteness.

The proximity to midnight did not appear to me to be significant, for it seemed too much of a cliché. Yet that hour is not without its significance in certain magical processes. I had just located the statue and begun the banishing ritual when I noticed a change in the statue. In the space immediately around it, the snow was not falling, and the carved figure was turning black. The steady drip of water told me that it was shedding its cape of snow. Then what Hillyer had seen as smoke began to rise. But it was not smoke; it was steam. On the face of the pedestal the Theban Letters glowed so clearly that I could have read them, though I knew well enough what they heralded. The demon Effrigis was coming forth.

That was a moment of real terror. My mind conjured up all the images of horror I could conceive. Or would it be beautiful and seductive, and all the more dangerous for that? I could even have believed that the statue was about to come alive and step down from its pedestal. At such moments, the mind functions on the level of the Penny Dreadful.

What did happen was in its way even more disturbing. The air was filled with a rustling sound. It might have sounded like flames to Hillyer, but to me it brought to mind the shifting and rubbing together of countless dry wings. The letters on the face of the pedestal were partially obscured by a moving, crawling mass of blackness.

I did not perform the banishing ritual, and I do not think it would have achieved anything if I had. I shouted aloud some words of divine

[145]

invocation and threw the dagger at the patch of blackness on the pedestal. There was no sound of steel on stone. The dagger disappeared into the mass, and the rustling ceased. The stone lay plain and cold in the moonlight. I hastily buried the amulet in front of the pedestal and left that place. The shock set in as I was walking away, and I felt old and frail.

The next day was Christmas Eve. My niece had invited me to spend the day with her family. I am not usually the most sociable of souls, but as you have gathered I do enjoy Christmas, and I felt that I needed good company, because the chill of that encounter had got into my heart. If anything could have been calculated to work a healing spell, that day was it: building a snowman in the garden with the children, singing old songs by the Christmas tree, enjoying a wonderful lunch and a lazy afternoon with brandy and cigars by the fire. During the evening we were entertained by a neighbour who was an amateur conjurer. His act was intended for the children, but as someone who has never been able to master even the simplest trick, I too was enthralled and delighted. Particularly impressive was a miniature version of the vanishing-lady illusion, in which he made a child's doll disappear from a small cabinet and reappear. Close as I had been to the proceedings, I just could not see how the trick was done.

My niece seemed amused to hear that I had been so impressed by this, and teased me, saying 'I don't want to shatter your illusions, uncle, but just because only one door is visible, it does not mean there is not another, you know. These cabinets have two-way doors.' These words did not quite have the effect she had intended.

I looked at the clock. It was eleven-thirty. What I did next caused some consternation among the family. I rose, put on my overcoat and left the house.

There were a surprising number of people out at that time; some perhaps on their way to midnight mass, or on the last stage of journeys home for Christmas: devout worship or joyous greetings. I was out walking for a very different reason.

It took more than fifteen minutes to reach Hillyer's lodging. I rang Hillyer's bell and stamped impatiently up and down on the step. It was ten minutes to twelve. Hillyer was stunned by my unexpected appearance. There was no time to explain. I bundled him up the stairs and into his room.

'Answer me one question, Hillyer,' I shouted. 'Are you developing any pictures at the moment?'

'Of course not, I was getting ready for bed.'

'I thought not. Look.'

There was red light in the doorway to the kitchenette. Across the blocked-in window with its loosely replaced stone, the letters of the Theban Alphabet were glowing cherry red. The stonework was rippling, and like a rotting log rising up through the surface of a draining lake, a head and an arm came through the wall, black and quivering with strange movement. At once the air was full of that loathsome dry rustling. And I knew that the power was greater than it had been on the previous night. I was struck down and the head came down over me. There was no face, just the seething of a million crawling things.

In my hurry to get to Hillyer, there had been no time to think what I might do to defend him. I lay there helpless, and heard a strange voice:

'Ilasa gahé Effrigis bajilenu iehe noco gono adana od bajilenu iehe totza das dorebesa n-e-el od qua a on; eca gohusa: uaunilagi pujo faoregita dorepesa ohorela das e ola, ge kiaisi nore-mo-lapi—'

It was Hillyer who stood over me, his face red and contorted with effort. As the words boomed out, the head and arm drew back through the wall and the room fell silent.

For a moment I was just grateful to be alive. Then I became angry. Hillyer had not been the innocent victim after all. Mere dabbling would never have given him the knowledge he had just displayed for he had recited the licence of the spirit to depart, from the Book of the Goetia. More than this, he was reciting it in the Enochian language John Dee claimed to have received from the angels. I was determined to get an explanation, but as I stood up, a change came over Hillyer. Not so much a physical change as a subtle alteration of expression. One moment I was looking into the face of a grim and ruthless man; then the spirit behind the eyes changed, and became that of the superficial if amiable young man I had known. He seemed to be waking from a dream. As I stood struggling for something to say there came faintly the sound of bells, chiming midnight. So I said, 'Merry Christmas, Hillyer.'

And that is my story. I was terribly slow, you know. The first time I saw the window I should have known that brick would have been sufficient to block it up, that stone must have been there for another purpose. Both Hillyer and I had been confused by that story told by the old priest. We only thought of shutting something out, not of forming a gate to let something in. Bellman had never been protecting himself, but creating a gateway of his own. If it had not been for that most innocent of entertainments, the conjurer's cabinet, I should not have begun to think about second doors, and doors that let things in as well as out. I like to think that at that last moment Ripley took a hand in the matter. Why? Who can say. Perhaps a kind of restitution or penance. Still, we were fortunate that Hillyer's foolishness only stirred up *one* of the demons listed by the *Dictionnaire Infernal*: Effrigis, 'the one who quivers in a horrible manner'. It could have been so much worse. There is Ramisen, who moves with a particular creeping motion; The Burasin, destroyers by stifling smoking breath; and the one who tears asunder—but let us change the subject to a more pleasant one.

WISH YOU WERE HERE

Basil Copper

Basil Copper (b. 1924) has been
described as 'unquestionably one of the
greatest living macabre writers', with several
novels (*Necropolis*, *The Great White Space*, *The
Curse of the Fleers*, etc.) and six fine collections to
his credit: *Not After Nightfall* (1967), *From Evil's
Pillow* (1973), *When Footsteps Echo* (1975), *And
Afterward The Dark* (1977), *Here Be Daemons*
(1978), and *Voices of Doom* (1980). His latest
novel, *The Black Death*, was published earlier this
year. We are now pleased to present 'Wish You
Were Here', a new story by this fine writer,
written specially for this anthology.

1

The cards started arriving early in October, long before
Christmas. They were old-fashioned things, of the type
Wilson had never seen before. He had inherited Hoddesden
Old Hall from a wealthy aunt and it was his first winter in the place. It
had been a vile autumn so far as weather was concerned, and a
sulphurous yellow fog hung over the village and the marshes beyond.

But there was still a blaze of colour from the banked flowers in the
garden and the neglected lawns were beginning to shape up under the
scouring of the sit-on motor mower that Wilson had recently purchased. He was a writer who had previously lived in a cramped flat in

London and he was expanding in the luxury of large beamed rooms and spacious attics. Though the grounds had been let run wild the interior of the house had been well kept up and the furnishings were in keeping with the age of the building; it dated from the sixteenth century in its oldest parts, and the paintings and the contents alone must be worth a fortune, Wilson thought.

Not that he had needed the money; a long run of successful books, despite his comparative youth—he was now thirty-five—had enabled him to live in some style—but as the Old Hall was only half an hour by fast train from London he had the best of both worlds and he had decided to keep the place. Currently he was sharing early days of renovation with a friend, Barry Clissold, a departmental head of one of the great London museums, who was coming down at weekends to give him a hand and who would be staying over Christmas.

But the two were not the final arbiters of where everything should go; that was up to Deirdre. She was Wilson's fiancée and she too was coming down at weekends to keep an eye on things. This was not, of course, the interpretation put upon it by people in the village. Not that they were narrow; they were remarkably broad-minded and up to date, in fact. Though Mrs Savage, the lady who did daily cooking for him and some of the major cleaning jobs in the house, had relayed with relish some of the more amusing pieces of gossip that were going the rounds.

What it boiled down to was that Barry Clissold was imported at weekends to 'add respectability to the arrangement'. Wilson was amused in turn and so was Deirdre when she learned of it. She tossed one lock of blue-black hair back from her eyes and looked up at him, her strong, clear-minted face alive with impish humour. Wilson was at the top of a ladder at the time, trimming a mass of overgrown foliage away from trelliswork near the front door.

'They probably think we're very old-fashioned, John.' She smiled again. 'But it's certainly an idea.'

Wilson was so startled that he almost pitched from the ladder. Deirdre was an extraordinary girl; she held an important position in the design department of one of the biggest advertising agencies in London and though her talk was racy and sometimes extremely risqué she had decided views about sex before marriage and Wilson was not inclined to press her on the point. She had a fantastic temper when roused and they were so deeply involved emotionally that he would

[150]

never have risked turning her against him by transgressing their unspoken, unwritten rules.

It was a Friday today and Wilson was looking forward to the advent of the two in the early evening; Clissold would probably travel with Deirdre in her car; otherwise Wilson and his fiancée would collect him from the six o'clock train. The station was less than a mile from the house. He was still unpacking his books in the big study he was making for himself under the eaves; Deirdre had given him carte blanche over certain areas and she would decide later about decoration and colour schemes for the rest of the place.

After all, they were not to be married for almost another year and there was plenty of time to decide on these finer points. Wilson had finished one huge segment of shelving next to the fireplace he had reserved for various editions of his own books and now he washed his hands and descended to the ground floor to seek out Mrs Savage in the kitchen for his mid-morning coffee and biscuits.

She was in the hall as he descended the graceful oak staircase with its brightly polished treads and handrail, and the post had apparently just come for he could see Mr Dunnett, their local postman, through the side window, walking back down the path to the front gate.

Mrs Savage handed him the bundle of letters with a pleasant smile but she wrinkled up her nose as though something distasteful had happened.

'There's something musty,' she said. 'I can't quite place it. It wasn't there before Mr Dunnett came. I hope it isn't dry rot.'

Wilson gave her a wry look.

'So do I. You say the most cheerful things sometimes, Mrs Savage.'

The tall woman with the close-cropped iron-grey hair shook her head.

'I'm a realist, Mr Wilson. Better to take these things in time.'

She was right, Wilson thought, as he followed her out to the kitchen. He then realized he had put the bundle of letters down on the small demilune at the bottom of the stairs. It was a long way through to the entrance hall so he merely sipped his coffee, munched the sweet biscuits and engaged in chit-chat before again returning to the study.

He put the bundle of letters down on the surface of his green tooled-leather desk and finished arranging his own books in date order. There was an empty shelf at the bottom but he would leave that for future editions and reserve the other big bookcase in the further alcove for the same purpose. In the meantime Deirdre would fill in the empty spaces with ornaments and bowls of flowers. She was rather good at the latter, he had to admit.

When he had finished he sat down in the big leather swivel chair behind his desk and went through the mail. There was nothing of vital importance, though a couple of royalty statements and the accompanying cheques were a welcome bonus. There were still three or four large white envelopes but as he sifted them he became aware of their provenance from the printed originators at the tops of the envelopes. At the same moment he caught the musty smell of which Mrs Savage had spoken and he realized it was emanating from the pile of correspondence on the desk. He went through the last two envelopes somewhat gingerly.

As he did so, a glossy brown card fell face uppermost. It was from this that the odour was coming. Wilson slid it round toward him with a hesitant forefinger. It was a postcard with a sepia view of Aberdeen which must have been at least a hundred years old. The card had a deckle edge and there was some hand-tinting which gave the scene, depicting imposing granite buildings, gardens and a distant view of the sea, an almost ethereal quality.

Wilson at first thought it was one of the rather luxurious reproductions that some card manufacturers were now affecting but he soon realized his mistake. He turned the card over and saw by the mottled brown patches on the back that it was an original. And he understood something else; the odour was not only mustiness but was combined with another essence; something like a woman's stale perfume. It must have been some mistake, Wilson thought, but the card was addressed to him at the Old Hall, in a spidery writing he did not recognize. It looked as though it might be a woman's handwriting, though he was no expert on those things.

On the right-hand side of the card, in the space reserved for messages, were just a couple of sentences. The ink was black and faded as though with time but that could not be, because the thing had just been delivered. The stamp at the top had been obliterated by a heavy postal franking die; the ink on that was so thick he could not make out the date or the office of origin. The message itself commenced abruptly, without any prefix or his name. It merely said: '*Enjoying the season and the band concerts immensely. Wish you were here.*' There was no signature, merely an initial, and that in such a distorted curlicue script that he could not make it out.

It must be some joke, surely. Perhaps one of his friends in London.

But his amusement soon gave way to exasperation. No one he knew would send such a thing. Certainly not Deirdre, even as a joke. But for the fact that the card was addressed to him firmly and legibly at his new address he would have dismissed it out of hand.

Later he went down to the dining room for an excellent cold lunch Mrs Savage had laid out. He took the card with him, propping it against a salt cellar near his plate, studying it with growing irritation as he poured himself a glass of chilled white wine. When Mrs Savage came back with the dessert and coffee he pointed at the card, an object so banal and yet so mysterious.

'What do you make of that?'

Mrs Savage took it delicately, using the edge of a teacloth to avoid contact with her fingers, he noticed. She sniffed delicately, her eyes wide.

'That was it, Mr Wilson. The mustiness . . . Where did you get it?'

Wilson felt faint surprise.

'You gave it me,' he said. 'It came with the post this morning. It was in that bundle of letters.'

The housekeeper slowly shook her head.

'Was it really? I didn't notice it. But surely not. This is a very old card. Like something they sell in those specialist dealers' shops for collectors. It might even be valuable.'

'You surprise me,' said Wilson drily. 'But it's addressed to me all right. And it certainly came through the post. Do read it, please. There's nothing personal and I can't make out the sender.'

Mrs Savage turned the card over and studied it with growing interest.

'A lady's perfume all right,' she said at length. 'Though stale. The mustiness comes from the card, of course. It's a very old one. And a lady's writing too.'

She screwed up her faded blue eyes. Presently she pursed her lips and put the card down delicately near the edge of the dining table, still holding it by the napkin.

'Some sort of a joke, perhaps?'

Wilson shook his head.

'I don't think so, Mrs Savage. That's why I'd value your opinion.'

The tall woman shrugged, leaning forward to pour out the first measure of black coffee into the blue china cup.

'I'm afraid I shan't be much help. The stamp and office it's been posted from are obliterated by the franking. And the initial could be a C, perhaps.'

'You have nothing to add, then?'

The tone of his voice momentarily roused her.

'I don't see we can take things much further, Mr Wilson. But you could ask Mr Dunnett about it when he delivers the post tomorrow morning, if you wish. He may have some ideas. And of course you may hear from this person again.'

Wilson sat back in his chair and picked up his coffee cup. The brew was excellent, as always.

'That's a point, Mrs Savage. It hadn't occurred to me. The post office may be able to trace its origin. I don't suppose it's very important really, but I must confess I was intrigued.'

Mrs Savage smiled mysteriously.

'Leave it to me, Mr Wilson. And in the meantime please finish your sweet. It's getting cold and I took such trouble with it.'

2

It was almost dark before Wilson heard the car; the days were beginning to draw in more noticeably now. Mrs Savage was getting ready to leave but she came out of the kitchen to greet the arrivals as he left the study. He could hear Deirdre's high heels rat-tatting on the parquet of the entrance hall and then the sound of her voice as she greeted the housekeeper. Barry's more measured voice joined in a few seconds later. Wilson lingered at the stairhead until Mrs Savage had left and the conversation died away. Apparently Clissold had gone back to the car because he could hear doors slamming.

Still Wilson stayed on in the gathering dusk of the massive staircase as the hall door again slammed echoingly and then the girl's footsteps, softer now, came swiftly up the stairs. They were locked in a deep embrace in front of the long gilt-framed mirror on the landing when there came a dry cough from the hall below.

'Haven't you any greeting for me?'

Clissold's eyes were wide and ironic as the two hastily broke away. Wilson gave the other an easy smile.

'Not in that way, my dear chap.'

He went down a few steps as Clissold came up to meet him and the two men shook hands, Deirdre's suppressed giggle sounding behind them. She joined the two a moment later and put her arm affectionately round the writer's shoulders. Wilson was aware at that moment

[154]

of his good fortune; to be young and comparatively well off; with a marvellous fiancée; good friends like Barry; and possession of a magnificent house. Life stretched unendingly before him in the rosy glow of the setting sun that came in from the big stained glass window at the stairhead.

The three went down the hall together, to where the luggage was piled in the centre of the silk Tabriz carpet that Deirdre had imported from London a week or two before. Again Wilson was conscious that he had with him the two people he most cared for in the world. He was an orphan, as was Deirdre, and like most engaged couples they felt that pre-ordained fate had brought them together to find happiness.

But he expressed nothing of all this, merely mouthing the banality, 'Had a good trip down?'

Deirdre nodded, tossing a lock of blue-black hair from her eyes in the gesture with which the novelist had long become familiar.

'Not too bad. The traffic was awful, of course, until we cleared the suburbs. Anything to eat?'

Wilson laughed, leading the way across to the big pine door that led to the dining room.

'Never mind that. Let's have a drink first. Not too cold after the drive?'

Deirdre shook her head. Today she wore a smart tailored suit of some dark grey material and her face was shining with health and suppressed excitement. Barry Clissold had made a move toward the luggage but Wilson stopped him.

'Don't worry about that, Barry. I'll take the stuff up later. I hope you don't mind cold things tonight. Mrs Savage leaves early on Fridays. And we'll eat out tomorrow, of course. I've found an excellent place about ten miles away.'

Clissold shrugged and joined the others at the doorway. It was a big, long, low-ceilinged room with massive oak beams and a huge bressummer above the fireplace, in which a blazing fire of logs gave out a fierce heat. There was full central heating in the house but Wilson hadn't yet turned it on because the weather continued warm in the daytime. He poured large goblets of sherry from the decanter on the sideboard and shovelled in chunks of ice with the silver tongs. Deirdre watched him with detached amusement, her blue eyes pensive.

'What about the car?' she said.

'I'll take it round after we've eaten. Plenty of time.'

The three sat sprawled in big leather armchairs ranged in a semicircle round the fireplace. At the far end of the room, in an alcove overlooking the ruined garden, the Sheraton dining table, its surface reflecting the gleaming flames of the fire, was ready laid. It was a contented, luxurious world and Wilson reminded himself that he might find it more difficult to work here than he had in his London flat.

'How are things at the museum?' he asked.

Clissold shrugged.

'Booming. Just booming', he said. 'Shoals of visitors. But pretty dead in some of the more esoteric departments.'

'Not that again,' Deirdre sighed.

She was used to Barry's dry sense of humour but his oblique references to mummies and Dead Sea scrolls were becoming a little wearing. Wilson looked at her in surprise and even Clissold stopped in the middle of his next sentence, which would have contained the punch-line, his dark brown eyes owl-like beneath the horn-rimmed spectacles he wore. His face looked a little hurt beneath his thick shock of reddish hair. With his stocky build and corduroy jacket and trousers he looked more like a successful gentleman farmer than a scholar and authority on various obscure fields of learning.

'Oh, come on, Barry,' said Wilson, getting up to replenish his friend's glass. 'Deirdre was only joking. Weren't you, darling?'

The tall girl flushed.

'Sorry,' she said shortly. 'It's just that I've heard that one so often before.'

Clissold got up from his chair, holding out his hand somewhat erratically for the proffered glass.

'Apology accepted,' he said. 'I promise not to crack that one again during the entire weekend.'

He went over to stand by the fireplace.

'What's the drill for tomorrow? You want me to help you finish off filling up the study shelves?'

Wilson shook his head, aware that Deirdre's eyes were fixed upon him critically, as though she were annoyed at something. There was an atmosphere building up that he could not quite place. He decided to ignore it.

'I've something special prepared for you, Barry. You wouldn't know where the books go. I like to do those things myself. But we won't talk about it now. If you've had enough sherry, let's go and eat, shall we? Everything's prepared. I only have to fetch the stuff from the kitchen.'

[156]

There was a long silence during the meal and it wasn't until Wilson had brought in the second course and opened another bottle of wine that general conversation resumed. They all agreed that Mrs Savage was an excellent lady and that the wine had more than come up to expectation.

'What's been happening your end?' Barry asked as they reached the coffee and cognac stage. He knew that John and Deirdre spoke together on the phone almost every day and that she would be *au fait* with local happenings.

'I've been making pretty good progress,' Wilson said slowly. 'But something rather funny happened today.'

He felt Deirdre's eyes upon him and plunged on.

'Trivial but quite curious all the same. It might be in your line, Barry.'

Clissold sat back in his chair, savouring the bouquet of the cognac in his big balloon glass.

'How do you mean?'

'Collecting old postcards is one of your interests, isn't it?'

The eyes behind the thick lenses were absorbed now.

'Well?'

'I had a strange old card come in the mail this morning. It smelt musty and looked Victorian. It was a very old view of Aberdeen. It was addressed to me here and it had a banal but nevertheless cryptic message on it, written in a woman's spidery handwriting.'

Clissold exchanged a satirical smile with Deirdre at the other side of the table.

'A woman, eh? This sounds exciting.'

'I'll ignore that,' Wilson said. 'I didn't know the person or at least I couldn't place her. There was only an initial and I couldn't make it out.'

Clissold put a finger up to the side of his nose.

'A mystery woman now. This is even better.'

'Don't play the fool,' said Wilson rather more sharply than he had intended. 'I'm being serious now.'

'This we had better see,' Deirdre cut in. 'Where is this mysterious missive?'

'Up in the study,' Wilson said. 'I'll fetch it when I've finished my coffee. Help yourself to more and there's plenty of cognac if you want a refill.'

A few minutes later, as he gained the landing that led to the study, he was aware that there was a changed atmosphere between the three of them. All the old, familiar, jokey friendliness seemed to have been temporarily dispersed. Why, he couldn't think. It was as though some subtle form of invisible blind had been silently drawn between the three so that they had difficulty in communicating in the usual manner and when they did the little intimacies fell flat and intended jokes, long-established between the trio, merely irritated, instead of being greeted as cherished old friends.

Wilson abruptly brushed the thoughts away. This would not do. The weekend must not be spoiled. He saw Deirdre only for the two days, because she invariably returned to town on the Sunday night, having much work to prepare for her studio on the Monday. He resolved that when he returned downstairs he would do what he could to restore normal relations. He switched on the light, crossed to draw the curtains and then returned to the desk. The letters had been answered and they and the carbons of his replies had been filed away in the big indexed cabinets in the corner. He had left the postcard on the middle of the desk, together with a couple of circulars and the notice of a forthcoming village concert.

The card was not there. He bit his lip with vexation. He hunted around for several minutes, aware of the other two in the dining room, listening to his muffled progress overhead. He heard Deirdre's footsteps in the hall as he descended the stairs.

'I can't find it anywhere . . .' he began.

Deirdre smiled.

'I don't wonder,' she said drily. 'You left it over there.'

Wilson followed her pointing finger, and saw with another stab of irritation that the card was on the demilune at the bottom of the staircase. He had no recollection of bringing it down from the study and fought his rising irritability.

'I left it on my desk upstairs,' he said stubbornly.

Deirdre looked nonplussed. Wilson was aware that Clissold was leaning easily against the jamb of the dining-room door, engrossed in their conversation.

'You can't have done,' Deirdre persisted.

She had the card up now, her delicate nostrils wrinkling as she too caught the faint musty odour.

'Funny sort of thing,' she added. 'Perhaps Mrs Savage brought it down during the day without you knowing.'

'Yes, that must be it,' said Wilson with relief. 'See what you make of it, Barry.'

[158]

The three went back into the dining-room and took seats by the fire. Clissold waited until Deirdre had finished her perusal of the card and then adjusted his glasses as Wilson handed it to him.

'Definitely a woman's writing,' Deirdre said. 'Subject to your expert opinion, Barry.'

Clissold grinned. Somehow, Wilson felt, the atmosphere had lifted and the three of them were once again on the old easy terms.

'Certainly, Deirdre. No doubt about that. Mystery or no, this thing could be valuable.'

'You don't mean it.'

Clissold gave him an amused look.

'Oh, no, I don't mean your man in the street. I'm talking about the dealers and the dedicated collectors. Now, do you two know anything about the history of the postcard? Not to mention the Christmas card.'

Wilson shook his head.

'No, and we don't want a learned dissertation from you now. We want to know about this particular card. Apparently it's been posted quite recently but to me that looks like an ancient franking mark.'

Clissold held it up to the light, his eyes squinting ferociously beneath the glasses.

'You're right. This beats all.'

He sat for a moment, the card in his left hand, the right raking through his red-tinged hair.

'And yet there is an element of doubt. This could be a joke, you know.'

'What makes you think that?' Deirdre put in.

'For one thing the frank has obliterated the office of origin and the date.'

'My thoughts exactly,' said Wilson.

'And then,' Clissold went on, his eyes dreamy and his voice far away, as though he hadn't heard the interruption, 'there is the matter of the correct address, while the writer hides her identity by a single initial, so badly written that it's almost impossible to make out.'

'I have my own thoughts about that,' said Wilson.

'Let's hear them then, darling,' Deirdre said. 'I plump for C.'

Clissold nodded.

'Good girl. I incline to that initial myself.'

He turned back to Wilson.

'Have you got a powerful magnifying glass, John?'

'I believe there's one in the lounge,' Wilson said. 'I was trying to make out the detail of some of the panelling in there a couple of days ago. I'll go and get it.'

When he returned the three stood together, Wilson holding the card under the overhead light while Clissold studied it beneath the magnifying lens. Presently he put it down with a baffled expression.

'What's the matter?' said Deirdre sharply.

Clissold stroked his chin.

'I'd rather not say for the moment,' he returned enigmatically.

3

Wilson was about early the next morning and was in the garden burning a huge bonfire of rank weeds when the postman arrived. Dunnett was a wiry man in his fifties with a thick head of grey hair that looked like steel wool clustered to his scalp. Wilson took the small sheaf of letters from him, sifted through them quickly, with a suddenly heightened pulse rate. The postman was regarding him curiously.

'Something wrong, Mr Wilson?'

The latter shook his head.

'It was only that I wanted to ask you something. Do you remember delivering an old postcard to me yesterday? It had a rather musty smell and looked Victorian somehow.'

The postman was smiling now. He ran a thick finger through his mat of grey hair.

'Nothing that I can recall. But then the stuff is now bundled up in our sorting office and secured with an elastic band. So I wouldn't have seen it anyway. If there's any complaint . . .'

'No, no, Mr Dunnett, of course not. Nothing like that. It was just curiosity on my part.'

'If I could have a look at the card, perhaps I could recall something . . .'

'It's of no importance, really,' Wilson said quickly. 'Besides, it's right at the top of the house and I don't want to hold up your round.'

The two men were on their way back to the front gate by now and Wilson thanked the postman again and walked slowly back to the bonfire. He went in to breakfast with Deirdre and Clissold with a certain resolution forming in his mind. Later, when the other two were in the garden, he went quickly up to the study. He took the postcard from the desk and brought it back downstairs and into the open air. There was no one about, though he could hear the voices of the others beyond the far hedge. He burned the card quickly in the glowing mass of the bonfire, somehow feeling guilty.

He said nothing to the others and the matter was not mentioned again during that weekend. Deirdre went back on the Sunday night and Clissold stayed on until the Monday evening as he had a day off from his duties at the museum on that occasion.

Several weeks passed and the subject of the postcard receded into the background, and it gradually faded from Wilson's mind, though occasionally he regretted his rash act in burning it. As Clissold had said, it had a certain historical value; perhaps he should have offered it to his friend for his private collection. However, it was too late now.

The even pattern of life at the Old Hall was resumed as the days advanced; workmen came and went, tackling the scheduled renovations with skill and competence. The weather was worsening now and Wilson had temporarily ceased operations in the garden. He was tackling the house from the ground floor upwards, sensibly filling the reception areas and first-floor bedrooms with his personal things, before proceeding to the more difficult and dilapidated rooms in the upper reaches. The attics and lumber rooms were in a horrific state and he was not really looking forward to that aspect. Though Clissold had offered to give up some of his annual winter leave on a concentrated effort, Wilson did not wish to impose too much.

It was early November now and the weather had closed in, though this particular morning, as sometimes happens in winter, an orange sun, low in the sky, cast a deceptively warm glow over the autumnal trees and the sheaves of golden leaves that strewed the garden, the village lanes and the surrounding fields. Mrs Savage had lit big fires in the principal ground-floor rooms and the central heating, set low, was nicely warming the upper floors of the old house. Wilson was typing business letters this morning; the ribbon was growing faint and frayed and he found to his annoyance that he had used up the last one.

He decided to stroll down to the village to buy another at the local stationer's; he called out his destination to the housekeeper and then set out down the lane, the breath smoking from his nostrils in the cold air. It really took one's breath away and he huddled deeper into his thick, fleece-lined driving coat. Even though he had been in the neighbourhood some time he had hardly set foot in the village, so busy had he and Deirdre been in transferring his things from London and settling in.

A few hundred yards away was the old Norman church which was the most imposing public building in the village. It looked friendly and well-cared-for in the rich autumn light and the turf between the ancient gravestones had been recently mown. Certain thoughts had been forming in Wilson's mind and, on sudden impulse, he turned aside through the old lych-gate and walked up the path to the imposing main entrance. But instead of going in he turned along the gravel path to the left, skirting the church and eventually coming across the newer part of the graveyard where faded wreaths and sodden bunches of flowers denoted more recent burials.

He went down the newer gravestones, looking for a familiar name. He was crouching to read the inscription on one of the nearest when a sudden shadow falling across it momentarily startled him. He looked up to see a thickset man in his mid-forties, with a friendly face and wearing dark clothes with a clerical collar, advancing down the path toward him.

'Mr Wilson? I thought I recognized you.'

Wilson rose and shook the extended hand.

'I'm sorry. You have the advantage of me.

The cleric smiled, revealing strong, square teeth. He waited until the sudden clamour of rooks from a nearby coppice had ceased.

'Roger Anstey. Rector of this parish, for my sins. I left a card at the Old Hall when you first moved in, but I expect you've been far too busy . . .'

'Of course,' Wilson said. 'I'm sorry.'

He realized he was repeating himself; the other laughed then.

'Please don't apologize. Most newcomers probably feel I'm soliciting for donations. But I have to do it. I'm a sort of general factotum around here. Though the people are good and very helpful when the church needs something, so I can't complain.'

He stared enquiringly at Wilson.

'You were looking for something as I came down the path just now. Is it anything I can help with?'

Wilson felt momentarily awkward and at a loss.

'All this seems rather ridiculous, Rector.'

The other laid a hand upon his arm.

'Call me Roger, please. Everyone else does. We don't stand on ceremony down here.'

'I don't even know if she's buried here, of course, but I was looking for my aunt's grave. It sounds absurd but I know very little about her.

[162]

We only met a few times when I was a very small child and after the death of my parents we lost touch. In fact I didn't even know where she lived until her solicitors contacted me.'

A shadow had passed across the Rector's face and he turned back down the path, motioning the other to accompany him. As he remained silent Wilson prompted him.

'Miss Hollamby? My aunt, I mean.'

Anstey cleared his throat.

'Ah, yes. Then you didn't know?'

Wilson was puzzled.

'I'm afraid I don't understand.'

'Perhaps you'd like to come to the Rectory and join me in a glass of sherry? It's only across the field here.'

The two men walked through another ancient gate and along another path which led to a large, tile-hung house, comfortably appointed and with elegant furniture as the writer saw as soon as his companion had opened the front door. A good-looking young woman, and a small boy who clung to his mother's hand, turned out to be the Rector's wife and son.

After the introductions were over and Mrs Anstey had brought the decanter and glasses on a silver tray, she excused herself and left to resume her domestic duties. The big, book-lined room with its stone fireplace and crackling fire exuded a friendly, scholarly atmosphere but Wilson was aware that his companion seemed somewhat stiff and constrained as he poured the sherry into the big crystal goblets. But he sat down at last and the frank eyes in the strong face were very steady as he toasted his guest.

'So you know nothing about your aunt's circumstances?'

Wilson shook his head.

'The solicitors merely wrote me; said that she had left me the Hall. I called at their offices of course, and they read me the will and supplied me with the necessary documents. I was not curious. As I said, I had not met my aunt since I was about five years old and I'm afraid that I was so excited at getting such a splendid country house that I asked no particular questions about her circumstances; though I should imagine that was all spelled out in the mass of documentation they gave me.'

Anstey nodded, tapping the rim of his glass with a broad, spatulate finger. Wilson noticed that his nails were a little ragged, as though he did a lot of manual work about the church and graveyard.

'The solicitors were in London, I presume? I know Miss Hollamby preferred that to leaving her affairs in local hands'.

Wilson nodded and waited for the other to go on.

'The fact of the matter is that your aunt disappeared quite a few years ago. It was a great mystery at the time. She was seen in the garden one afternoon and after that, nothing. She had her own housekeeper then and a distant relative who visited her regularly but we in the village knew little of her relations or circumstances. The solicitors in charge of the estate kept up the house and garden on your aunt's behalf—there was a full-time housekeeper and gardener then'.

He held up his hand before Wilson could interrupt.

'The police were called, of course, but nothing was ever discovered. And then her relative—a distant cousin, I believe—turned up and claimed the estate under the terms of the old lady's will. He took possession of the house. Some years ago he was found drowned in an old well in the garden. Apparently it was at ground level, covered with rotted boards, in a part of the grounds that had been left to run wild. Undergrowth had obscured it and the gentleman, whose name I can't recall—he was buried somewhere on the Sussex coast—went through the covering and must have been killed instantly. It was in all the local newspapers at the time.'

Wilson was astonished. He had listened with growing apprehension as the Rector went on and now he had to clear his throat several times before he could speak.

'But I gained the impression that Miss Hollamby had died only a few months ago . . .'

Anstey shook his head.

'Oh, dear me, no. I should imagine the administrators of the estate had to wait a statutory number of years before the old lady could be declared legally dead. And it may be that another will was then discovered. Perhaps an earlier one, which favoured you after the cousin. That man had visited Miss Hollamby frequently and had helped her in a number of ways. Probably the solicitors did not wish to rake up old scandals and gave you the impression that your aunt had died. You know how close-mouthed lawyers can be about these things.'

'I quite see that,' said Wilson, trying to put his thoughts together. 'Where could I find out about all this?'

'We have an excellent local library. If the bound volumes of the newspapers have not been sent to the county library for storage you should be able to find everything you need there. Miss Gillespie is an excellent librarian. I think you will be able to get what you want locally. I understand they keep all the bound volumes for 20 years, until they take up too much space. They then go to county level.'

Wilson kept his face turned down to the table as the kindly figure of the Rector refilled his glass.

'You have given me much to think about,' he said. 'Thank you for your frankness.'

Anstey reseated himself opposite his guest, turning his face toward the study door as the excited shouts of his little son could be heard. Then the front door slammed and the child ran out excitedly into the garden.

'I'm afraid I have troubled you,' the Rector continued. 'Please forgive me, but when I first saw you in the churchyard I thought you were *au fait* with the history of the Old Hall.'

'There is no need to apologize,' Wilson said. 'You have been extremely helpful. What do you think happened to my aunt? Could she herself have met with some accident about the grounds, such as that which later befell her cousin?

The Rector shook his head, the yellow sunlight falling in at the window accentuating the strength of his clear-cut features.

'Very unlikely, Mr Wilson. The police made extensive searches. And the well itself was dragged and concreted over after the accident to the cousin. Just to make sure . . .'

He was silent for a moment. Then he rose quickly and drained his glass.

'You ask me what happened to your aunt. Who knows? Old people are sometimes forgetful. Their minds wander or they become mentally confused. Perhaps she got some idea in her head and simply walked a long way away and died in an obscure place like an unfrequented wood. Or took a railway journey to the coast, walked into the sea and drowned. That is a common form of suicide.'

'You have not considered the alternative,' Wilson said.

'And what is that?' Anstey asked sharply.

'That she may still be alive somewhere,' said Wilson.

He got up in his turn.

'But I am extremely grateful for what you have told me this morning, and I will certainly take your advice and look out those newspaper files.'

It was very quiet in the library, only the ticking of the big cased clock against the opposite wall and the occasional rustle as someone turned the pages of a newspaper disturbing the silence of the reading room.

As the Rector had said, the librarian, Miss Gillespie, an attractive woman of about thirty, was very helpful and efficient. Wilson had three thick bound volumes of newspaper files in front of him, covering three consecutive years. It looked like being a long search but it still wanted two hours to lunch and he had only to collect his typewriter ribbon on his way home. He searched for half an hour before his meticulousness was rewarded. Anstey was right; it had been quite a few years back. He was first alerted by the large heading of the local newspaper which spoke, predictably, of an 'Elderly Widow Missing'.

But the facts were accurate enough, judging by the quotations from county police sources, and as Wilson slowly turned the yellowing pages a pattern began to emerge, hardly discernible, but clarifying as his search progressed. The police had certainly been diligent in their searches. There was a photograph of Miss Hollamby in the second report he unearthed but the lady bore no relation to the image he recalled from his childhood. But then that was to be expected. The cousin the Rector had mentioned, Edward Povey, had soon put in an appearance but he had been no more helpful than other local people; less so, in fact, as he lived a long way away on the Sussex coast.

Wilson became more fascinated as he worked his way through the thick volume and he soon had all the salient facts at his finger tips. He jotted down notes in a small pocket-book he always carried, in which he amplified story ideas as they came to him from time to time, but he hesitated as to whether to impart all his new-found information to Deirdre and Barry. He put a question mark against his notations and decided to leave it until later: he needed a few more days in which to sift the facts in his mind. Anstey's confidences had come as quite a shock, and he even noted that his fingertips were trembling slightly as he put the pencil down on the open page of the third volume.

He would go through the whole sequence in the afternoon, when he had finished a few more study improvements. There would be time enough. He closed the book and, after a short talk with Miss Gillespie, walked out into the bright sunshine of Hoddesden High Street. It wanted merely a quarter of an hour until one o'clock. Just time to reach the stationers and make the short walk back.

He had been puzzled by the first headline he had come across in the newspaper file; the fact that Miss Hollamby was a widow. But it emerged that the marriage, many years earlier, had not been a good one and there had been a divorce. Her former husband had later died and she had reverted to her maiden name before coming to live at the Old Hall. Wilson did not really know why he was going to all this trouble. But he was becoming intrigued by the shadowy figure of his benefactor and there were the faint stirrings of a plot for one of his novels. He was between books at the moment and embryonic ideas were beginning to take shape.

Mrs Savage was desultorily clipping back foliage from the front door with a pair of secateurs.

'Lunch will be ready in ten minutes,' she said as he came up the path.

'I'm just going up to wash my hands but I'll be down directly.'

He thought the housekeeper had a somewhat subdued look on her face and she said somewhat jerkily, 'There's more mail on the table inside.'

He noticed the large bundle on the demilune as he went up the stairs and when he returned he took the letters and circulars into the dining-room with him to read over lunch. He was amused to find an early Christmas card among them, from a literary friend in Australia, but he was at the same time aware that Christmas would soon be on them and he and Deirdre had made no firm plans except that the two of them, together with Barry, were to celebrate their first yuletide in the house together. He hastily ripped open the letters, digested their contents briefly before passing on. He would try to reply to the more urgent ones in the afternoon before returning to his work on the house.

As he turned the penultimate letter over he saw there was another of the ancient postcards, still exuding the same musty smell. He now understood the strange expression on Mrs Savage's face and the reason why she had left the dining-room so abruptly as she brought each course, without lingering to make her usual salty observations on life and local people. Wilson stared at the faded image of Edinburgh for a long moment before turning the card over. Again the same spidery writing and the illegible initial. The abrupt message this time read simply: '*Taking in the sights. Looking forward to seeing you again. Perhaps for Christmas?*'

Wilson felt a faint tightening in his chest and his lips were dry as he looked at the thing. So the woman knew him? Wilson racked his

[167]

memory but could come up with nothing that made any sense. As on the previous occasion the heavy franking on the card made the date and postal details illegible, though he could make out the letters 'Ed', which could only mean Edinburgh. Whoever she was, he did not want a stranger descending, especially at Christmas. A sudden thought struck him; perhaps this was an elaborate joke by one of his readers who thought well of his books.

Wilson had written a couple of highly regarded fantasy novels some years back, which had brought him a shoal of admiring letters at the time. Yes, that must be it. Though it would be a nuisance, he need only see the woman for an hour or so if she ever turned up at the house; he could sign a book or two for her and perhaps present her with a volume from his spare copy shelf. Much relieved, he finished his lunch and went up to his study.

But something had disturbed the tenor of the day and around four in the afternoon, when he had cleared the backlog of mail, he rang up Barry in London and told him the latest development.

'You may well be right, John. But that doesn't explain the antiquity of the cards.'

He was being facetious now, Wilson knew, but he could not keep the irritation from his voice.

'I was relying on you for support. This thing is becoming a nuisance. Have you any ideas?'

He could imagine his friend in the big panelled curator's office in Kensington, the tranquil life of the great museum going on around him, and he felt a sudden stab of envy for the other's more ordered routine.

'I shouldn't worry about it,' Clissold went on. 'It will unravel itself in due course, no doubt. And if this woman should turn up I shall probably be there. We'll give her a quick glass of sherry and send her on her way.'

Despite himself, Clissold's brisk dismissal of the minor mystery made him smile.

'Let's hope you're right.'

'Art imitating life, old chap. You shouldn't grumble. May give you an idea or two for a new book.'

'That's not the point, Barry.'

'Well, we can discuss it at the weekend. I've got rather a lot of work on this afternoon and there's a Japanese party due in half an hour.'

'Sorry to disturb you,' Wilson said drily. 'But I just thought you'd be interested.'

[168]

'I'm certainly that. First thing is to compare the two cards and look for similar factors.'

Wilson bit his lip.

'Afraid I can't do that, Barry. I threw the first one on the garden bonfire.'

There was a muffled implosion of breath at the end of the line and then a long silence.

'Why on earth did you do that? I told you the thing could be valuable to a collector. That view of Aberdeen may have been unique. I haven't seen such an image in my life.'

'I'm sorry,' Wilson said. 'I just got annoyed with the damn thing. I hate mysteries in real life.'

'Oh, well, it can't be helped,' Clissold said philosophically. 'We'll discuss it in detail when I come down. Till tomorrow night then.'

There was a click as he put the phone back and Wilson was left with a feeling of frustration and annoyance, though he could not have said why.

5

He put the half-empty teacup down in the saucer with a sharp clinking noise, sat back at the desk and went through his roughly pencilled notes. A pallid mist hovered at the window today, making the dim outlines of trees seem ghost-like and ethereal. But inside, the central heating—he had had a new boiler put in at Deirdre's insistence—creaked comfortingly as the radiators gave out their warmth and the shaded lamps shone blandly down on every modern comfort, from the internal telephone system linked with almost every room to the latest in computers which sat on its own special desk near the window.

Though Wilson still preferred his heavy manual standard typewriter he had had the computer installed as Deirdre was expert in its use and had promised to key in and print out the typescripts of his books after they were married. It was an offer he had been unable to refuse. Now, he sat on the desk, absorbing, as though by some subtle process of osmosis, the mysterious, not to say bizarre circumstances of his aunt's disappearance.

Not that there was a plethora of information. The county newspapers had made quite a running story of it, it appeared, but a friend of Wilson's in London who ran one of the capital's biggest cutting agencies had failed to find any reference to it in the national news-papers. Not surprising, really; one old woman's disappearance, which was almost a daily occurrence on a nationwide scale, would hardly be considered important enough. Before he had left the library last week Wilson had taken the precaution of asking Miss Gillespie if she would run off photocopies of the items regarding his aunt and her cousin, and had given her the page numbers.

He had told her there was no hurry for them but as it had been several days ago he might look down there later and see if they were ready. He glanced at his watch quickly. Fridays seemed to come round with amazing speed and Barry and Deirdre would be there again tomorrow evening. It might be an idea to have the fresh information ready for them. He had, after all, decided to confide in them. They would both be interested, he knew, but there was a doubt growing at the back of his mind that the story might put Deirdre off the house altogether.

He would decide finally tomorrow. In the meantime the cuttings would fill out the story more satisfactorily and then he could spend time clearing up one or two of the rooms above the study. Incredibly, Hoddesden Old Hall had four storeys, if one counted the attics, which he had hardly penetrated, so full were they of old furniture and the debris of many years. There was nothing in the vaulted cellars but modern concrete floors; bunkers full of coal; and a very respectable collection of choice wines which he had been delighted to discover. The cellars were not, in any event, very extensive for a house of this size and he had plans to get rid of the coal and construct a small cinema and shelving on which to store his extensive archive of 16 mm film classics and erect suitable seating for himself and his guests, so that he could view the films in comfort.

With these and other thoughts coursing erratically through his mind he went swiftly through his pencilled notes; he did not think he had missed anything vital but the printed stories about his aunt, shorn of the journalistic verbiage and concocted melodrama, would fill in and add colour to the bare facts. Presently he got up from the desk, extinguished the lamps from a single switch at the door and went back downstairs to let Mrs Savage know his movements.

The thin rain had stopped as he slammed the massive front door behind him but the mist lingered and it was difficult to make out the far edge of the garden through the thick swathes of vapour. He turned toward the village, keeping well back from the pavement because some of the cars crawling through the mist were behaving in an erratic manner. He reached the library within a quarter of an hour, relieved to find himself back in warm and comfortable surroundings. The sounds from the road outside were muffled now as though they were coming from the far distance. Miss Gillespie was at the reception desk with her assistant and smiled brightly as he came up.

'Glad you looked in, Mr Wilson. I was just going to ring you. I have that material ready for you.'

She slid forward a large brown envelope which Wilson took with muttered thanks. He saw that she indicated the extracts and page numbers in red ink on the face of the envelope. She was certainly efficient.

'Many thanks, Miss Gillespie. What do I owe you?'

'Shall we say a pound?'

Wilson looked dubious.

'It doesn't seem very much. There's a lot of stuff here. Better make it two.'

The smile on the smooth face beneath the dark braided hair widened.

'Many thanks, Mr Wilson. We'll put the extra toward the tea money.'

She took the coins from him and was placing them in a drawer when she caught sight of someone over Wilson's shoulder.

'I think there's a gentleman you should meet, Mr Wilson. He's a mine of information on Hoddesden's affairs.'

A tall, broad-shouldered man in his late sixties, with silver hair and a well-trimmed Vandyke beard, was greeting the librarian in a jocular and affectionate manner. He was dressed in something that looked like a green hunting jacket and he wore a green felt hat with a gamebird's feather in the band. Wilson was vaguely amused. The newcomer looked like a character out of *The Prisoner Of Zenda* but he kept the thought to himself.

'This is Dr Broadbent. He's a distinguished historian and has written many books about historical subjects. Allow me to present Mr John Wilson, a well-known writer himself and we have many of his books on our shelves. Mr Wilson has just come to live at Hoddesden Old Hall.'

'Indeed!'

The smile was open, genuine and welcoming.

'Delighted to meet you, Mr Wilson! I must say I envy you your

[171]

possession of the Old Hall. My humble dwelling is eighteenth-century but yours goes back to the mists of time. I must say I would love to look inside your house on some mutually convenient date. The timber construction there is most remarkable and there are two unique crownposts in the upper chambers.'

Wilson returned the other's vigorous handshake, smiling in his turn. The doctor's enthusiasm was infectious.

'I should be delighted to invite you round for a meal one evening, doctor. Preferably when my fiancée and my good friend Barry Clissold, the museum curator, are in residence.'

Broadbent's face expressed even greater pleasure.

'Ah! You are a friend of Mr Clissold! Better than ever.'

Wilson concealed his surprise.

'I didn't know you were acquainted with Barry.'

The tall man in the rain-flecked garments wagged an admonitory finger.

'Kindred spirits, Mr Wilson. Fellow scholars. I am a doctor of philosophy not a medical man. Call me mister! The world does, though Miss Gillespie here—a very good friend, by the way—is meticulous about people's titles.'

She had turned away by this time but Wilson could see her shoulders shaking with suppressed amusement. He was warming to this new acquaintance by the minute and he might be a source of useful information. The two men had moved back and were now in an odd corner of the library building where shallow steps led to a small balcony and bookstacks hemmed them in so that a *sotto voce* conversation would be unheard by others using the library premises. Another useful factor was that they could, from their raised vantage point, see if anyone was coming in their direction.

Wilson was not quite sure why he was being so secretive this morning but some inner voice was enjoining caution. He skirted the topic most heavily on his mind.

'You met Barry where, Mr Broadbent, if I am not being too curious.'

'Oh, by no means!'

The big man stood with one massive hand on the polished teak railing and casually surveyed the crowded shelves below them. His dark eyes were clouded and dreamy beneath his shaggy eyebrows but there was nothing dreamy or indeterminate about his manner.

'There is no secret, Mr Wilson. I use his museum facilities in London a good deal and we naturally saw one another from time to

[172]

time and a friendship developed. As I said, we share certain esoteric interests. We used to compare notes in the library there. He's an avid collector, like myself, as you must know.'

Wilson nodded, deliberately keeping his voice casual.

'So you know the Old Hall.'

'Not as much as I should like to. It's quite the oldest extant dwelling in the village but the previous owner did not exactly keep open house and I glimpsed the interior on only two occasions when she grudgingly allowed the local historical society to look round certain selected rooms while one of our members gave a lecture.'

His eyes were focused to sharp points now, as though recollecting the scene vividly.

'Yes, Miss Hollamby. A very strange woman, if I may say so.'

'So I understand,' said Wilson, as though he had heard the comment before. 'I inherited the place, you know. She was my aunt.'

Broadbent turned an embarrassed face to his new acquaintance.

'My dear sir, I had no idea! I offer you my abject apologies . . .'

Wilson began to laugh, waving aside the other's remarks.

'There is really no need, Mr Broadbent. I never knew the lady and apart from a brief acquaintance when I was about five years old we had never met.'

The other's features cleared.

'Oh, I see. Yes, well, that makes a difference. I take it I may speak quite freely, seeing that you intend to live there. And as you have a fiancée, I also presume you will make it your married home.'

Wilson nodded, not quite sure what the antiquarian was getting at.

Broadbent lowered his voice, glancing around sharply once more.

'May I speak quite frankly?'

'I would be grateful if you would.'

'Good.'

The big man stroked his well-trimmed beard before proceeding.

'I meant nothing detrimental to Miss Hollamby, I can assure you. It was just that she was something of a recluse who kept apart from the life and activities of the village. Like most such people she was eccentric in her habits. Village gossip exaggerates, I know, but even allowing for that, some of her procedures were bizarre.'

'Such as?'

'Well, she was morbidly afraid of disease and wore gloves at all times, even indoors, I believe. She rarely, if ever, went out, at least, when she was living at the Old Hall. Her gardener used to do the

[173]

shopping for her on several afternoons a week. There were other stories but I won't go into them now.'

Wilson deliberately kept his manner casual though he was extremely interested in what Broadbent was saying. He eased out the sheaf of photocopies from the envelope Miss Gillespie had given him.

'Yet her disappearance was curious, wasn't it? And perhaps in keeping with what you have been telling me?'

'Ah, you have been doing some research in our archives, Mr Wilson. I approve of that.'

His face had clouded over now and the two men stood as though in some spell for more than a minute while the gentle mumble of voices and the civilized background noises of the library lapped around them.

'Yes, it was strange,' Broadbent resumed. 'But then elderly ladies do do strange things from time to time, unfortunately.'

'What do you make of that business of her nephew? That was somewhat bizarre too, I felt.'

Broadbent turned to face him on the narrow balcony, his gaze fixed over the other's shoulder to the floor below.

'Hardly bizarre. Something that could have happened to anyone. I hope it will not detract from the charm of your new surroundings. So far as I know that is the only violent occurrence in all the Old Hall's long history.'

Wilson joined in the other's smile.

'What was the cousin like?'

'Oh, Povey?'

For the first time Broadbent looked nonplussed.

'An unpleasant man, to put it no higher. His great good fortune did not seem to improve his manner or add to whatever happiness he got out of life. There was a lot of local gossip about him too. He lived here for only six months or so and that was quite a while back so I should not let these old newspaper reports cloud your coming, Mr Wilson.'

He tapped the bundle of photocopies which Wilson slipped back into the envelope.

'I hear you are making tasteful improvements up there. And with Christmas not so far away, the Hall should provide a charming background. Your fiancée will be there, I suppose.'

Wilson felt a sudden access of warmth toward this big, capable man. He was oddly comforting and his brisk manner was dispelling the vague aura of discontent that had been seeping into the author's thoughts lately.

[174]

'Oh, yes. And perhaps you would like to join us for dinner on Christmas Eve if you have no other plans. But we will make arrangements to show you over the house long before that.'

Again Broadbent looked embarrassed.

'I would be delighted, Mr Wilson! It really is too generous and kind of you.'

Wilson waved away his thanks.

'Think nothing of it. And as you are already an old friend of Barry's and I'm sure you will like Deirdre, you will be among friends.'

The two men walked back down the steps to the ground floor, conversing in normal tones now, and when they parted near the reception desk it was with a firm understanding that Wilson would phone shortly and make an appointment for Broadbent to come to tea and to see over the house.

His mind was full of conflicting impressions as he walked back to the Old Hall.

6

There was a savage squall of rain in the afternoon and Wilson descended to the ground floor with the library cuttings. There was a fire burning in the great stone fireplace in the lounge, though the central heating was on, but, as Mrs Savage said, the fire added cheer to the scene. Now he sat in a deep chair with his feet extended on the polished oak floor, which reflected the dancing shards of gold from the fire, and pondered his good fortune.

Mrs Savage's teapot and the tea things with a large tin of biscuits stood at his elbow, and the sheaf of photocopies on his knee occupied him intensely as the gentle ticking of another big cased clock went on in the corner. He was not really concentrating at this moment in time, lulled by the comfort of his surroundings; the vague feeling that he ought to be making greater efforts with the work on the house; and that there were many things to do regarding his preparations for Christmas. He went on sifting through the old newspaper reports of his aunt's disappearance and gradually again felt his attention becoming focused.

He was now on to the inquest on the body of the cousin, Edward Povey, following its recovery from the well. There was an arresting exchange between the police surgeon, a Dr Arnold Strang, and the coroner, Cedric Knowles, himself a medical man:

'"The cause of death of Mr Edward Povey was consistent with him having fallen through the rotten boarding of the well-cover."

'The Coroner: "Yes, I have your post-mortem report here, doctor. Death due to severe head injuries, bodily contusions, shock following the impact, plus a broken neck. Almost any one of these injuries would have been enough to cause death. Yet there was something else implied in your report, Dr Strang."

'"There was something beyond that, sir. The expression on the deceased's face was one of great shock and horror."

'The Coroner: "Surely anyone falling through a well-cover to his death would express on his features such shock and horror as you have described in your report?"

'Dr Strang went on to say that there was something beyond the normal. He continued, "I have carried out many such post-mortems during the past fifteen years and I have found in most cases of violent death, where that death was unexpected, that the victim showed surprise or mild shock. Usually the person is killed before he has had time to register such a realization upon his features."

'The Coroner: "I do not follow you, doctor."

'Dr Strang: "Well, sir, it is difficult to describe."

'The Coroner: "You are not implying that the deceased was pushed into the well or that there was any suspicion of foul play in your mind? Because, if so, there has been no evidence adduced at this inquest to support such a theory."

'"I am not saying that in so many words, sir."

'"Well, what exactly are you saying?"

'"I am not, of course, suggesting murder. But there is something beyond my experience in this case. I can only say that I have never seen such a shocking expression on a dead person's face in all the years I have been performing post-mortems in cases of sudden death. It is just a feeling I have and I would like it to go on record. Perhaps we had better leave it at that".

'The Coroner: "As you say, doctor, perhaps we had better leave it at that. But my clerk has it all on record."'

There was a good deal more in the photocopied stories of Miss Hollamby's disappearance and Povey's sudden death where the inquiries had been conducted in a similar sober and civilized manner but Wilson put the sheaf of papers down and stared into the heart of the fire, only vaguely aware that a slightly sinister dusk had fallen in the shrouded, rain-swept garden outside the ancient, small-paned win-

[176]

dows. The disquiet at the back of his mind had again returned, yet it was all so intangible; slightly less diaphanous than the mist outside the windows. He was now resolved to say no more about these matters to Deirdre.

Though he would discuss it fully with Barry when the pair arrived tomorrow evening, probably after Deirdre had retired for the night. He felt a certain guilt at this for Deirdre was a strong-minded, sensible girl and her refreshing commonsense would no doubt have thrown cold water on some of Wilson's more fanciful suggestions. He was long familiar with her arguments; mainly based on the exotic imaginings of a writer, of course.

No doubt Wilson was allowing his imagination to run away with himself but he did not want to cast any shadows on their happiness and he was determined that she should love and appreciate the old house as much as he did; he knew she was of that mind at the moment but she might not feel the same if he went into all this business of Miss Hollamby and the sudden and tragic death of the cousin.

Wilson was anxious to get Barry's opinion on these topics and his conversations with the Rector and then with Dr Broadbent had reduced the trivial matters of the postcards to their proper level. He withdrew his eyes from the misty garden and got up abruptly to draw the curtains, aware of the sudden clatter of Mrs Savage's activities in the kitchen, sanity again returning to the ancient beamed room with its atmosphere of comfort and culture.

He gathered up the cuttings and replaced them in the envelope. He would re-examine them again when he was in a less sombre mood. The weather did not help; the dreary atmosphere outside with the approach of winter was not conducive to cheerful thoughts. He wondered for a moment whether he was wise to bury himself in such a rural location. It was all very well in summer with London only half an hour away but what would it be like during the winter gales and, even more depressingly, when snow and ice made the roads impassable and he would be marooned down here? After all, life with Deirdre was almost a year away.

He finished his tea, ate another biscuit and took a turn or two about the room, his thoughts still slightly confused. He was interrupted by the entrance of Mrs Savage.

'Post is late today,' she said shortly.

She put the packet of letters down on the arm of Wilson's easy-chair.

'Getting closer,' she said enigmatically as she left the room.

Wilson soon saw what she meant for as he turned over the bundle, another of the old, musty-smelling cards fell out. He bit back the exclamation of annoyance that sprang to his lips and bent to retrieve it.

It was an ancient, tinted photograph of Carlisle and once again, with a quickening of the pulse, he saw that the postal details were obliterated and the initial indecipherable. The message was again short and cryptic: 'Still enjoying the sights and coming closer all the time.' His first impulse was to throw the thing in the fire together with the previous card but Barry Clissold's advice stopped him. Instead, he took the thing up to his study and put it on the desk with the other, both secured by a heavy brass paperweight.

Irritating and incomprehensible as this series of cards was, they were thrust into the background by the conversations he had had with the Rector and Broadbent; the material in the newspaper reports, much of which he had had no time to go through, had only emphasized his feelings. The thoughts they had engendered were beginning to tinge the whole atmosphere of the Old Hall with dark and shadowy forebodings and the damp, misty weather outside did not help.

But he was much cheered as he went in to dinner by Mrs Savage whose down-to-earth commonsense he was learning to cherish. Without being asked she herself broached the subject of the cards. He had asked her to take coffee and a cognac with him this evening before she cleared up and went home. She had obviously sensed his unease but was not aware of the reason for it.

'About those cards, Mr Wilson,' she said almost apologetically. 'I shouldn't take them too seriously. Perhaps someone you know, who's a fellow collector of such old things as Mr Clissold, is pulling your leg.'

'I don't quite follow you, Mrs Savage.'

'Well, Mr Wilson, perhaps it's someone in your life you've forgotten. A lady, perhaps, or possibly a man who's got a woman to help him.'

'But to what purpose?'

The housekeeper pursed her lips as though she were dealing with a backward child.

'Perhaps some sort of a joke and eventually he or she will turn up at Christmas and you can both have a good laugh about it together.'

'But would anybody spoil valuable old cards like that?'

[178]

Mrs Savage sipped delicately at her coffee and put the cup down before replying.

'Mr Clissold might feel they're valuable, but then he's a collector. I've seen such cards in boxes on market stalls and in London going quite cheaply. Anyone who knew about such things could obliterate postmarks and destinations.'

'But then how do you explain the fact that there are no modern stamps on the cards, and that the postman seems to know nothing of them?'

'Ah, you have me there, Mr Wilson. But there are ways . . .' She paused mysteriously. 'I expect they will be more frequent now.'

Again Wilson was nonplussed. But he had no need to put the question.

'Well, Mr Wilson; Aberdeen is quite a long way away, isn't it? Edinburgh is nearer and Carlisle nearer still. So whoever is sending the cards is obviously travelling towards us!'

Wilson made no reply and Mrs Savage got up with a quiet air of triumph and took her coffee cup and glass out to the kitchen. Wilson sat on, listening to the rain pattering against the window panes, quite uplifted. There was quite a lot in what she said but that still did not explain his last two points.

He shrugged and put the matter from him for the time being.

7

'Hmm. Interesting.'

Barry Clissold put the magnifying glass down and looked enthusiastically across the table at the other two. Deirdre pushed back the recalcitrant lock of black hair from her eyes, and gave an elegant little sniff.

'In what way?'

'In lots of ways.'

Clissold turned back to Wilson. It was Friday evening and the trio sat amid the debris of the dinner things. Clissold was quite a good cook and as a concession to the current cold weather he had provided his hosts with a hot main course. The rain still whispered at the windows but it was warm and luxurious in the dining-room with its blazing fire and shaded lamps.

'Name one.'

It was Deirdre again.

Clissold gave a stifled snort but his eyes were dancing with mischief.

'Mrs Savage is right in her suppositions about distance and her theory of the sender coming closer, but that still doesn't explain those old postmarks and the lack of modern stamps. I'll swear these never came through the postal service. Maybe the person lives here in the village or hereabouts and is hand-delivering them as though they'd come from afar.'

'The thought had occurred to me,' Wilson admitted.

Deirdre looked incredulous.

'But what's the point?'

'Mrs Savage thinks it may be someone I knew years ago and who wants to surprise me at Christmas time.'

Deirdre shook her head impatiently.

'She's certainly baffling you. Not to mention us. But I just don't believe it. It's too preposterous for words.'

'Well, let's leave it, shall we?' Clissold said. 'In the meantime, I'd like to borrow these two cards.'

'What for?' Deirdre demanded.

Tonight she wore a tight-fitting red sweater and white linen trousers, an outfit in which she looked boyish and at the same time infinitely desirable, Wilson thought. Perhaps she had read the expression in his eyes because he noticed a slight heightening of her colour; though it may have been due to the wine and the heat of the room. Clissold reached over to pour himself another glass of the rosé.

'We've got a lab at the museum. I'd like to have an analysis made.'

'By all means,' Wilson said. 'I'll be glad to see the back of the damn things.'

Clissold shrugged, got up and went over to put the cards in the briefcase he'd left in a corner of the room when they'd first arrived.

'Talking of museums reminds me of something,' Wilson continued when the other had reseated himself. 'I met an old friend of yours at the local library yesterday.'

Clissold gave him a sharp look.

'More old friends turning up,' he said. 'This sounds like an interesting village. Who was he?'

'It might have been a she,' Deirdre put in impishly. She gave her fiancée a slow, secret smile which was, however, not lost on Clissold, though he said nothing.

'It was a he,' Wilson said. 'A Dr Broadbent. A great historian and author of books on history. A big noise around here.'

Clissold broke into a smile.

'Good God! I didn't know old Arnold lived here. I must hunt him up'.

'No need,' Wilson said. 'I've invited him to have a look round the house soon. And he's coming to dine with us on Christmas Eve.'

He looked at Deirdre apologetically. 'I hope you don't mind, darling.'

She smiled brightly.

'Why should I? Mrs Savage and Barry will be doing most of the catering and one more will make little difference.'

Both men knew that Deirdre was an excellent cook but they also realized that she did a lot of cooking for herself and guests in London and did not want to be too closely involved with the catering arrangements at the Old Hall until she was mistress there. Wilson quite saw the point and had never pressed her on the matter.

'Good, that's settled then,' Wilson said, ending the topic as he thought. But Deirdre missed very little and her eyes had never left his face the past few minutes.

'And what interesting things did he have to tell you about this house, John?'

Wilson shifted uncomfortably in his chair.

'Oh, its incredible age, the wealth of pargeting and that Hereward the Wake once ate toasted tea-cakes here,' he lied humorously.

There was muffled laughter but Wilson could tell by Deirdre's face that she was only half-convinced of the truth of his earlier statement. He would have to be very careful in imparting what he had learned about his aunt and her cousin when speaking to Clissold later this evening. He changed the angle of the subject.

'Strange you not knowing Broadbent lived here.'

Clissold made a deprecating little movement of his shoulders, his reddish hair glistening in the lamplight.

'There's no mystery about that either, John. We always met in London, at functions, various libraries and at the museum. I knew he lived in the country, of course, but I didn't know exactly where. I never had any reason to enquire.'

The conversation drifted on to other things and it was almost midnight before the girl broke the silence which had fallen on them. The three were grouped round the fire in their armchairs as was their recent habit, and Wilson sipped appreciatively at the remainder of his second cognac in the big balloon glass, strangely

[181]

content despite the events of the past few days.

Then Deirdre got up abruptly.

'Well, you can stay down here all night if you like. Don't forget the bricklayer is coming to do that repointing at eight in the morning and the carpenter wants to look at those attic floors.'

Wilson got up too.

'I'd forgotten that. You're quite right, darling. Do you want me to see you to your room?'

Clissold gave a muffled snigger and Deirdre turned a laughing face to the two men.

'I think not,' she said primly. 'I know the way by now. And it might lead to complications. Don't forget to lock up.'

Her moist mouth brushed Wilson's in a familiar way and he again felt the subtle erotic thrill of the contact. He went out with her to the hall on the pretence of locking up and they were glued together in a brief, hot embrace before she ran lithely up the stairs, her heels beating a brief rat-tat on the oak treads.

Wilson went on to secure the house for the night, feeling somewhat unsteady and he realized the sensation was not entirely due to the wine and cognac he had imbibed. He bolted the massive front door which was the only one of the three entries to the house not yet secured for the night, extinguished the main hall light and returned to where Clissold sprawled contentedly in front of the fire. He went to stand by the fireplace, looking down at his friend.

'You know, we soon ought to be making some firm plans regarding Christmas,' he said. 'I have to book several meals out and we don't want to spend all our time cooking.'

'You've got lipstick all over your face,' Clissold said irrelevantly, his eyes dancing.

Wilson made a mouth at him, scrubbing vigorously with his handkerchief.

'Never mind about that,' he said. 'It's only about six weeks away.'

He went to sit down in one of the ancient seats actually inside the massive fireplace.

'You sure you've got the time off?'

Clissold stirred in his chair, fully opened his eyes.

'For Christmas? Of course. I've got a week's annual leave coming up and I've added three days to it, which will take us over into the New Year.'

He looked in the direction Deirdre had taken.

'That is, if the two of you can put up with me that long?'

'Don't be silly,' Wilson said. 'You know we love to have you around. And where should we be when it comes to the heavier manual work?'

He got up from the fireplace, not quite sure how to start the conversation.

'Another cognac?'

Clissold looked over at the big cased clock in the corner.

'Why not? It's only twelve-fifteen now, and I shan't be around at eight for the bricklayers in the morning. Deirdre's promised to bring me tea and toast in bed.'

Wilson raised his eyebrows.

'Really? As long as that's all she's providing.'

The two young men laughed, the sound echoing sonorously round the silent room with its massive beams and the huge bressummer over the fireplace.

'She's a lovely girl,' Barry said. 'And you're a lucky devil. You certainly don't deserve her.'

'I know that, old chap. But I do appreciate her.'

'I'm sure you do,' Clissold said warmly, taking the big balloon glass from him. He in his turn went to stand leaning against the fireplace while Wilson sank into a chair.

'Why don't you take the plunge too?' Wilson said after a bit, still looking for an opening.

Clissold frowned.

'What, get married?. Never yet met the right girl. Lots of possibilities and I've been playing the field pretty heavily.'

He laughed, showing strong white teeth.

'I notice you're not too much in a hurry, despite all the attractions lying in wait.'

Wilson smiled.

'Well, that's really Deirdre's doing. I respect her wishes. And there is still a hell of a lot to do before we get this place looking exactly as we want it.'

Clissold shrugged again.

'Well, don't leave it too late, that's all.'

The other looked at him sharply.

'What exactly do you mean by that?'

'Nothing, really. Except that there are a lot of counter attractions in London, you know.'

[183]

Wilson got up and joined the other so that they were both standing close to the fire.

'I take your point. But Deirdre's really not like that. If you knew her as I do . . .'

Clissold nodded, appreciatively tasting his cognac.

'Damned good stuff, this. I must make a note of the label.'

'Take a bottle on Monday, if you like,' Wilson said. 'I've got another three or four down in the cellar. Part of the inheritance so I shan't miss one.'

'I may take you up on it.'

Clissold looked as though he were ready to go to bed but his host gently waved him down into a chair.

'Listen. I want your advice.'

For the next ten minutes Wilson poured out his story, voicing some of his forebodings. Clissold sat silent and absorbed. He did not interrupt once but waited patiently until his friend had finished the history of the house as it concerned his aunt and her cousin. There was a long, brooding silence in the lamplit room as Wilson finished. Clissold said nothing for a while, his eyes absorbed and sombre. The firelight made a mottled mask of his face as he turned to the other.

'Well?' said Wilson impatiently.

'Interesting, John.'

'But no more?'

'Perhaps. For the imaginative. But I shouldn't tell Deirdre if I were you.'

Wilson bit his lip.

'Then you do think there's something bizarre about the house?'

Clissold got up, cracking his knuckles; the small reports in the shrouded silence of the room suddenly irritated Wilson, though it was a long-standing habit with his friend.

'Bizarre? About the house? No. No more than any other ancient building with a long and varied history. Povey's death was sudden and tragic, certainly, but as I've said before, these things do happen. You're surely not still worrying about those cards? A minor mystery but one that will probably be readily explained when the joker behind them eventually turns up.'

Wilson stepped nearer.

'What do you really think, Barry?'

'I've just told you.'

There were notes of fraying temper in Clissold's voice now.

[184]

'But why did you say not to tell Deirdre?'

Clissold had merely voiced Wilson's own thoughts but he could not resist pressing his friend.

'Just being circumspect. You know how sensitive and apprehensive women are about such matters. You don't want to put the girl off the house even before you're married, do you?'

Wilson's mood lifted and he put his hand on the other's arm.

'No, of course not. I expect you're right. And you know how I value your opinion. I'm not worried about those silly cards any more. I expect there will be a perfectly logical explanation in due course. But do let me know what your people find out at the museum.'

'Of course.' Clissold glanced at his watch. 'My God! It's almost half-past one. And we have a lot to do in the morning.'

Wilson felt his mind greatly eased as he extinguished the lights and prepared for bed.

8

'Anyone for coffee?'

Deirdre's banging on the tin tray with a spoon as she put the things down on a low stone wall adjoining the terrace startled Wilson momentarily. Incredibly, it was a brilliantly sunny day today and winter seemed to have temporarily departed, though a faint misty haze still lingered. The bricklayer had turned up on time, had erected his scaffolding and was busy pointing brickwork on one of the ancient stacks.

He had smilingly declined the coffee, which he said gave him indigestion and had brought his own thermos flask of tea, which he would drink aloft. Deirdre glanced up at him as he worked with the smooth precision born of long practice.

'You're lucky to get people to work on a Saturday down here, John. You wouldn't get that in London.'

Clissold, who had been hacking at the undergrowth with a sickle, joined them on the terrace, wiping the perspiration from his forehead with a blue and white striped handkerchief.

'Too right, Deirdre. Only fools work on Saturdays.'

The grin he gave the other two was infectious.

'You'll get your reward at Christmas, Barry,' Wilson promised him. 'Let's go farther down and I'll drag the teak seats out from the summerhouse. It's too fine a day to waste.'

The three were soon comfortably ensconced in an angle of the old house, where two walls met; it was quite a suntrap there and Wilson guessed that this had been a favourite summer spot of his aunt's. The three sat contentedly blinking at the sunlight and consuming the coffee and biscuits the girl had brought out, when she suddenly said, 'That reminds me. Do you chaps realize Christmas will soon be on us and we haven't got any presents, cards or anything else sorted out yet.'

'Don't bother us now,' said Barry rudely. 'I haven't finished with July.'

Wilson screwed up his eyes against the sun.

'The girl has a point. What with all this work I haven't had much time to think about it.'

'Well, it's about time you did,' said Deirdre decisively. 'After tea. It gets dark early now and we can make lists and things before supper.'

Clissold groaned and Wilson himself screwed up his eyes again. Like most men, and Barry in particular, he didn't like being reminded of urgent tasks that needed doing when he was taking his ease.

'We'll sort something out,' he said unconvincingly and Deirdre cast him a sudden glance of impish insight. She looked particularly enticing today, Wilson thought, with her blue jeans buckled in tightly against her flat stomach and a man's thick red sport shirt which only emphasized her tanned features beneath the mass of tangled black hair. He felt a sudden surge of joy and pride of possession.

'Don't forget the carpenter's coming at two o'clock to look at those attic floorboards,' Clissold said warningly.

'An attic tragedy,' said Deirdre, waiting for the groans which failed to come.

Wilson grinned wryly.

'It will be when the bill comes in,' he said.

He had been clearing out junk from the summerhouse, preparatory to burning it on the bonfire and he reached the end of this task at about midday. Deirdre was busy somewhere inside the house and Barry was still attacking the undergrowth in the neglected part of the garden. It ran to about two acres with thickets of dark fir and sycamore on the boundaries and Wilson had privately decided to leave the area where the sealed well lay as wilderness. He did not want to be reminded of such things and he thought he would erect a high board fence there, isolating the spot from the rest of the grounds.

He was musing in this way as he opened the inner front door and in the glass he suddenly saw an image reflected. It was that of a man and as he glanced back over his shoulder he recognized the local postman,

Mr Dunnett, disappearing down the drive. There were several letters lying on the mat. Among them was the familiar oblong of a postcard. Wilson turned it over.

Strangely enough, he was not worried about them now. This one showed a yellowed picture of the city walls in York. It appeared as though Mrs Savage's suppositions had been right. And the cards had been coming at increasingly short intervals. Only a day in this case; or perhaps two as the one from Carlisle may have been posted some time earlier, though it had only arrived yesterday.

Wilson trembled slightly but outwardly his manner was unruffled as he took the rest of the mail over to the demilune at the foot of the stairs. He glanced at the message side of the card, saw that some of the delicately formed handwriting had been smeared and partly obliterated as though by rain or damp. But he made out the end of a sentence, which read: 'Interesting perambulations. Still coming in your direction. Hope to be in the neighbourhood by Christmas.'

He could hear Deirdre moving about in the kitchen; then he was startled to hear sudden footfalls in the hall behind him. But it was only Barry, coming in to clean up before lunch.

Wilson handed him the card.

'Add that to the collection for your analysis. And please don't mention it to Deirdre.'

Clissold took the card without a change of expression.

'Right,' he said laconically, and put it in the pocket of his jeans and went on rapidly up the stairs. Wilson then saw that Deirdre was in the doorway. He did not know how long she had been there but she had apparently just come through from the kitchen because she said, 'Aren't you going to open your letters?'

'You do it, darling,' Wilson said, handing them to her. 'I don't think it's anything important.'

He went into the downstairs cloakroom to wash his hands and tidy up and when he came out she was still by the table, glancing at the opened correspondence. She handed it to him.

'Royalty statement. Request to address a women's club. An invitation to sign books.'

Wilson smiled.

'Routine stuff. But it's nice to be remembered. Royalty cheque reasonable?'

Deirdre smiled too, showing flawless teeth.

'More than reasonable. At least, I shan't be marrying a pauper.'

[187]

'Mercenary wench.'

They were locked in a fierce embrace when they heard Clissold hurrying back down the stairs. Deirdre tidied her blue-black hair in the oval mirror and shot him an amused but warning glance.

'I'm preparing a cold salad as the weather is so beautiful, I thought we could eat on the terrace. A bottle of chilled white wine and some of that angel cake from the village patisserie. I think I can just about manage coffee, too. All right?'

Barry had joined them now.

'More than all right. Eh, John?'

'Great. And there won't be too much clearing up to do before the carpenter comes.'

A clattering noise from the half-open front door made Wilson jump. He realized his nerves were becoming a little on edge.

'What was that?'

Deirdre gave him a strange look.

'It's only the bricklayer knocking off for lunch. I expect he's going down to the pub.'

A moment later they saw his grey-painted van glide past the end of the driveway.

'As long as he's in a fit condition to finish that stack afterwards,' Wilson said. 'I want to get the outside weatherproof before the winter sets in.'

'Plenty of time,' Clissold said. 'How many pubs are there in Hoddesden anyway?'

'Five in the village itself,' Deirdre said, turning back toward the kitchen. 'We've sampled them all. Three are pretty good and the other two really excellent. I expect he's gone to the Red Lion. That's the nearest.'

Clissold looked at the girl and then back to John.

'You two seem to have been making the rounds.'

The girl laid a hand on his shoulder.

'We're here more often than you, that's all. You'll catch up in time.'

'Perhaps we could try another some evening?' suggested Clissold. 'I only know the two nearest, at the entrance to Hoddesden proper.'

'Why not?' Wilson said. 'You've worked hard. And I don't want to strain your good nature, Barry.'

The strong teeth flashed in a ready smile.

'You'll never do that, John. But I must see this vast attic I've heard so much about.'

Deirdre had gone back to the kitchen now and the two men were alone.

'Don't expect too much,' Wilson said. 'There's an incredible amount of junk up there. And it's really a series of long, interconnecting rooms. There are some magnificent hammer beams. Later, we could make some superb reception rooms up there. Just the place for dancing.'

'Old Arnold will be interested,' Clissold said, resting his chin on the ancient oak balustrade as Wilson started ascending the staircase. A thin shaft of sun coming in from the stairhead window turned his hair a reddish gold.

'You look like a crucified saint,' said Wilson irreverently. Clissold laughed.

'Some hope of that! That's something Arnold won't be interested in. But returning to the subject of the attic, I can't understand why you don't put your cinema and film collection up there instead of the cellar.'

Wilson paused on his way up.

'Well, for one thing the cellar is bone dry, with enormously thick walls. I'm a late bird as you know. And if I use the attic I may disturb guests sleeping on the floors below, especially when I'm running late-night sound films. The attic rooms are far too good to waste in such a way, as you'll see after lunch.'

'Well, it's your house, John. I'm going to have a pre-lunch drink and then join Deirdre in the kitchen. See you on the terrace.'

Wilson was crossing the lounge after lunch when he heard the sound of the carpenter's van outside and he went to the front door to let him in. Tom Blake was a sturdy man in his thirties, with a mop of black curls and a frank, open manner.

'It will be nice to see The Old Hall in proper use again,' he said, as the two ascended to the upper floors. 'It had been badly neglected in Miss Hollamby's time.'

The two men had paused outside Wilson's study and a sudden flush suffused the carpenter's cheeks.

'No offence, sir. Seeing that she was your aunt.'

'That's all right,' Wilson hurriedly assured him. 'I'll just get the keys.'

He quickly hunted out the bundle from his desk drawer and rejoined the other on the dusty landing half a flight up. The stairs grew narrower as they reached the third floor, which Wilson guessed had been formerly occupied by maids and other indoor servants. Wilson had been briefly over the top floors but nothing had yet been done here as he was anxious to get the main part of the house habitable first. Most of the rooms contained old furniture and china in tea-chests, together with bundles of books tied with string and slowly mouldering away; while the dozens of large sealed cardboard boxes contained God knew what, he told himself.

There were two bathrooms on this floor also but he was undecided as to whether to have all these rooms brought back into use. After all, there were eight bedrooms below, as well as three more bathrooms. A large wooden door with a latch barred the way to the attics and the smell of mould and the accumulated dust of years grew more oppressive as they ascended the final flight. There was electric light, fortunately, and the dusty bulbs, giving only half light, revealed a more melancholy scene with every step they took.

'What do you think of these treads?' Wilson asked.

Blake had brought a small case in with him which the writer guessed contained tape measures, set squares and other such instruments. Now the former bent to the treads with a sharp, appraising eye.

'Solid enough,' he announced, going carefully up and down the narrow stair. 'There are a couple of places in the corners there. I shall use inserts and strong bracing for those. All in matching oak, of course.'

Wilson nodded absently, his thoughts elsewhere.

'I haven't spent much time up here, of course, since I moved in. Too busy elsewhere. But from a cursory glance I should think there would be much more for you to do in the attic itself. The boards seem quite rotten in several places, mostly in the corners.'

They had come to the top landing now and Wilson was fumbling for the keys. Blake shifted from one foot to another, his massive frame seeming to burst out of his dark blue shirt and matching jeans.

'That would be damp and water penetration over the years. Probably leaky tiles and shrunken window frames. As you know, we've put everything to rights up aloft.'

He was referring to the earlier work he had carried out with the co-operation of a larger firm. He was noted in the neighbourhood as a fine and conscientious craftsman with an excellent reputation in the surrounding area and Wilson was well pleased with his work so far. He put the key in the lock, turned it, tried another.

'There will be plenty more to do here,' Wilson said to cover the awkward gap while he found the right key. 'If you can spare the time.'

'Oh, I'll find the time, Mr Wilson,' said Blake easily. 'You have only to phone and I'll always be up within a day or two to give you an estimate.'

Wilson had the door open at last, stepped back as the smell of choking dust met him. It was hot up here under the eaves on such a sunny day and he asked his companion to open the small landing window. The two men were in the first of the big, shadowy attics and Wilson fumbled for the light switch. The illumination seemed to make the place darker as the only sunlight was filtering in through heavy green canvas blinds that appeared to be in the last stages of disintegration.

'I'll get those things down and the windows open,' Wilson said. 'Better let me do it because I've been up here before and know the bad places.'

Blake stood to one side of the open door, slowly appraising the contents of the vast rooms; noting the sheeted piles of ancient furniture; the glass and chinaware heaped at crazy angles in their tea-chests; parcels, bundles, statuary, tarnished brass oil lamps, and piles of hundreds of leather-bound books, stained and shrunken, that had been sitting on the dusty oak boards for perhaps the past forty or fifty years.

'Phew, what a mess!' he couldn't help exclaiming.

'You now see what I mean,' said Wilson, perspiration beading his forehead, as he wrestled with a rusted window catch. He'd torn the first blind down; it gave way with an ugly ripping noise and thick motes of dust danced in the shafts of strong yellow sunlight that only emphasized and reinforced the squalor of the place. He had the window open at last and relished the sweet afternoon air, with an undertone of autumn coolness that wafted in.

Blake had moved forward as the light increased.

'I see those places you mean. I'll take care.'

He moved down the enormous length of the four great connecting rooms, whose doorways had long been removed, leaving just ancient beamed bracing helping to support the roof, and the two men tore down blinds and opened windows until the freshing breeze at that height danced through, flapping the stained edges of the pages of books and sending trailing cobwebs spinning and spiralling, to the startlement of their owners. When they had finished, the two stood near the biggest central window as though deep in thought. From the corner of his eye, Wilson could see Clissold, a minute figure far below, crossing the garden on some errand. Wilson was the first to break the silence which had fallen between the two.

'What did you mean about Miss Hollamby earlier? You can speak your mind frankly. I never knew the lady, except very briefly when I was a small child.'

The big man shrugged, his eyes drifting across the jumbled chaos around them.

'Nothing, really. I was only going on to say that she was one of the most eccentric people I'd ever come across. That's if only half the local stories are correct.'

'So I've been told,' Wilson said. 'May I ask what else you may have heard?'

Blake paused and looked uncomfortable. The expression of unease on his face gave way to determination.

'Just gossip, really,' he said slowly. 'Some people said that the old lady's cousin had made away with her to get the inheritance. But that's only hearsay, you understand. You know what village people are and Povey was much disliked in Hoddesdon. I must say some local people thought Miss Hollamby was in the well too. It's enormously deep and the police couldn't dredge it properly. They were only able to recover Povey's body because it had lodged against a big iron bracket near the surface. But I shouldn't repeat that in front of your young lady, Mr Wilson. It would only make her uneasy. It was for your ears only.'

'Of course,' said Wilson, but the other's words had given him a strange feeling. 'You don't think she is in the well?'

Blake shrugged. 'If she is no one could ever find her there under thirty feet of rubble, topped by a three-foot concrete capping.'

Wilson fought down his ragged nerves as he looked the other squarely in the eye.

'You're not implying that the cousin's death in the well was the old lady's revenge?'

The laughter of the two men echoed hollowly beneath the great rafters and beams of the roof and started echoes from the corners.

'I have heard it suggested,' Blake chuckled. 'But I don't hold with such rubbish myself. However, I'd better get on with your commission.'

He got out the rule and a pencil and wandered about, testing the floorboards with a hammer and making notes in a small black book he

[192]

produced from his hip pocket. Wilson noted the absorbed interest of the professional and was careful not to disturb him. Instead, he walked up to the far end of the series of long rooms, thinking that it would take an enormous time to sift, sort and evaluate all this old furniture and other material, much of it would have to go on the bonfire or out for the dustmen but from what he could see there would still be an enormous residue. Fortunate that there were all those empty or half-empty rooms on the floor below. Some of the stuff would go nicely there along with some halfway decent oil paintings stacked against the wall, far from the light of the windows. Clissold's opinion would come in useful in evaluating them.

'So there you are!'

Wilson jumped at both the voice and the sudden footfall that reverberated on the bare boards of the attic. It was Deirdre who thrust her smiling face round the shrouded bulk of an old chest of drawers. She pushed back the lock of hair from her forehead, leaving a faint cobwebby streak. Wilson guessed she had just brushed against something coming in.

'You look startled, John. Whom did you expect to see?'

Wilson laughed.

'It was nothing, Deirdre. I was just in a brown study, that's all. Thinking principally what a lot of work we're going to have to do before we're finished.'

Deirdre gave a bright smile in the direction of Blake, who was dubiously testing the floor beneath one of the big windows.

'But it will be worth it, John. This could make a magnificent place when it's put in order. Even now we could clean some of this stuff and take it downstairs.'

Wilson gave his fiancée a sceptical look.

'Such as what?'

'Well, those are genuine Georgian silver candlesticks in that box over there. They'll look beautiful once they're polished. In fact I think I'll take them down now.'

'Hullo, hullo! Treasure-hunting already?'

It was Barry, who had crept up silently on rubber soles, hoping to catch them in some compromising situation, Wilson thought with an inward smile.

'Come in, Barry. You haven't been up here before.'

Clissold looked round slowly, acknowledging the carpenter's greeting with a brief nod. His voice sounded weary when he replied.

'No, and I'd rather not come again, judging by this mess. But I expect you'll find me plenty to do. It's time and a half on Sundays, remember.'

Wilson left the two of them and went back on down toward Blake, anxious to get his professional opinion. The latter lightened his mood at once.

'Nothing to worry about. I've located about a dozen boards that need renewing. I can saw a couple and use them across other joists when I've reconditioned them. And I have a stock of old oak floorboards in my workshop that will match perfectly. I can't give a firm estimate at the moment, of course, because it depends what we find when we get the worst ones up.'

Wilson felt relieved.

'Don't worry about that. Nothing major, then? That's fine.'

The two men chatted on for a few minutes longer and then Wilson left Blake to his measuring and rejoined the others, who were now rooting about among dusty wooden boxes in the centre of the floor in the second large room.

'What have you found?'

'Oh, this and that,' said Clissold but his eyes were filled with suppressed excitement. 'We'll take the stuff downstairs so we can dust and clean it.'

Wilson then saw that Deirdre had brought up a big plastic shopping bag, which was filled with salvaged material, while Clissold had a bundle of things wrapped in canvas under his arm.

'Come down for some refreshment when you've finished up here,' Wilson called to Blake.

He could hear the others chattering animatedly as he followed them down the stairs. But he could not get Blake's words out of his mind. What if the old lady's body was still at the bottom of the well? Then he relaxed. After all, tragic as it was, it hardly mattered now. It was years ago and the well had long since been filled in, as Blake had said. And concreted over. He tried to put it from him as he followed on behind the others.

9

A misty dusk had enveloped the garden when the three of them gave up work for the day and trooped in from the outside. The air was chill now and the sun hung an angry orange ball through the vaporous

them from London in the first week of December and by next weekend they would hope to have the rest done. In addition they had fixed a day for Dr Broadbent to come to look over the house and had actually telephoned and fixed details with him and for Christmas Eve also.

As he walked into the kitchen to make some coffee for the three of them, Wilson felt as though they were at last getting on top of things. And Blake would be coming on Monday to start work on the attic. Wilson had promised that the three of them would begin clearing the floor on Sunday morning and the carpenter had indicated very clearly the sections where he intended to start work. These were near the door and pretty sensible places to begin, Wilson felt. Far better than shifting a great mass of stuff from one end of the vast rooms to the other and then repeating the process in reverse.

He had forgotten Deirdre's earlier remarks and when he entered the big beamed kitchen with its massive Aga and modern steel sink units he was astonished to see how much she and Clissold had brought down from the top rooms. Most of it was piled on plastic sheeting in two huge bundles on the floor. The Georgian silver candlesticks were obviously the major find of the day and Deirdre had already dusted them and put them down on one of the granite working tops, together with a soft cloth and a tin of silver polish.

Somehow, Wilson felt touched by this little proprietorial gesture and once again he felt a small flash of remorse; Deirdre did so much for him in quiet, unobtrusive ways, and he felt he had never really adequately thanked her. He picked up one of the massive objects, marvelling at the intricately chased workmanship beneath the grime of years. He wondered why old Miss Hollamby had secreted such treasures away in a neglected attic. Perhaps they were relics of people who had lived at the Old Hall many years before or possibly she had simply put them in store and forgotten about them. That was the most likely supposition.

There was an impatient call from the lounge area—Deirdre with mock complaints about the lateness of the coffee—and a moment later Clissold poked his tousled head round the door jamb.

'No peeking!' he said in an affected voice. 'That's the *pièce de résistance*, you know, and we wanted to astonish you.'

Wilson laughingly put down the candlestick on the working top and bustled about with a pretence of great activity. Ten minutes later he made his way back to the lounge with the coffee and biscuits to find the others studying gift catalogues.

'Heavens!' he said protestingly. 'Christmas isn't for over a month yet.'

'You can't start too soon,' Clissold said. 'And I've seen a lovely pair of wool mittens that would just suit you.'

Deirdre had collapsed in front of the log fire, her shoulders shaking.

'You know what you can do with them,' Wilson said. 'Why do you play the fool so?'

Clissold put on a mock-crestfallen look.

'Try and get into the spirit of the season, old man,' he said. 'We'll just finish the coffee and then Deirdre and I will go out to the kitchen and put the treasures on display.'

'Why not bring them in here?' Wilson asked.

Deirdre shook her head, the blue-black sheen of her hair glinting in the firelight.

'Too mucky,' she said decisively. 'Tomorrow, perhaps, when I've had a chance to clean some of them up.'

Wilson said nothing further but settled himself at an oak side table and went over Blake's estimate again. He noted that all the joinery would be of the old, seasoned oak that the contractor had already mentioned. He was so absorbed, both with that and some drawings he had made for further improvements to the house, that he was only half aware that the girl and Clissold had left the room, though he could hear them faintly giggling as they went down the far corridor.

A comfortable silence ensued for about half an hour and Wilson was completely absorbed in his calculations, the only sounds the creaking of boards as the building settled, and once a log fell from the fire to the massive stone hearth, sending a small chain of sparks dancing.

Then he heard Deirdre's voice and rose quickly, putting his pen and the documents aside on the dark table surface. He made his way to the kitchen where the others waited with veiled expectancy.

'Well?' said Deirdre at last.

'Well, what?'

'Don't be obtuse, man,' said Clissold. 'Haven't you even noticed the candlesticks?'

He moved away as he spoke and Wilson was dazzled. They were indeed magnificent now that Deirdre had polished them and he was taken aback by their splendour.

'They must be worth a fortune,' he said.

Clissold nodded. 'Solid silver and genuine Georgian too.'

[198]

'That's what I can't understand,' Deirdre said with a little frown running across her forehead. 'Why hide them away in that dusty old attic?'

'Why indeed,' said Clissold. 'Maybe the lady used them to light her way around there.'

'Impossible,' Wilson said. 'I noticed before Deirdre cleaned them that they hadn't been used for years. There was no candle grease and certainly no trace of candle stumps in the sockets.'

Deirdre looked thoughtful.

'Yes. And didn't you tell me the agents said electric light had been run up there more than thirty years ago.'

'That's right,' said Wilson. 'Hullo, what's this?'

His attention had been taken by some exquisite animal carvings in rare wood. To him they looked like eighteenth-century Eastern European work but he was not expert enough to be sure.

'This is more your line, Barry,' he said. 'Genuine stuff, I presume? Like that jade there.'

Clissold looked quizzical.

'Can't you see the green in my eyes?' he asked. 'We didn't bring any rubbish down, I can assure you. I can get you free valuations any time at the museum if you wish. Some of this stuff is a bit out out of my field.'

'Later, perhaps,' Wilson said. 'But don't think I'm not grateful.'

Half an hour passed as the three rummaged among the agreeable treasures unearthed from obscurity.

'There are a few other smaller things that may be interesting,' Deirdre said at last. 'But we haven't had time to get to them yet.'

'Tomorrow will do,' Wilson said. 'Just look at the workmanship on that Japanese sword . . .'

He turned back from the big pine table on which the refurbished artefacts had been placed, set out with almost mathematical precision on the plastic sheeting. As he did so he kicked against something wrapped in plastic that stood near the table legs.

'What's this?'

'I haven't had time to see yet,' Deirdre said. 'Some very nice things in leather mostly.'

Wilson bent down to look. He stood up with a very heavy volume bound in expensive brown leather, with gilt lettering on the spine. He took the duster from Deirdre and wiped the leather clean before placing the book on the table. As he did so there came a musty, somehow familiar odour from the thick linen-backed pages.

'It's an old photo album,' he said in a somewhat unsteady voice.

He turned over the pages, almost reluctantly, aware of the beautifully mounted deckle-edged photographic prints, depicting the sensuous faces of long-dead Victorian beauties shaded by large-brimmed hats. There were scenes by the riverside, with picnic parties; punts gliding along what looked like the Thames at Marlow; and one extraordinary scene with young men and women intertwined in the rapture of the dance, as they waltzed in what looked like a Viennese tea-garden, beneath the soft glow of Chinese lanterns looped among tree branches.

'These look interesting,' Clissold said, moving closer. 'Does it say to whom the album belonged?'

Wilson shook his head, turning the spine of the volume to the overhead light. The gilt curlicue lettering merely winked back: *Photographs.*

'It's definitely an English album,' Clissold said. 'For a moment I thought it might have been Continental. Some of these studies have that feel about them.'

'I agree,' said Deirdre, craning over the two men's shoulders. She gave a little gasp. 'What's this?'

She had turned to the back of the book and Wilson now saw identical postcards to the ones which had arrived for him through the post during the past week. The resemblance was uncanny.

'This is remarkable,' Clissold said, enthusiasm in his voice. 'Yes, I have noticed. I'll go up and get those other cards from my valise so that we can compare them.'

'No need,' said Wilson, a deadly certainty settling over him. He had turned back the leaves. There, at the beginning of the sequence of pictorial views were the empty spaces where the original cards had been taken out. The next, where they resumed, was a view of Nottingham.

Clissold gave a rather foolish, wavering laugh. 'The lady's getting closer,' he said with an attempt at jocularity. And then, more slowly, 'It almost looks as though she must be sending them from here.'

'Don't be ridiculous!' Deirdre broke in sharply. 'There must be some perfectly logical explanation. How on earth can cards locked in an attic for years get into the British postal system for delivery here?'

'You have a point,' Clissold conceded. He avoided his host's eye.

[200]

Wilson guessed that he had been itching to see the interior of the house for many years and he hurried back to the kitchen to ask Mrs Savage to prepare some refreshments for eleven o'clock. Broadbent was punctual almost to the minute and as they went over the house together, the antiquarian explaining abstruse points of architecture and historical anecdotes regarding the structure, Wilson gradually began to be fired by the doctor's enthusiasm. It was almost as though he were the visitor and Broadbent the host, showing him facets of his own dwelling that he had never even noticed.

Before they descended to the lounge for their coffee break, Wilson took his guest up into the attic rooms to show him the progress they had already made. Broadbent looked round with approval, his eyes missing nothing.

'These will be magnificent, when finished,' he said. 'I envy you, sir, though I am not exactly short of space myself.'

He walked up to the far end of the vast rooms, threading his way between ranks of sheeted furniture that Wilson had not yet explored. He grunted with satisfaction as he knelt to inspect the new work on the floor and window surrounds.

'Yes,' he said, rising to dust his trousers. 'Tom Blake is a good man. One of the best craftsmen hereabouts. Had him in to do some of my own renovation work.'

'He's promised to come back this afternoon,' said Wilson as they descended to the ground floor. 'He's gone somewhere this morning to discuss the renovation of a tithe barn.'

Broadbent nodded, stroking his beard. His kindly eyes looked reassuringly at the other.

'The owners are in good hands, then.'

After the coffee they continued the tour, taking in the cellars, and when Broadbent eventually left, declining all invitations to stay on to lunch, Wilson felt curiously deflated. He went out into the front garden, where thin swathes of mist still hung above the frosty grass, all stained a rust colour by the red ball of the sun low down in the winter sky. There was still much to do before Christmas, Wilson mused, both in the renovation of the house and in his personal affairs. His thoughts were interrupted by Mrs Savage calling him in for lunch.

Another of the cards came in by the early afternoon post which Hoddesden still enjoyed. It depicted the Goose Market or some such place in Nottingham; the same view as that in the card upstairs. Wilson hardly noticed, he felt such constriction of the heart. The reverse said: '*Still coming to meet you, John.*' It was the first time the unknown writer had used his name but the other particulars were the same. He threw the thing almost savagely on to the hall table and went out for a long walk, turning away from the village and striding through the bleak countryside that lay beyond; the bare branches of the trees and every individual twig stood out silvered by frost, like some exquisite artist's conception, but he was in no mood for such fancies this afternoon.

His first thought was to visit the Rector and he made a wide circle back toward the village, but then he decided against it. He did not really need spiritual advice at the moment but a layman's common-sense. He longed for Barry's solid expertise and the reassuring comfort of Deirdre; it was true there was her call tonight but she would not be returning for another four days. It seemed a long time to get through. Back at the house he found that Blake had arrived and that work was steadily progressing in the attics while the bricklayer was again at work on the stacks.

He had put the card away in his desk and gradually, in the press of making decisions about the house and in preparing for Christmas, his mind emptied itself of the subject, though it was never far from the surface. The following weekend passed in a much lighter atmosphere and though Wilson showed Barry the latest card in confidence while Deirdre was in the kitchen one afternoon, the latter made little comment and put it in his suitcase.

'There's been a big run of work on at the lab lately,' he said. 'But I hope to phone you with a report on the cards by next Wednesday.'

The next week three more came, each bearing the ancient views that Wilson had come to hate and fear. The first was from Leicester, the second from Aylesbury and the third, on Wednesday morning, from London. Each one bore the cryptic message: '*Coming closer.*'

He had put the latest on his desk and was staring at it obsessively when the jangling of the phone exacerbated his already eroded nerves.

It was Barry.

'I've got that lab report back,' he said in a rather restrained voice. 'Not very good news, I'm afraid.'

Wilson cleared his throat with difficulty.

'What do you mean?'

'Well,' Clissold began diffidently, 'it's against all the odds; against all reasonable scientific proofs, of course, but those cards . . .'

His voice trailed off.

'Well?' Wilson asked almost savagely.

Clissold plunged on.

'I didn't tell our lab people, of course, what exactly we had in mind—just asked them to date the cards and give me their opinion on the writing. As we know the cards must have been posted a few days before you received them, the thing's a scientific impossibility. Our chief scientist says that the writing and the ink used date from many years ago.'

Wilson could not speak for a moment and blackness seemed to envelop him. He must have felt dizzy for a second or two because he next heard his friend's anxious voice issuing tinnily from the mouth-piece and he realized he had dropped it on to the desk. He picked it up with a trembling hand.

'My God, I'm frightened!' he burst out before he could stop himself. 'I've just had another three of those beastly cards, the last posted from London. Each one says simply: "*Coming closer*".'

'Now hold on,' said Clissold hurriedly. 'No need to get upset, John. We'll be with you shortly, and I'm coming several days before Christmas. Then we can face this thing together.'

'So you are beginning to take it seriously?' Wilson said.

'There has to be some logical explanation in the end,' Clissold persisted stubbornly. 'We've just got to work this through. And it mustn't spoil Christmas.'

'But the last card came from London,' Wilson said wearily. 'This means the woman will be here shortly. But what sort of woman, who writes with ink fifty years old or whatever your lab people say?'

'It's too fantastic for words,' Barry said. 'There's got to be a logical answer, as I just said. And we mustn't let Deirdre know.'

'For God's sake don't say anything to her. Not even about the new cards.'

'Quiet as the grave, old man. Don't let it get you down. I'll try and get there on Friday afternoon if I can. I'll take an early train if Deirdre can't get away in time.'

'Thanks a lot,' Wilson said. 'I greatly appreciate it.'

The two friends said goodbye and he hung up. Then Wilson put the three latest cards in his desk drawer. As he did so a sudden thought struck him. He got out the heavy leather album and opened the musty leaves. He looked incredulously at the pages. There were three extra spaces where cards had been before. He checked again on all the empty places, extending over two pages. They tallied with the number of cards he had received. All had inked captions and the last of the missing set indicated Leicester, Aylesbury and London.

Then he noticed that the very next card, after the interrupted series, showed a faded old view of a village only ten miles away. When he left the room half an hour later he was walking like a drunken man.

11

For some days Wilson could not concentrate on the work on the house and wandered the great beamed rooms as though in a somnambulistic trance. Mrs Savage noticed immediately the change in him but was unable to draw anything from her employer, despite her solicitous questioning. Wilson left Blake to his renovation work above and locked his study, retreating to one of the smaller ground-floor rooms overlooking the garden, where he installed his typewriter, his note-books and a fresh ream of typing paper. Here he made a pretence at work as the shock of the most recent events slowly began to recede.

He dreaded the arrival of the post and often took long walks about the village when the mail was due in, returning only when he was satisfied that none of the sinister postcards were on the hall table. In the meantime he made discreet inquiries at the library, reread the photocopies of the newspaper cuttings as though he might, somehow, by a process of osmosis, arrive at the truth of the bizarre events that he felt were beginning to enmesh him. He longed only for the arrival of Deirdre and Clissold when the house would be again fully inhabited and a more normal atmosphere would prevail.

His self-sought solitude was broken on two occasions by the arrival of the Rector, who came to bring him Christmas greetings and to invite him and his guests to a midnight carol service on Christmas Eve, which Wilson gladly accepted; and the second time was a more social call when Anstey stayed on for sherry and biscuits and a long chat.

Wilson was greatly taken with his strong character and common-sense by this time and though greatly tempted, kept his mouth tightly shut on the subject of the postcards and particularly the death of Povey and the disappearance of Miss Hollamby all those years ago. He craved the comfort of Deirdre's encircling arms and her sturdy com-monsense but at the same time he was worried in case his haggard face, withdrawn manner and edgy nerves would quickly lead her to the truth.

But as day followed day without any more cards being received he began to recover; he slept better and rediscovered his appetite. Mrs Savage noticed the change in him and put it down to the imminent arrival of his fiancée. In fact things were so back to normal that Wilson took to using the study again on Friday morning, though his desk remained locked. Blake was still hard at work and Wilson was frequently in and out of the attic rooms, admiring the carpenter's skill and craftsmanship as he shaped and restored window frames and gradually replaced all the defective boards. One of the roof-beams was found to be in a dangerous condition and he renewed that with no help other than that afforded by a portable sling hooked to one of the great king-posts; and the next time Wilson looked in he found that Blake had even shaped the massive timbers to match the adjoining adze marks on the ancient originals.

At the weekend Wilson was so far himself again that he entered fully into the Christmas preparations, inaugurated by Deirdre, who looked dazzling in a dark blue evening dress on the Saturday night when the three went out to dinner at a fashionable roadhouse some miles distant. Though Wilson and Barry discussed the strange situation in which they found themselves into the small hours each night, they came to no probable solution to the mystery.

'Perhaps you ought to sell that album,' Clissold had muttered one night as he mounted the stairs. But, Barry, true to his word, had said nothing to Deirdre and gradually the two men put their sombre thoughts behind them and entered fully into the spirit of Deirdre's arrangements.

On Friday night they had trimmed and decorated the tree which had been brought into the great beamed lounge, though it was really a hall house which had been fitted with a lower ceiling at some period of its history to create more accommodation upstairs.

Carol singers were round early on the Saturday evening, as the three finished sending out the last of the cards, and when Wilson had left lists for Mrs Savage on Monday for the various provisions for Christmas week he was quite himself again. They arrived back to find a few flakes of early snow falling, but on the Sunday morning the expected blizzard had not materialized, though the ground sparkled with frost.

'And a very good thing too,' said Deirdre firmly. 'I wouldn't have fancied driving back along these narrow lanes in heavy snow tomorrow morning.'

'I think it might be better for you to take the train Christmas week,'

Wilson said seriously. 'Just in case there is a heavy snowfall over the holiday period.'

'We'll see,' Deirdre said. 'I like to be independent, as you know, and I don't fancy crowded trains at this time of year.'

'Nevertheless . . .' began Wilson, interrupted by a warning glance from Clissold. He dropped the subject abruptly. Barry was undoubtedly right; if he got into an argument with Deirdre it might lead to other things. His nerves were in shreds beneath the surface. If he got irritated she'd soon know something was wrong.

'Only a few days to Christmas,' said Clissold cheerily. 'We really ought to sort out the itinerary. And what about presents . . .?'

Wilson smiled a genuine smile.

'That's a restricted subject. There are certain locked cupboards in this house.'

Deirdre came up behind him and put her arms round his neck. The tip of her pink tongue tickled his ear. Wilson was embarrassed in front of his friend and tried to wriggle away but she only held him tighter.

'Secrets, eh?' she breathed. 'You said there were to be no secrets between us.'

'Only at Christmas,' Wilson said shortly. 'You'll spoil the surprises.'

Clissold laughed, breaking the sudden little tensions that had begun to grip Wilson.

'He's using the plural, Deirdre,' he said. 'So there are more than one. A generous chap. It's a good augury for the marriage.'

Deirdre smiled too and gave Wilson an affectionate little kiss on the back of his neck before moving away.

'It's Christmas time,' she said, giving her fiancée an enchanting smile. She looked round the big, beamed room, shining with lamp-light and firelight; taking in the brilliantly decorated tree and the sprigs of holly festooning the tops of pictures, the old clock and the doorcases. To Wilson the berries suddenly seemed like little dark flecks of blood.

'We don't want to talk about balls and chains and lifelong commitments,' Deirdre went on. 'We're going to enjoy ourselves.'

Clissold made a knowing little grimace at Wilson which Deirdre intercepted. She laughed again.

'No need to worry, gentlemen,' she said gravely. 'I shall fall into line like everyone else when the time comes.'

'It won't be that bad,' Wilson promised. 'Now, when are you two coming down?'

'As I told you, I've got quite a bit of time off,' Clissold said. 'I'll be here next Wednesday. That's six clear days before Christmas and I can give you a hand with the renovations or whatever.'

'I'd greatly appreciate it,' Wilson said. 'What about you, Deirdre?'

She frowned, which didn't affect her beauty at all, Wilson thought.

'I can't make it as soon as I would have liked, but I'll manage Friday afternoon. That's still four days before Christmas Day.'

'Fine,' Wilson said and gave her arm a little squeeze as he made his way to the liqueur cabinet.

Next morning, when they were both gone, he had the same old sinking feeling. But Mrs Savage's bustling presence soon restored his spirits.

'I'm making some nice things that you can store in the fridge, Mr Wilson,' she said. 'They'll keep nicely for Christmas and you won't have too much trouble over the holiday.'

'Excellent,' Wilson said. 'And I greatly appreciate your kindness in coming in on Christmas Eve.'

The housekeeper gave him a knowing smile.

'Well, you do have a dinner party and an important guest. But I'd like to leave by three o'clock to make my own arrangements. I'll leave everything ready. Your young lady will be able to manage all right after that.

'Great,' Wilson said. 'I'll make it worth your while, Mrs Savage.'

'I don't do it for that, Mr Wilson.'

'I know,' Wilson said gently.' That's why I like to do it.'

When Mrs Savage had left the room he sat for a long while, feeling an unaccustomed glow of contentment. Presently he went out for a walk. There was a ferocious edge to the wind but a fragrant smell of woodsmoke in the air. It looked as though it was going to be seasonable weather. Contrary to his expectations the next few days passed quickly and agreeably, and he ate and slept well, free from all the things that had been troubling him.

He attended an antique market in the village and a carol concert at the local school, exchanging greetings with people he was coming to know. On Wednesday morning Clissold had phoned to say that he was detained longer at the museum than expected but would definitely be there late that night.

That was the morning the penultimate card came. It lay on the demilune and he picked it up with fear and loathing. It was an old card depicting Gosford, the village only half an hour's drive away. The message was as clipped as the illegible initial. It merely said: '*Be with you soon.*' On impulse he took it into the dining room and threw it savagely on to the great log fire. It burned with a curious greenish glare that set strange shadows dancing on the panelling and to his over-heated imagination it seemed as though the sudden upsurge of flame was accompanied by a faint screaming sound. Then he realized it was merely the sap burning in the logs and used the poker vigorously, forcing the jumbled wood into silence.

He debated for some time whether to tell Barry. In the end he decided he would share the knowledge. And after all there appeared to be more at stake here than his wanton destruction of potentially valuable old postcards. Despite his doubts and fears he forced a strained smile at the thought. Contrary to his habit he walked down to the station to meet Clissold off the half-past ten train.

He could not bear the clotted silence of the great house on this winter night. Mrs Savage had, of course, long gone home; she had said nothing about the card but now Wilson wished he had spoken to her about it. She had probably brought it in from the hall and had tactfully avoided the subject. In some ways he wished she had herself thrown the card on to the fire but he realized that given her trust-worthy and upright nature that would be the last thing she would do.

His feet crunched heavily over the frozen paving as he went down the shadowy lane between the yellow glare of the street lamps, his shadow flung swiftly before him on the powdery white surface of the road. There was little traffic about tonight and the inhabitants of Hoddesden were obviously at home busily preparing for their own Christmas celebrations, though there were a few late-night shops such as grocers and chemists which still kept open.

The train was only a few minutes late and Barry's welcoming face was soon evident among the surprisingly large crowd of passengers that debouched from the eight-coach diesel. The two men shook hands. Clissold carried with him a heavy suitcase and a large canvas bag and Wilson took the latter from him as the two fell into an easy stride.

'Forgive me for not bringing the car,' Wilson said. 'It seemed hardly worth it for such a short distance.'

The other shook his head.

'It doesn't matter at all. The exercise is good for us. And since we're going to be heavily over-eating at Christmas . . .'

He broke off suddenly. The two men were passing beneath a street lamp and the guest had noticed the expression on Wilson's face.

'You've had another card,' he said quickly.

Wilson nodded, unable to speak for a moment.

'It came this morning,' he said. 'Apparently posted from Gosford. That's only a few miles off. I'm afraid I burnt the horrible thing this time.'

The two had paused for a moment and Clissold put a reassuring hand on the other's shoulder.

'It will be all right,' he said soothingly. 'There are two of us now. Mrs Savage will be back in the morning and Deirdre arrives the day after tomorrow. Full house again.'

Wilson forced a smile.

'That's true.'

The two men moved on, their shadows dark and mysterious against the frosty white tracings on the pavement. They did not mention the matter again and once at the Old Hall they flung themselves into small tasks, interspersed with hurried conversation, as they prepared to make a fitting reception for Deirdre when she arrived. It snowed in the night and when they woke in the morning there was a deep oppressive silence everywhere, a dazzling whiteness in the garden and Mrs Savage complaining banteringly of the difficulty she had had in walking in.

To Wilson the snow came as a welcome diversion, though he was a little worried in case Deirdre was unable to get there. For it snowed all the next day and by Friday, when his fiancée was due to arrive, it lay in thick drifts, banks of fog between the distant trees giving a spectral aspect to the landscape. Wilson phoned Deirdre and persuaded her to take a train and then he and Clissold dug out a path to the garage and while Barry cleared the driveway with some difficulty, he put chains on his tyres in order to drive Mrs Savage home.

The main road had been partly cleared by the local council but later snow, drifting, had been compacted by the sparse traffic and the surface, with its thin coating of ice, was treacherous.

When they arrived back at the house it wanted only an hour to Deirdre's arrival. Clissold tactfully volunteered to stay behind and prepare their evening meal while Wilson drove down to the station. In the event the train was half an hour late and he had a miserable time stamping about the badly heated waiting room before the one face in all the world, with its crown of blue-black hair, now with a faint dusting of snow, came flying through the crowd, its owner, heavily furred, bearing suitcases and mysterious packages.

[211]

The melting into each other's arms and then the silent drive to the house; glances passing from one to the other; quiet contentment in the joy of possession; minds at rest and exhilarated with the prospect of a whole week or more of Christmas festivities ahead; cut off from the outside world by a brittle coating of snow and ice, ghostly white as the headlights glanced across the latticework of trees that fringed the road.

Back at the house Clissold was presiding, beaming over a fully laid dining table, glass in hand as he welcomed them both.

'Dinner in twenty minutes! And here's a toast to the new master and mistress of Hoddesden Old Hall!'

12

The next few days passed swiftly and though the blizzards continued, little seemed to disturb the well-ordered routine of the household. Even Tom Blake continued work on the attic rooms until just before Christmas. He had now covered about half the space and Wilson promised him they would shift more of the furniture ready for the next phase, which he intended to start around the 28th of December.

The Tuesday before Christmas Wilson rose early, his mind at rest. He had phoned Broadbent the previous day regarding the weather but the latter had said he was well able to walk the short distance to the Old Hall for the Christmas Eve celebrations. Surprisingly, most of the post and milk deliveries were getting through and radio and television reports indicated that public transport was still working at seventy per cent capacity.

Early as he was, Clissold was already up and working in the kitchen and the agreeable smell of toast and coffee drifted out as Wilson went down the corridor. He fancied there was a somewhat strange expression on his friend's face and a moment later he saw what had caused it when Barry handed him another of the now detested postcards.

'This just came. Though it's miles too early for normal deliveries.'

Wilson stared at it dully, his thoughts turning uselessly.
Then he made out the faded sepia view. It was Hoddesden High Street at the turn of the century. He turned the card over with deadened fingers. Mechanically he glanced at the inked message, barely taking it in.

'At *last!*'

'She's here!' he told his companion, dry-mouthed.

'And so are we,' said Clissold grimly. 'We three. Four of us, when Mrs Savage gets here. There's nothing to be afraid of, man.'

His reassuring words steadied Wilson a little.

'Someone's having a diabolical joke,' said Clissold savagely, pouring coffee.

Wilson sat down automatically, hardly conscious that he did so.

'I wish I could believe that,' he said, ashen-faced.

Clissold pointed with a spatulate finger at the inked initial.

'I've just thought of something. That could be an O.'

'Well—'

'Your aunt. Old Miss Hollamby. Her christian name was Olive, wasn't it? Someone's having a dreadful game with us. I wish I could get my hands on the perpetrator.'

'And I wish I could believe you,' said Wilson, the hot coffee bringing some of the colour back to his cheeks.

'What other explanation is there?' said Clissold in a matter-of fact-voice. 'Such things cannot be. Dead people don't come back. And if she was in the well she could never get out in a million years.'

'That's true,' said Wilson slowly. Just what Blake had said.

His heart had stopped hammering and he felt a little more normal now. He accepted the slice of toast Clissold pushed toward him.

'Even so, we must think of Deirdre. Burn that thing before she gets down. We don't want to spoil her Christmas.'

Clissold took the card from him and put it straight in the boiler; again, there was the strange greenish flare and the musty odour. Wilson went over to the sink to wash his hands before starting on fresh toast.

'So what happens now?' he said dully.

Clissold smiled.

'If someone does turn up we shall be ready for her,' he said in a deceptively mild voice. 'There are laws to deal with such things.'

Wilson felt more at ease now.

'A bit difficult to prove in a court of law, wouldn't it?'

Clissold shook his head.

'I wasn't speaking about a court of law. I just want to put the fear of God into her.'

'She sounds more like someone out of a lunatic asylum,' Wilson went on as though talking to himself, all the time aware that their pat explanations could not touch the core of the matter; how the cards were delivered or why the messages were written with ink half a century or more old.

'What were you talking about?'

It was Deirdre in the doorway, looking radiant and rested.

'Oh, this and that,' said Barry casually, not knowing whether she had heard anything of their conversation or not. 'Chiefly my superb culinary gifts. Voilà, mademoiselle! Coffee and toast!'

Deirdre laughed obediently but her eyes were darting shrewd glances at Wilson. He made an effort to appear normal and joined in the conversation, relieved a few minutes later by the arrival of Mrs Savage, welcomed by Clissold with an invitation to a second break-fast, which she gratefully accepted.

The day passed in a whirlwind flurry of last-minute activities and towards dusk the snow stopped and stars blazed out of a deep velvet sky. The three were agreeably tired but satisfied with their exertions and went to bed fairly early for them—before eleven o'clock—as the following day was Christmas Eve. Wilson slept well and on waking found his mind cleansed of all his previous forebodings. He found Deirdre already busy in the kitchen. She broke away from his arms with a flushed face as Clissold's footsteps sounded on the stairs. He poked his head in at the door.

'The mail's just come,' he said brightly. 'Nothing but bills by the look of it!'

This was for his host's benefit, as Wilson's face had momentarily changed alarmingly. Deirdre was bent over the sink so the moment passed unnoticed. Mrs Savage arrived at the appointed time and the day passed without incident. There was the crisp sound of church bells coming from the nearby village; the occasional rumble of a passing car, its driver cautious with the steering wheel as he traversed the treacherous road surface; once, some last-minute carollers; the faint barking of a dog in the thin air.

Wilson felt extraordinarily happy as he went up to his study to do some last-minute packing of presents for Deirdre and Barry. He busied himself with coloured paper and string, vaguely aware of muffled laughter and preparations for the coming feast going on below. When he came downstairs he found Mrs Savage ready to depart and pressed into her hands a thick envelope and a very expensive bottle of wine, suitably wrapped. Clissold drove her home and returned in twenty minutes to say road conditions were much better.

Dusk was falling when there was a sudden ominous click and the whole house was plunged into darkness. Wilson was replenishing the lounge fire at the time and he heard Clissold swear as blackness descended; he had evidently cut himself during one of his kitchen tasks. As Wilson hurriedly crossed the hall he could hear Deirdre throwing light switches to no effect.

'It's a power cut,' she called. 'This would happen on Christmas Eve!'

Clissold loomed up, a shadowy figure, putting a small plastic bandage round his little finger; they kept a kit in the kitchen.

'Where are the candles?' he said.

Wilson looked at him hopelessly, his face worried in the faint light of the snow filtering in through the hall windows.

'We haven't any,' he said. 'Though there may be some in the cellar somewhere. This is something I never thought of.'

'But we can't be without light tonight,' Deirdre said. 'This might last for hours and we have a guest coming. Thank God we have a gas cooker so the meal won't be affected.'

She went over to the hall rack and reached down her anorak.

'Where are you going?' Wilson asked.

She gave him a pitying look in the dusky hallway.

'To the village to buy some candles, of course. It's only four o'clock and the shops are still open.'

'I'll go with you,' Clissold said decisively. 'I'm out of cigars anyway. Besides, you can't go alone in this weather. You might fall into a snowdrift. And it's not worth getting the car out again. I put it in the garage for the night.'

'As if I would fall into a snowdrift!' the girl said contemptuously but there was an affectionate look in her eyes which was not lost on Wilson.

'Barry's right,' he said.

Clissold was already shrugging on his overcoat.

'We'll only be about half an hour at the most. Anything you want in the village?'

Wilson shook his head.

'Not that I can think of. But be careful, the two of you. It's pretty treacherous underfoot.'

The two waved, the front door slammed and Wilson was left alone in the muffled silence of the dying of the day. He went back into the lounge and poked the burning logs in the fireplace, sending great flickering shadows over the furniture and on to the walls. The radio was still switched on in the kitchen; it worked off batteries and it was comforting, as he went in, to catch the latest bulletin on the weather. It sounded pretty glacial over the whole of the country.

Wilson went back into the lounge to check the fire and from there into the dining-room. He had just realized that the central heating would be off too and if the power cut lasted all evening as it well might, given the severe weather conditions, they would have to rely on the two big fires for warmth. Fortunately, Barry had brought in a huge supply of logs for the iron baskets each side of the great beamed fireplaces in the two rooms and they would last the evening at least.

He returned to the hall and was hesitating, wondering whether to try any more light switches, though he knew it was a fatuous exercise, when he heard the footsteps. They were a woman's, he thought, slow and delicate across the snowy flagstones that ran round the front of the house. He held up his watch to the faint light creeping into the hallway; it was too early for Deirdre's return; only ten minutes had gone by since she and Barry had set out for the village. He waited, suddenly gripped by strong emotion. Could this be the person who had been sending the cards? If so . . .

He took a deep breath and started toward the massive studded front door. Then he saw the faint shadow of a figure passing the old bottle glass-panes that formed the lower half of the window. There was fantastic distortion and the traceries made by the frost rendered it impossible for him to make out who was passing at a stately pace along the terrace. He stood immobile for a few seconds more until the dragging footsteps had died away. He cautiously opened the front door. An icy blast of air came in.

Then he noticed two things. Light shone clearly from the curtained windows of a house several hundred yards away, farther down the road that led to the village. And there was a street lamp still alight at the far end of the street leading to the station. He rushed back and flipped the hall light switch angrily. Nothing happened. Now he saw the delicate set of footprints in the snow that led along the terrace and round the angle of the house. He hurried on, anger and apprehension mingling within him. If there had been no power cut . . .? Though there could have been a fault in the main fuse box of the Old Hall. But what was this intruder doing in the garden and behaving in such a furtive manner?

He was round the end of the house now, saw that the set of footprints ended abruptly within a dense mass of laurels. He went forward cautiously, noticing that nothing had emerged from the other side. There was no sound anywhere except a faint crackling as though someone were moving about in the small coppice that bordered the garage at this side of the house. Then the noise stopped and he was suddenly conscious of the great silence; the falling dusk; and the loneliness in his own heart. He went quickly back to the front door, careless of the icy surface underfoot. He had just slammed the massive oak behind him when there was another click and all the lights came on and with that sudden brilliance normality flowed in.

As he gained the lounge he could hear, through the open doors, the faint humming of the refrigerator and deep-freeze in the kitchen and all the other homely little sounds that a well-ordered house gave out when things were normal. He stared thoughtfully at the Christmas tree and the gaily wrapped presents heaped around it. The hammering noises started at that moment. They seemed to come from upstairs and they reverberated throughout the ground floor rooms. Wilson felt anger mixed with his exaggerated fears. An insane idea that Blake had again started work on the attic rooms crossed his mind. On Christmas Eve? Surely not. And yet . . .

He turned swiftly, energy returning. He mounted the staircase two treads at a time, noticing then the wet imprints and the melting snow left by some recent visitor. The hammering noise was louder now; a steady, monotonous thumping that started echoes from every corner of the ancient house.

Wilson forced himself to go on, some unknown energy infusing his actions, the adrenalin coursing through his veins. He was on the second attic flight now and the noise was so loud it seemed to split his head. The lights burned steadily and he fumbled briefly with the switch to the last flight. Then he was before the attic door. He took a deep breath and flung it open. The noise was now almost like a physical barrier; the loud, regular thumps like some giant pulse.

Before his courage failed he forced himself into the great room, operated the switches there. As he did so an enormous silence fell. He noticed then that perspiration was streaming down into his eyes, noticed too the wet footmarks that went on until finally they started getting fainter as they threaded between the sheeted furniture. He was aware of the same faint odour, like a woman's stale perfume.

This was the far end where Blake had not yet commenced working and it was equally obvious that the carpenter had nothing to do with the bizarre manifestations here. For one moment Wilson wavered;

[217]

what if the lights again failed, leaving him alone at the top of the house at the mercy of whatever intruder had just passed up these stairs? For Wilson knew that the figure he had glimpsed passing the hall windows was the same person who had just climbed the stairs and was responsible for these shattering banging noises.

He looked round quickly for some sort of weapon, aware of the dark shadows to the left, up in the darkest corner of the attic; the place to where the footprints led and to where the electric light had never penetrated. He seized a metal shaft at his elbow, lifted it quickly. It was heavy and he then became aware that it was a golf club, he must have cut a ridiculous figure had there been anyone there to see.

But there must be someone here, he realized. He went swiftly round the sheeted furniture but, as he had hoped, there was no one there. That left only the dark corner. He was advancing, club upraised, when there came a sudden rattling on the stairs.

He whirled fearfully, relief bursting in as he made out the anxious figures of Deirdre and Clissold. Then the girl was in his arms and he felt all the strength ebbing from his body.

'I saw the lights down the street,' Clissold said. 'So we decided to come back because it was obvious the power cut was over.'

Wilson turned to face the dark corner, explained the situation in a few broken sentences.

'You'd better go back down,' he told the girl.

Deirdre tossed the dark curls from her forehead; her face was set and stubborn and revealed no sign of fear.

'Certainly not, John. We must get to the bottom of this.'

Before either of the two men could protest she had dragged the dust sheet off a big pier glass and tilted it so that the reflected light from the nearest overhead bulb shone into the corner. To Wilson's relief there was nothing there, though he could see the faint outline of a footprint near the wall.

For some reason this end of the attic had been covered in a yellow patterned wallpaper and the ancient boards creaked and trembled as the trio walked down toward it. There was a shadowy angle there where four of the old beams followed the outline of a gable and Wilson saw that the paper was all cracked and split with age.

Clissold suddenly bent excitedly.

'Hullo! There's a cupboard or door somewhere here.'

He picked up a rusty carving knife from an old set of kitchen cutlery

[218]

that lay open in a faded velvet-lined canteen on the floor and started stripping the paper. He turned an apologetic face to his host.

'Hope you don't mind?'

'God, no. Go ahead.'

A thin crack had appeared in the paper set against the angle of the wall. Soon, as Clissold worked round, the outline of a door appeared. He went down the middle so that his companions could see the two panels and then enlarged an area round the lock. A keyhole was now visible.

Clissold applied pressure on the knife-blade.

'Locked,' he said in a disappointed voice. 'What shall we do?'

'Break it down,' Deirdre said decisively.

The two men exchanged glances and then Wilson had his fingers round the door-edge. They pulled and then there was a violent cracking noise and dust flew about. Wilson was suddenly engulfed by the same musty odour he had smelt before. Part of the left-hand doorway opened and Wilson had just time to see that the door had been bolted from the inside. He was now able to get his fingers round the right-hand door and it began to creak ominously. To his astonishment that also was bolted from the inside. It suddenly gave with a shriek that jarred the nerves.

Deirdre jumped back with a cry of alarm but it was too late. There was a strong odour of decay and fragments of something loathsome flew about the attic. Clissold was now trying to hold back some weight which sagged forward. With a cry of horror Wilson saw a withered hand thrust toward him as though in some fearful greeting.

Between the mummified fingers protruded a postcard; even by the subdued light he was able to read the jocular greeting in block capitals: HERE I AM!

Deirdre screamed then as the vile thing came out of the cupboard. Wilson found an obscene, yellowed face with blackened tongue thrust into his own, the ligament round its neck brushing across his face with a shock that was almost electric in its impact.

He and Clissold were borne inexorably backward as the wizened, mummified creature, a beetle scuttling from the empty eye socket, clasped them in a ghastly embrace as they went down to the floor in a flurry of dust and decay.

The stench of death was in their nostrils and some frightful liquid drenched the floorboards as the two men, with hoarse shouts of fear and disgust, thrashed about in their efforts to escape the loathsome contact.

Deidre was already pulling them clear as Christmas bells were sounding in the frosty air. Miss Olive Hollamby had at last come home.

TO DANCE
BY THE LIGHT
OF THE MOON

Stephen Gallagher

Stephen Gallagher (b. 1954)
worked for a number of British television
companies before moving on to become a full-
time freelance writer in 1980. In the past ten
years he has produced an impressive number of
acclaimed fantasy and psychological horror
novels: *Chimera* (recently dramatized as a four-
part television series), *Follower*, *Valley of Lights*,
Oktober, *Down River*, *Rain*, *The Boat House*
and *Nightmare, With Angel*.

At eleven o'clock on New Year's Eve, Mercedes Medina read the news.

She was the only newsroom staffer on the station at this hour, and so the bulletin was no more than an update from the IRN teletype; she was off the air at three minutes past, the red light in the news studio dying as the all-night DJ pulled the sound fader out. Mercedes could see him through the double-thickness window along with his tech operator, Derek, who'd got his chair tipped right back against the wall by the door. As she stood, Derek rocked forward and signalled to show that he wanted to speak to her; so she mimed holding a coffee cup, and then she went out.

There was an empty-office silence out in the corridor, and the musty-new smell of carpets recently relaid. Mercedes had been with the radio station since its second year of operation when money had been tight and everything had been run on a shoestring, and she wasn't sure that she liked the new image that the place was now taking on. It had all started to happen when they'd swung into profit; everybody started getting more image-conscious with the next round of franchise competition only two years away, because in a field where most people were newcomers there was an edge to be gained in becoming the establishment as quickly as possible.

Everything considered, Mercedes didn't like the new situation much. But she doubted that she'd be saying so.

She stepped into a small room beside the promotions office. It had one low vinyl settee, a drinks machine, a food machine, and one bag-lined waste bin. Mercedes dialled the code number for a black coffee, and decided to stick at that because the drinks were free whilst the crisps and snacks weren't. The second machine also had a habit, seemingly inherited from its predecessor which had been around the corner before the big overhaul, of keeping money and delivering nothing—a tendency which had earned it the nickname of the Diet Machine.

'Had someone on the line for you before,' Derek said from behind her as a cup dropped and something that would (hopefully) be coffee started to run. 'I told her to ring you back.'

Mercedes turned. Derek was unbelievably tall, around six-four, and unbelievably thin. His sweatshirt sleeves had been rolled back to show arms that looked as if they'd just been cut out of plaster casts.

She said, 'When was this?'

'Just as you were getting ready to go on-air. She said she'd call you on the newsroom line right after the bulletin.'

'You didn't give her the number, did you?'

Derek held up his hands in a kind of defence. 'Not me,' he said. 'She already had it, but don't ask me how. You going to talk to her?'

Mercedes half-shrugged. 'What was it about?'

'Could be a hot tip. Deep Throat stuff, you know.'

'Yeah, I bet,' Mercedes said disbelievingly, and she bent to raise the machine's perspex gate and take out her coffee. It seemed to be more or less what she'd wanted, not counting the slight odour of chicken soup. 'What's happening at your end?'

'Don's usual bunch of rough schoolgirls due to arrive any time now. He's put on something long and slow so that he can run down and let them in.' Something long and slow, in this case, meant an album track which would play to an empty studio during the time that it took for the DJ to race down to the ground-level fire door where his friends/associates/ hangers-on would be waiting. Don's taste seemed to be for noisy, knowing, under-age girls. Derek shook his head, and said, 'I don't know where he finds them.'

'I don't know how he gets away with it.'

'Only because the ones with the big tits get passed along to the boss. You think if I had a perm and got some tinted glasses, I'd have the same kind of luck?'

'No,' Mercedes told him as she shouldered the door open to leave. 'Those are just accessories. It's the basics you're missing.'

'Like what?'

'A total lack of discrimination, and an ego bigger than a telephone box. See you later.'

Derek held the door as she slid through it, her cup in one hand and the yellow flimsies of the eleven o'clock bulletin in the other; and then, as she started off down the empty corridor towards the newsroom, he called, 'Hey, Mercedes!'

She turned to look back; he was still in the doorway, a huge stick-insect less than a year out of college, mousy-haired and with something that, in better light, might have been the beginnings of a beard. He said, 'In case you're busy. Happy New Year.'

'I'll be seeing you at midnight,' she told him, and walked on.

The newsroom corridor was low-lit and silent, and windowless like the rest of the complex. In the background was the murmur of the late-night show being relayed through corridor speakers turned as low as they would go. The station was in a tiny corner of a huge plaza of shops, offices, a multi-level car park and a high-rise hotel; at this time, when all of the office staff had gone home and there was barely more than a handful of people in the entire building, it was possible to detect a once-a-minute vibration that rumbled through the floors and the walls as if the whole plaza structure was in tune with the deep heartbeat of the city.

The phone had started to ring even before she was through the door; half-hoping that it might cut out before she had to answer it, she went over to the big table that ran down the middle of the room and put the bulletin sheets on the spike for the office junior to sort out and file in the morning. Over by the window, the IRN teletype was already hammering out updates for the midnight news; the full-length glass behind it looked out into the main concourse of the darkened plaza, a goldfish-bowl effect that all the staffers hated because of the crowds of kids who gathered in the afternoons to gawp and to tap on the glass as if they were trying to wake the lizards in a reptile house. Now Mercedes saw only herself, a half-real reflection in a room that was a mess of half-read old newspapers, dead press kits, and stacks of directories: a ghost-girl that stared back at her, the skin of a dusty olive and hair of the blackest jet.

And the phone was still ringing.

She hitched herself onto the side of the desk, and moved aside somebody's discarded pullover to reach the receiver. 'Hello?' she said cautiously, expecting to find herself landed with some long and involved message for one of the other staffers. They weren't supposed to give out this unlisted number for personal use, but they all did it.

'They said to call back,' a woman's voice said. It was a terrible line. 'Can you talk to me now?'

'How did you get hold of this number?' Mercedes said. Not a message for someone else, after all; her interest began to warm a little.

'That doesn't matter. What I need to know is, can I trust you?'

'That depends. What are you going to tell me?'

'You're recording this,' the woman said suspiciously.

'We don't record calls. We're just a small station and this is just an ordinary phone. Is it something you've done?'

'No. But I know someone who has.'

'Tell me about it,' Mercedes said. 'Perhaps I can help.' Or perhaps you're just going to waste my time as you try to make trouble for somebody you've decided deserves it; and then you won't give me your name, and then I'll forget all about it. She lowered herself into one of the well-worn typist's chairs, and reached for a noteblock. Just in case.

'It's about that girl,' the woman's voice said. 'The student who was killed. You did a story on her last week, and tonight you said that the police aren't getting anywhere. Well, I know the person who did it.'

Mercedes was bolt upright now, looking desperately around for the portable UHER recorder that was supposed to be kept on permanent standby in the office. Either it was buried under the rubbish some-where, or else someone had taken it home. 'Do the police know about this?' she said, swearing to herself that she'd find whoever was respon-sible first thing in the morning and dig out selected internal organs with a rusty fork.

[224]

'I can't trust the police,' the woman's voice said. 'The question is, can I trust you?'

'Yes, you can,' Mercedes said firmly. 'I've never let down a source yet.' Or even had a source worth letting down, she thought as she hitched the chair in close to the table and started to jot down verbatim everything that had been said so far. 'What's his name?'

'I can't tell you that. He's someone close and it would come back to me, you see what I mean? He needs to be caught, I think he even wants it. But he mustn't ever know that I had anything to do with it.'

'Is he your boyfriend? Your husband?'

'I'm going to hang up,' the voice threatened, and Mercedes scrambled to give reassurance.

'Wait wait wait,' she said. 'All right. I'm not going to push you. But with something like this, you get calls from all kinds of people and they aren't always one hundred per cent genuine. Now, I'm not suggesting that this means you . . . but you see my problem? You've got to give me something I can show around. I'm talking about credibility.'

A breath. Then: 'She was wearing powder-blue underclothes. A matching set. He took a piece away with him.'

'Okay,' Mercedes said, soothingly as if a big hurdle had just been overcome here. The truth of it was that she had no idea whether the information was accurate or not; the body had been discovered only half a mile away across the city centre and she'd been the first of the press to reach the scene, but the actual information that she'd received from the investigating officers had been the same as that in the official release. The important thing was that her caller didn't know this; and if the detail was as genuine as it sounded, it already gave her an edge on the competition.

Big time, here I come, she thought, and she prepared to apply the squeeze. 'So you're not giving me your name,' she said, 'you're not giving me his name, you won't even say what your relationship to him is. Why exactly are we talking, here?'

'I told you, he *needs* to get caught. I know he left things, and the police didn't even see them.'

It really was a lousy line; and the woman seemed to be trying to disguise her voice as well, which didn't help. Mercedes said, 'What do you mean, *things*? You mean clues?'

'He even wrote on the wall, right there where it happened, and they didn't even *see* it. They probably thought it was kids. You could make them listen, though.'

'And what exactly did he write?' An even darker possibility occurred to Mercedes. 'Were you *with* him?'

'I've got to go.'

'No, I didn't mean . . .'

'He's coming. He'll hear me.'

'Well, let's work out some way that we can talk again . . .' she began, but she was wasting her time; the line had already gone dead.

Mercedes hung up; gently, reverently, as if the receiver was of thin glass and filled with gold dust. And then, alone in the newsroom with just the quiet clatter of the teletype as background, she took a moment out to think.

She knew as well as anybody the dangers of believing in hoax calls in a case like this. That would be how she'd have to treat it, until she knew better; but it was the detail about the powder-blue underwear that already had her halfway convinced. She couldn't confirm it, but it hadn't sounded like an off-the-cuff invention. Now, to keep it one hundred-per-cent legal and by the book, she ought to call the police and tell them what she had.

Which meant that they'd move in and take over. And what would *she* get out of it? She was the one who'd been singled out for the call, hadn't she?

By the clock on the wall, she had forty-five minutes before her next on-air appearance. She started to move.

First she dug out the contract list, and phoned for a taxi to meet her out in front of the plaza right away. She knew that they'd all be busy so late on the eve of the New Year, but she also knew that contract work took precedence over casual bookings and that they'd probably bounce back some party pick-up for a half-hour or so in order to fit her in. Then she went around all the desks, opening their drawers and looking for any kind of torch or flashlight; she found one belonging to Bob King—it was in with the rest of his stuff, anyway, amongst the pens and the stale cough drops and his dirty-book collection—and she took it out and checked it. It wasn't much, just a cheap plastic thing running off a couple of pencells, but the batteries were good and it would be better than nothing. Then she took her heavy winter coat from its hook behind the door, and put it on.

She was in the middle of winding her long scarf around her neck when the phone rang again.

[226]

She almost strangled herself in her haste to answer it this time, snagging her scarf on the door handle and jerking herself up short; she snatched up the receiver and said a breathless 'Hello?', but all that she could hear was the electronic echo of her own voice on a dead line.

After waiting a while and hearing nothing, she hung up.

Don's regular soirée—cheap wine as well as cheap women—would probably be well under way by now, and since Mercedes didn't want to interrupt or even to get too close she decided to call Derek via the talkback system from the adjacent news studio. She stood in the narrow booth and leaned across the microphone to the talkback switch; 'Derek?' she said, and through the soundproofed glass she saw his attention snap around to her. He'd been sitting with his chair tilted back against the studio wall again, well apart from Don and his friends and with his face a careful mask of nothing. The main desk was out of the line of sight from where she was standing, but she could see a reflection in the window of the music studio opposite; Don was sitting with one of the girls on his knee, showing her how to run the desk and how to trigger the sequence of loaded cartridges for the commercial break. Mercedes wouldn't have cared to guess exactly how young she was, but she made Don look *very* old.

She told Derek, 'I'm going out for half an hour to check on a late story. I'll be back in time for the midnight bulletin. I'll ring you from the box outside to let me in, okay?'

Derek signalled okay through the glass, but otherwise he didn't move. Nobody else paid any attention. She felt sorry for him; he could get up and wander around the empty station every now and again, but his job required him to base himself in the main studio to act as technical troubleshooter on the show and to handle the incoming calls when the DJ decided to open up the lines for requests or a competition. There was nothing much more for him to be doing at the moment than to sit in as witness to the spectacle of a middle-aged man trying to camp it up like some juvenile stud.

Mercedes left them to it. She had forty minutes left, or half an hour in realistic terms because she'd still have to time and prepare the next bulletin when she got back. She hurried down the whisper-quiet corridor, past the Managing Director's office and the sales suite, and let herself out through the door that was the boundary between the private working areas of the station and the public-access, public-arena zone of the foyer. People could come in here from the plaza to drop off requests, pick up station merchandise, or get signed photographs of the presenters; they came through an outer glass door that could only be unlocked by remote control from behind the receptionist's counter, so that the worst of the weirdies could be kept at bay. The counter was unmanned now, the small switchboard lit up and locked through to an answering machine. Once out of the foyer, she'd be effectively sealed out of the station until Derek emerged in response to her call to let her in.

Stepping out through the door into the chill of the big enclosed mall, Mercedes was thinking ahead. The first and most obvious scenario that had come into her mind—apart from that of the whole thing being a motiveless hoax—had been one in which the sicko who'd killed the student persuaded an accomplice to phone and set up his next victim for him. But what did they think she'd do, walk the half-mile alone in the middle of the night? As she moved out past the boarded gaps of the plaza's unsold shop units, she made a firm decision that she wasn't even going to step out of the locked cab if she could help it.

There was almost no light out here, but she was sure of her way; at the far end of the mall stood a half-hearted attempt at an indoor garden, and beyond that a bank of escalators that would take her down to ground level. The escalators wouldn't actually be running at this time, but there was rarely more than one of them in service anyway. At the bottom, an outward-opening fire door would let her out into the plaza's service road where her taxi would be waiting. Derek would have to make the same trek, remembering to wedge open the foyer door with a chair on his way out, in order to readmit her. It was an informal system and something of a pain, but what else could they do? The high number of unlet units in the plaza meant that the management couldn't afford round-the-clock security. They were lucky if they got a nightly visit from a man and a dog.

The contract minicab was waiting outside, its engine running and its headlights steaming faintly in the cold. Mercedes recognized the driver, who'd picked her up several times to run her home after night shifts; the big saloon was his own, its seats shiny and worn and the side pockets stuffed with colouring books and other children's debris. She settled gratefully into the back, the warmth of the heater already seeping into her as they rolled out of the alley and into the main street before the plaza.

'Where to?' he said. 'Home so early?' But she said no, and gave him the first direction that would take them through an area of old

[228]

warehouses and old pubs and nightclubs that changed names and nominal owners every few months. Gradually the pubs would get rougher and rougher, and more of the warehouses would be standing empty, and then finally true dereliction would take over.

What a place to die, she thought. The last sight your eyes ever see.

'You have a good Christmas?' the driver said over his shoulder, which brought her attention back to the present.

'Working for most of it,' she said. 'Was okay, though.'

'Yeah, me too. To be honest, I don't mind it. Glad to be out for a bit. Couldn't move in our house without getting a frisbee in your ear.'

The driver lapsed into silence again, and Mercedes sat back. The urban landscape outside was already beginning to deteriorate; the suppressed excitement of all those New Year parties boiling away behind steamy lit windows was starting to thin out and disappear, giving way to the blind shells of Victorian buildings marked for demolition and, with increasing frequency, open tracts of wasteland where demolition had already begun.

They called it an Enterprise Zone; there was a big hoarding some-where around here to say so, a desperate sign of a too-late attempt at renewal. The businesses that were supposed to be forced to relocate in the city centre developments had somehow dropped out of sight along the way, scared off by the high rents and the overheads. And now this . . . a nineteen-year-old girl, student at the Poly, fan of Bronski Beat and Spandau Ballet, smashed over the head with a length of railing and her already-dead body dragged into an empty sidestreet to be stripped, stabbed and slashed twenty-three times, and then partly re-dressed and covered over with her own coat. Or maybe this wasn't the kind of enterprise that they'd had in mind.

Mercedes now leaned forward again; the first turn-off was coming up soon, and a number of the sodium lights along the road were either out or else giving the dull cherry glow of a failed element. 'Here it is,' she said; and she could sense the driver's sudden confusion as they made the turn and the saloon's headlight beams swept across a cobbled street that was strewn with rubbish.

'Isn't this where they found that kid?' he said, slowing and watching for anything that might rip at the tyres. The carcass of a thirty-year-old washing machine lay on its side in the road, rusty works spilled all around it.

'This is the place,' Mercedes confirmed. She'd only seen it in daylight before, and hadn't thought that it could look any worse than it did then; but it was possible, she had to concede, it was definitely possible.

'You're not getting out here, are you?'

'Not if I can help it. Can you just cruise down slowly with your lights full on?'

It was a slow, careful, bumpy ride over bricks and glass and rotten timber. The houses on either side were roofless shells, sometimes with entire walls pulled out so that upper storeys hung in mid-air. Mercedes was watching the shadowplay of light over brickwork, watching for the evidence that she'd been led along here to see; she wasn't entirely sure of where she ought to be until they passed a couple of plastic traffic cones and some flapping shreds of barrier tape that had marked the sealed-off zone of a careful police search. Suddenly she could see it, that grey morning reconstructing itself in her mind.

'Just stop here,' she said, 'for two seconds. And whatever you do, don't go away.'

'Roger-dodger,' the driver agreed as the saloon came to a halt, and Mercedes got out.

She shivered in the night chill after the warmth of the car. But there was more to it than that; evil still lay over this place like a radiant imprint slow to fade. She could sense it, read it, feel its touch. The tiny pencell beam stabbed out into the darkness. There was the spot where the dead girl had been lying, a second tarpaulin cover over her to keep off the rain but which couldn't stop the blood from washing out underneath; and here was the place where Mercedes had been standing, shakily recounting her impressions into the UHER's microphone until the officer from the Community Affairs Division had firmly guided her away as the screens had been brought in. It had all gone out, virtually uncut, the officer's words included.

She ran the light over the walls, looking for writing. There was a spray-canned 'GAZ' in four-foot letters, but it was old and already starting to flake away. Nothing else. Picking her way carefully over the rough ground, she went over for a closer check.

Halfway there, she glanced back at the taxi for reassurance. The interior light was on, her beacon of safety and retreat, but it seemed much further away than the few steps that she'd taken. *Shape up*, she told herself, and moved on.

Her first impression had been right; there was nothing written on any of the walls, anywhere, that looked either recent or meaningful. She was about to turn and head back to the cab when the figure in the

[230]

corner raised its head and stared at her.

It was sitting, shapeless and slumped like a tramp, and it moved with a stiff, crackling sound like a dead bird's wing. The head came up and two dim, spit-coloured eyes blinked as if coming awake; they lingered on her for a moment as if recognizing and remembering, and then the head slowly lowered and the eyes were gone. Mercedes turned the light towards it so fast that she almost dropped the torch.

What she saw was two black plastic trash bags, stuffed and loosely knotted and piled one on top of the other. The topmost bag had come undone, perhaps pulled open by some scavenging dog. As she watched, the breeze lifted a fold of the plastic like a sail.

She took a deep breath, and tried to will her hammering heart back to something like a normal rhythm. But her heart didn't want to know, and Mercedes had to concede that it was probably right. She turned her back on the scene, and made straight for her transport.

By the time that they were rolling out of the far end of the derelict street and turning back towards the main road, most of her panic had turned to anger. She was cold, she'd been scared, she'd probably messed up her boots. The driver said, 'Find what you were looking for?'

'Different kind of evidence,' Mercedes said.

'Oh, yeah? What of?'

'The fact that there are people out there with a pretty sick idea of what makes a joke. Fast as you can, will you? I've got another bulletin at midnight.'

'Yeah, midnight,' the driver said with a trace of despondence as the streetlights came back into view. 'Another year gone, and nothing to show for it.'

There was more life around here; some of the houses had been taken over by squatters before the vandals moved in, and even a couple of shops had managed to stay open. Beyond them were the outer-ring tower blocks, distant grid-patterns of coloured stars against the night sky. The buses stopped running to them at eleven; that was why the girl had been walking home, because somebody who'd promised her a lift back from a party had disappeared and she didn't have the money for a taxi.

'You were there, weren't you?' the driver said, breaking into her thoughts. It was like he'd just come up with something that he hadn't expected to remember.

'Not when they found her,' Mercedes said.

'But you did all those interviews straight after.'

'Yes. They went out on the network.'

'So did you see the body, or what?'

Mercedes looked out of the side window at the passing traffic. 'They'd covered it up by the time I got there,' she said.

The cab driver was shaking his head. She saw his eyes as he glanced in his mirror, but he wasn't looking at her. 'What makes somebody *do* something like that?' he said. 'To a kid, as well?'

'I can't tell you.'

'I mean, you see some of them . . . whenever there's a trial, the papers dig out their wedding photographs or whatever. And they're just ordinary blokes—you'd pass them in the street and you wouldn't even know. So where does it come from? Is it supposed to be in everybody, or what? Because I'm bloody sure it isn't in *me*.'

'Well,' Mercedes said, 'we used to be able to talk about evil. But somehow it went out of fashion.'

'Yeah, I know. Couldn't come up with anything to replace it, though, could they?'

She checked her watch. Fifteen minutes to the hour. This was going to be one hell of a tight squeeze, and all over a hoax. The plaza was coming into sight now, the dark mass of the shopping mall topped by the linked tower of the hotel; they floodlit the hotel at night, giving its concrete a warm golden glow that it didn't have in the day. A couple of minutes, and she'd be there.

In the meantime, she was still thinking about evil. She'd been thinking about it a lot in the past few days. She hadn't exactly led a sheltered life, but that morning's visit to the murder scene had been her first exposure to the after-presence of something awesome and real. That evening, when she should have been out celebrating her first major-league report, she'd sat at home in her bed-sit and begun to shake so much that she finally had to go and throw up in the basin. She felt tainted, she felt scared. She'd seen it in the faces of the detectives, that they were in the presence of an old, old enemy, and she now had the sense that she was an unwilling member of their circle.

The nearest thing that she'd ever known to it had been about seven years before, when she was still living at home. The house next door had been broken into and vandalized, everything thrown around and furniture smashed. Nothing had happened to their own place, but a shadow had passed over and changed all that it touched. What she sensed now was something even worse; the passage of a malign intelligence, something whose agents had names and lives and family backgrounds but which simply drew them on as a temporary human skin to carry out its work.

She'd sensed it, all right. And what now made it worse was that she felt that *it* had sensed *her*.

She had the taxi drop her by the phone booth at the front of the plaza. There was nobody in it, which was a piece of luck.

'All seems a bit dead,' the taxi driver said doubtfully. 'Is this okay for you?'

'I'll ring from here and somebody will come down to let me in,' Mercedes assured him. 'I'll be fine. You go on.'

He nodded, and reached under the dash for his radio mike to report in. Contract rides never tipped, Mercedes knew, and her excursion had probably cut into his sideline earnings for the night. 'Happy New Year,' he said, and as she slammed the rear door she said, 'Same to you.'

She was already in the booth as he was driving away.

She dialled the studio's unlisted number. It was engaged. So was the newsroom number, which would have flashed a telltale in the news studio that Derek would have been able to see. In desperation she tried the request line, and hung up when she heard the beginning of the usual recorded message.

What were they *doing* up there? Didn't they know that she had to be on the air in—she checked her watch—just under ten minutes? To miss the broadcast would be the absolute pits of unprofessionalism, whatever the reason . . . and the reason she had wasn't even a good one. She tried the studio number again, once, for luck, but her luck was out.

Mercedes stepped from the booth and started towards the service road at the side of the plaza, half walking and half running. The pavement was a mess of grit and sand from a solitary and short-lived snowfall a couple of weeks before. Her only option was to try the door that she'd left by, to hope that perhaps Derek was already down there and waiting for her.

The service road itself was hardly more than a concrete alley, lit by a single bulb at its end and crowded with the bulking shadows of wheeled trash hoppers. She ran flat out, skidding and almost falling when she hit some sodden cardboard which had lain in the road for so long that it had greyed-down to its colour. She was half-expecting,

[233]

half-hoping for Derek to step out of the shadows and wave her in; but he didn't, and she arrived at the doorway panting and angry and completely at a loss for what to do next.

There was no official procedure for something like this. Nobody was supposed to enter or leave the plaza until the morning security shift clocked in at five a.m.; for any emergencies, the station crew were supposed to call a keyholder. Why couldn't she simply have passed the hoax message along to the police, as she undoubtedly was going to be told that she should have? Off-the-record approval might have been given if her information had turned out to be worthwhile, but she didn't even have that to look forward to.

Less than five minutes to go. Even if she went back to the phone and tried again, she still wouldn't make it. An hour ago, she'd been a competent professional on top of her job; now she was feeling like a child again, sick and awed as she realized too late that simple events were running quickly out of her control.

Shivering and unhappy, she leaned on the door.

It gave silently inward.

She clattered up the dark escalator, slowed by the unfamiliar pitch of its motionless steps. God, the timing of this was going to be tight! She couldn't even hope to grab a spare minute by cheating with the clock as she'd done at least once before on the graveyard shift, probably setting a few people rattling their quartz-crystal watches in puzzlement. This would be the one night of the year when everybody was counting down to midnight. Once inside the station she'd have no time to do anything more than to grab the eleven o'clock bulletin from the spike and repeat it.

There was the warm light of the foyer, a small pocket of welcome over in the far corner of a vast space of darkness. Her footsteps echoed flatly on the ridged plastic floor; the distance seemed to stretch even as she covered it, almost as if she were flying nowhere in a bad dream. She didn't dare to check the time again, but it must be down to under a couple of minutes. Don was probably getting ready to read out the teletype himself. Don was a lousy newsreader, even worse than he was a DJ.

Mercedes almost slammed into the glass door. It didn't give.

She tried again in disbelief, but it was definitely locked. She pressed the buzzer a couple of times to get Derek's attention, and then she backed off, hopping nervously from one foot to another like a duck on a hotplate, ready to go and animated by her frustration. As she waited, she moved along to take a look in through the newsroom window. She'd have bet anything that Don had been encouraging his schoolgirls to call up all their friends on the company phones. Looking through glass that was smeary with the prints of the noses and hands of daytime spectators—they called the newsroom the only zoo around where the animals were all on the outside—Mercedes saw nobody. The newsroom was as she'd left it.

So, where was Derek? She moved back to the foyer and, as she tried the buzzer again, saw the sweep hand of the reception clock covering the last half-minute to the hour. She started to pump at the button, wondering if it was working at all; it should be sounding right down in the studio corridor, and surely Derek would be listening for it. She put her ear to the glass, holding the button down as hard as she could; but she didn't hear any faint and far-off bell, just the muted sounds of the late-night music show on the reception speakers that couldn't be turned off. The track faded, and the drumroll jingle that always heralded the start of the news began.

The news at midnight, she heard the heavily-processed recording say, *with Mercedes Medina.*

She winced. This was terrible. Not only was Don about to screw up the news, but he'd now made it obvious to everybody that the regular newsreader wasn't even supposed to be missing. Thanks a million, she thought.

And then she heard her own voice.

The sound was blurred by the thick glass, but there was no mistaking it. She was too stunned to be relieved. She was past the headlines and into the first item before she realised that what she was hearing was a tape playback of the eleven o'clock broadcast.

It was unlikely that anyone would notice. News content tended not to vary much around this time of night anyway, and sometimes it could be a difficult job putting a new-sounding slant on items that were going around for the fourth or fifth time. What she couldn't understand was, where did the recording come from? Station output wasn't regularly taped—at least, not in any form that could be retransmitted—and she hadn't been aware of anything being done about this one.

Derek must have done it; he was the only technical operator on the station, and it was well within his province. Don probably wouldn't even know how to patch the signal into one of the studio decks. No, Derek it had to be.

But at eleven, Derek hadn't known that she'd be going out. Even Mercedes herself hadn't known it at eleven.

So what was the game?

Suddenly, Mercedes didn't like it. She didn't like it at all. She moved back along to the newsroom window and took another look, and this time she was almost prepared to swear that the chair and the phone and the mess on the desk were exactly as she'd left them. Never mind that she couldn't remember the exact details, she *knew*. Nobody had been in that office or used that phone, but still she'd been unable to ring in. There was only one possible reason for this that she could think of, an old journalists' ploy for tying up a phone line so that you could get to someone before the opposition could reach them; you dialled through, waited for the other party to reply, and then made some excuse about a wrong number so that they'd hang up. What you didn't do was hang up at your own end, effectively blocking the line for all other calls.

Over-sensitive? Perhaps. But the newsroom phone had rung a second time before she'd gone out, and nobody had been there. With that and the studio phone out of use, the station had been effectively isolated from all input.

Reasons: none that she could think of. A joke, perhaps. A really strange one.

Maybe she could ask Derek for the explanation now; because here was his shadow in the light from the foyer, and there was the sound of him opening the spring catch from the inside. The heavy glass door swung inwards, and Derek's gangling silhouette moved into the frame.

In the time that it had taken for him to unlock the door and emerge, Mercedes had backed around behind the nearest concrete pillar. She was barely aware that she'd done it until she felt the coldness of the untreated surface against her hands. Derek stood, bonily awkward and almost comically skinny, and he peered out into the darkness.

'Mercedes?' he said softly; so softly that it was almost impossible to hear. And then he moved out, letting the door swing shut behind him. From her place in the shadows behind the pillar she saw that this man of sticks and bones, this sudden stranger, was carrying a large insulated screwdriver from the electronics workshop. Its narrow shaft was almost a foot long. He let it swing by his side, a natural extension of his arm.

He obviously hadn't seen her, because after calling her name he was now walking straight out across the middle of the plaza, towards the escalators. Foyer music was seeping out as the glass door closed slowly on its spring; it was the sound of a Scottish accordion band, something traditional for the season, and it was growing fainter and fainter as the gap narrowed and Mercedes wondered if she could make a run for it and catch it before the lock could re-engage.

Several times she almost went, and each time she told herself to wait another second so that Derek couldn't dash back and reach her before she could get the door closed against him; until finally, the faint click of the door told her that the chance had slipped away with all her hesitation. She heard the distant echo of Derek as he started his descent of the escalator; he seemed almost jaunty, as if he was out on a job that was no more than routine.

But his eyes. His eyes had been like dead scales.

If the plan had been to give her a scare, then he'd done a first-class job. But she couldn't persuade herself that this was the explanation, partly because it was too much part of a sequence that linked back all the way to that bitter rainy morning in the derelict street. She'd been sensed, she'd been seen; and now she was to be gathered in. Derek—strange, gangling, skinny Derek—was the arm of the reaper.

What was he doing, down below? Perhaps he didn't know that she was already inside the plaza, and had gone down to wait for her. Or else—and this seemed more likely—he'd given her time to get in and now he was securing the door in some way so that she wouldn't be able to leave again.

There was only one way for her to go. Upward, to the rooftop car park. The prestige hotel's main entrance was on that level, reached from the street by a spiralling ramp. If you didn't come in a car, preferably one with a high showroom tag, then the hotel didn't want to know you.

At least she'd be safe up there. She'd find people, probably a big New Year party in one of the conference suites. She'd stay there until dawn, and to hell with explanations.

Moving as silently as she could, Mercedes set out to cross the plaza. She felt as conspicuous as a fly on a white rubber sheet. The entrance to the stairway was an anonymous pair of red ply doors situated between the frontages of a bridalwear store and a toyshop that had recently gone belly-up. The big shopfront sign with its bunnies and frolicking ladybirds was still in place, but the window beneath it was empty and drab. With a slight sense of relief and a prayer that the doors shouldn't creak, Mercedes let herself through into the stairwell.

It was narrow and undecorated, and it smelled of drains. She took out the small flashlight and shone it ahead to find her way; three floors up to the roof, she reckoned, and then another fire door with a push-bar just like the one to the service road. The flashlight, hardly stronger than a decent candle, threw out long, angular shadows and moving bars across the walls as she ascended. Somebody had used the middle landing as a toilet, more than once.

At the top, she had to put all of her weight against the bar. She didn't weigh much, and the bar didn't seem to want to move. It was waist-high, and it was supposed to hinge downwards under pressure to withdraw the long bolts at the top and bottom of the door; that was the theory, anyway, but the practice didn't seem to be working out. What was supposed to happen if they ever had a fire? Wasn't some-body supposed to check these things?

She tried to imagine smoke and flames, a panicking crowd. They'd come up those stairs at quite a lick, and they wouldn't be about to stop for anything; so Mercedes took a few paces back and then ran at the door, hitting the bar as hard as she could.

The door flew open, and hit the wall to the side of it with a crash that echoed all the way back down the stairwell.

But it wouldn't matter if Derek heard it, because by the time that he could get up the stairs she'd be across the roof and into the hotel. For the second time she emerged into the cold of the night, but this time it was like a release rather than a chore; the sight of stars and the low cloud that glowed faintly as if the city burned beneath it had never been more welcome to her. She was at a corner of the roof, the stairwell head being a brick tower close to where the station kept its radio car. She could see this in the shadows only a few yards away, grimy windscreen reflecting the neon tracery of a department store sign on the next block. Straight ahead, less than a hundred yards across the asphalt, was the painted-on driveway and the entrance to the hotel.

It was wide and glossy and glassy and bright. Automatic doors led through to the lobby, where expensively-carpeted steps climbed past display cases to a mezzanine level with reception desk, low sofas and coffee tables amongst potted plants. Hotel staff in dark suits or crisp whites could be seen moving around inside.

And between the hotel and Mercedes stood a roll-across metal gate.

She ran to it, grasped it, shook it; the barrier hardly moved at all. It was eight feet high and topped with spikes. A monkey might have made it over or a snake might have made it through, but Mercedes had no chance at all.

People were coming out of the hotel, and she called to them; 'Hey,' she shouted, 'Over here, help!' But as the automatic doors hissed open the group of seven or eight came spilling out with a party roar that drowned her completely, and within seconds they were at their cars and switching on their music systems in a kind of stereo war so loud and so discordant that she couldn't even hear herself. The cars started out in a jerky convoy, windows open and blasting as they drove off in a swirl of abandoned streamers and festive debris. As the last set of tail-lights disappeared into the downward spiral, they left behind a wind-blown silence in which Mercedes was calling hoarsely to the night air. Five floors below, somebody was sounding off as the traffic before him made a slow start at the lights.

Mercedes let go of the barrier. She'd been holding on so hard that it was now difficult to get her fingers to disengage. What was she going to do now? Go back below, and risk meeting Derek on the stairs?

Or was Derek up here with her already?

She moved to the nearest shadow; and just in time. She saw the stairhead door swing outward in silence. Derek stepped forward in the doorway and waited, listening. Mercedes held her breath. He turned his head slowly from side to side like a blind thing, as if trying to locate her with some deep radar sense that went beyond sound or vision; and then, moving with a stealth that looked faintly absurd in one so tall and so angular, he melted off to check around the back of the stairhead.

He'd left the fire door wide open. It wouldn't take him long to check around behind, and then he'd be back and he'd see her as she ran. She'd hesitated once already and missed an opportunity at safety; now she was on her way even before she was certain that her decision was a wise one.

He appeared so fast that he must have expected this, been listening for her; but even so he mustn't have been prepared for her to jump so soon, because she was just able to get in and slam the door before he could dive through after. She wrenched up on the bar as hard as she could; Derek's weight on the other side of the door actually helped her, because he unwittingly pushed it home that last vital fraction of an inch that allowed the long bolts to engage with a bang.

Mercedes was in darkness now, and again she fumbled out the flashlight in order to check that the bar was secure. As she ran the light over, a soft tapping that was almost a scratching began.

'Mercedes?'

The door began to rattle; just faintly, as if under no more than fingertip pressure.

'Mercedes?'

Three round, crashing blows against the door that echoed like explosions in the stairwell and made her step back in fright; but the door held solid, and then came that soft whisper again.

'It's *me*, Mercedes.' And then, slyly; 'You know who I mean, don't you?'

She began to descend, the flashlight showing the way ahead once more. The batteries were starting to fade now, the light yellowing and getting dimmer, but she couldn't bring herself to switch it off even for a moment. She wondered what on earth she was going to do when she reached plaza level again.

She'd be shut in, but Derek would be shut out. So far, so good. But she was guessing that he'd maybe pulled the wires on the buzzer, which meant that she wouldn't be able to get Don's attention inside the station; which left the option of perhaps trying to break into one of the shops in order to get to a phone and call the police. She'd never broken into anything before, and wasn't even sure how she'd go about it.

And suppose she got to a phone. What then? What exactly was she going to tell them? Because what had actually *happened*? She'd made an unofficial trip out, and she'd missed a broadcast. Derek had covered for her, and then emerged to come looking. He'd followed her to the roof, where she'd locked him out. There wasn't one element in the sequence where all the unreasonableness didn't seem to be on her side. All that she could offer was her fears, and her reading of the undercurrents of the situation. It was like a perfect melody with wrong harmonies that only she could hear.

It didn't help. She *knew*, deep down where it counted; there had been a mutual recognition between her and the presence at that derelict site, and now that same presence was wearing Derek like a glove. Perhaps it had even caused him to make that phonecall to the newsroom that had sent her out in the first place; the station's commercial production studio had harmonizers and equalizers that could turn a man's voice into a reasonable facsimile of a woman's, if the added on-line interference was bad enough to cover the deceit.

It wasn't Derek, not in the true sense; this was the sandman, and he was bringing her a dream. But it wasn't the kind of dream that anybody would want to lie half-awake for, in drowsy anticipation.

Down on the plaza again, she went across to the indoor garden near the top of the escalators. It was a half-hearted affair, with most of the borders just empty dirt because all of the plants had starved away from daylight; there were small trees in barrels, a few rustic benches for shoppers, and a wishing well for local charities which had a stiff wire mesh just under the surface of the water to stop kids from reaching down and helping themselves to the pennies. Mercedes chose a fair-sized stone from one of the border walls, and tried its weight. It was loose-laid, and so no problem to move, and she found that she could just about carry it.

Staggering along like the world's most heavily-pregnant woman, Mercedes headed for the radio station foyer. Halfway there she stopped a moment to rest, and that was when she heard it; the sound of a lift somewhere else in the plaza, a sound that would be lost during normal shopping hours but which was now like a warning signal in the cavernous silence. It said that Derek was back inside. It said that he was coming for her.

Her first attempt to smash the big foyer window had no effect; she couldn't believe it, but the stone simply bounced back in her hands and set the whole pane shivering. The second time, she threw it hard and let go; this attempt put a sudden and terrifying split into the glass that travelled outward from the point of impact like forked lightning. For one moment she stood in deep awe of what she'd done, and then she set about breaking enough of a hole out of the reinforced window for her to step through.

There was no time to feel guilty, or even to begin to enjoy it. The glass fell out in big plate-sized pieces onto the foyer's cord carpet, and she felt something catch and tear at her coat as she bent to crawl through the opening that she'd made. Inside, as she straightened, she was taken by the bizarre feeling that she'd squeezed out of one world and into another; here it was warm, and the lights were late-evening soft, and the foyer speakers were relaying *Here Comes Summer* at a low murmur. Odd choice, she thought as she pushed into the inner corridor, a degree of professionalism reasserting itself as she entered home territory; but then, as she moved down past the offices towards the studios and what she'd been certain would be a degree of safety, she heard the record ending and the DJ coming on-air to link into the next track.

The DJ wasn't Don.

In fact, he wasn't anybody who worked at the station at all; his name was Dave Cook, and he'd left six months before on the promise of a contract in television. The contract had never materialized, and now he was working at some really tiny new station over on the Welsh border. Mercedes started to run towards the studio, already half-knowing what she was going to find; the sound of the long-departed Dave Cook was a strong indication, and the absence of the red transmission light over the studio door seemed to confirm it.

She burst in. There they were, a neat triptych behind the sound console; Don and his two young ladies, one on either knee with his arms flung around them, their faces black as old iron and their necks wired together with a microphone lead. Their eyes were all bulging and their tongues were all sticking out; Yah Boo, they seemed to be saying, Sucks to the World.

The door behind Mercedes closed on its damper with a quiet thump, tapping her on the back and pushing her to go forward into the studio. She took one halting step, and looked around her in bewilderment. Her place of safety was suddenly old, bad news. Over by the big surprise behind the console was the sight that she'd been on the way to expecting; four full twelve-inch metal spools of tape in a stack, with a fifth playing on the deck. These would be the standby tapes, the emergency fallback material kept in a locked cupboard for occasions of serious equipment failure or evacuation of the station. It was supposed to be somebody's job to keep them up to date, but that somebody obviously hadn't.

It almost didn't shake her to walk around to the other side of the desk; Don and the two girls didn't even look real and their expressions were nearly comic, as if death was a bad joke that had simply jerked them away in the middle of its punchline. One outflung, long-nailed hand brushed at her coat as she carefully squeezed by them, and she delicately drew herself aside to avoid further contact.

Mercedes had been shown the basics of driving a desk on her first day at the station, but the details had gone whistling down the same hole as so much of the useless information that they'd been throwing at her around that time. She saw a long bank of colour-coded faders, another of equalizer dials, a row of needle indicators that bounced and bopped along with the outgoing music; there were pieces of masking tape making crude labels with messages like *off-air p/bk* and *tx* and *Do not use!*, this last with a small skull-and-crossbones added, and the whole array was topped with a mess of running order sheets and unsorted commercial cartridges.

The absurd thought that occurred to her, as she tried to make sense of the layout, was that at least she'd now have no problem in convincing anybody that she'd been in real danger. All that she needed to do now was to find a way to get a mayday message out, and fast. Derek might have tied up the phone lines somehow, but he'd had to leave the station's output running. She could make her plea for help live and on-air, and somebody would come.

Somebody would.

Wouldn't they?

None of the sliding controls on the desk seemed to be making any damn difference to anything; the transmission lights stayed dead, and the Beach Boys played on as the tape reels turned. She looked frantically from one side to the other, knowing that she had minutes or less to get her message out and then to find somewhere to hide. Every fader was up but the mike still wasn't open, which could only mean that Derek must have pulled the necessary patch-leads around the side of the desk. With no technical knowledge, Mercedes didn't have a hope of putting herself on-air.

He'd killed the studio. He'd tied up all the outgoing phonelines. What did that leave?

It left the incoming request line, the one that would be hooked up to an answering machine. The signal fed directly into the desk, but Mercedes had seen the TOs using a white phone to speak to callers off-air during tracks. She had to reach across Don to take it from its hook; it was an awkward manoeuvre because she didn't want to touch him, and managing this wasn't easy because she didn't want to look at him, either.

Lifting the phone had automatically switched the line to the handset. She broke in on what sounded like a couple of giggling kids phoning in for a dare.

'Listen,' she said, 'this is an emergency. I want you to put your phone down and then call the police. Tell them . . .'

'*Hello?*' one of the kids said.

'Yes, hello. My name is Mercedes Medina, I'm a newsreader here. Please call the police and say . . .'

But whoever it was on the other end of the line, she wasn't

listening; Mercedes heard the scuffling of a hand being placed over the mouthpiece, and an awed voice saying, *'It's her that does the news!'*

'I know,' she said, 'please! I need your help for something very important . . .'

'Hello?' the kid said, returning.

'Please listen to me! Don't talk and don't go away! People are *dead* here!'

But the voice which answered her then was not that of a child; it was one that she recognized instantly and with a cold, crawling sense of helpless fear. It was the heavily-processed facsimile of a female voice that she'd first heard only an hour before.

'Happy New Year, Mercedes,' it said. *'I've got a present for you. Want to come and see what it is?'*

Heard now and without the disguising overlays of fake interference, it wasn't so convincing; it didn't even sound human anymore. 'Derek,' she said, 'it's you, isn't it?' But the voice went on as if she hadn't spoken.

'All right then,' it said with faked resignation. *'I can see I'll just have to bring it to you myself.'*

She dropped the phone. She'd taken too long, allowed herself to be trapped; she looked around for a way out, a weapon, *anything*. With sudden inspiration, she moved to the tape deck and ripped the tape out from around the pick-up head; the music from the big speakers overhead ended with an ungainly squelch, and the big reels on the deck started to speed up as its tension control sensed a lack of resistance. Somebody might hear, somebody might wonder; perhaps even the Managing Director, who was notorious for calling people to account for fluffs and glitches which had happened at the most ungodly hours. Given time, somebody might even come to see what had gone wrong.

And then they'd probably find her, making up a foursome with Don and the others; because time was something that she was almost out of.

There was a soft thump from just outside; it was the sound of the studio's outer door as it closed behind someone. Someone who was about to open the inner door and step through into this one-exit, soundproofed killing pit. Mercedes was looking, but she couldn't even see any scissors or used blades from tape-editing.

The door opened with a hiss; he came in sideways with his eyes glowing like coals under darkened brows, a single strand of damp hair hanging forward over his face. He was hiding something from her, and it was as he turned to bring it into view that Mercedes found the will to move. She snatched up one of the metal reels from the stack beside her and, with a grace and an accuracy that wouldn't have been possible with forethought, threw it edge-on and frisbee-style towards Derek. It zipped through the air, spewing out tape as it spun, lifting in flight and making straight for his face. He ducked, but not fast enough. The edge of the reel clipped him neatly on the forehead and he staggered back.

He fell against the door, but the door gave only reluctantly as its damper resisted. He was pitched down onto his side as the reel clunked onto the floor and rolled away, still leaving a trail of tape behind it. Derek was struggling feebly. Mercedes came around the desk, sick at what she'd done and unable to resist her own feelings of guilt; she'd never killed anything, never even *hurt* anything before, and now here she was, plunging into the major league with a human target. She hesitated when she saw that Derek was moving to get to his feet again; she'd slowed him, but it seemed that she hadn't stopped him.

He pushed himself up against the doorframe. His movements were stiff, his eyes empty and dazed-looking; when he glanced down, it was with a thick, liquid slowness.

'Shit,' he said bleakly. 'You spoiled my surprise.'

He was looking down at his right hand; this was gripping a wooden plate that Mercedes recognized, after a moment, as the newsroom billspike. There was a lag in recognition because of the fact that only a couple of inches of the spike itself were visible. His hand was held out in front of his chest, just where the breastbone ended and the soft tissues began; the point was marked neatly by a dark stain that was beginning to spread through the material of his sweatshirt.

The fight to get upright was obviously proving too much for him. With a sigh of regret, he gave up and began the return slide to the floor. He hit it with a grunt, and his hand fell from the spike's wooden base; this stayed in place like some king-sized hatpin pushed into some life-sized voodoo doll, and now Mercedes saw that his eyes were fixed on nothing in particular.

It took her several minutes to raise the courage to step over him; time in which Derek didn't move, didn't blink, and didn't even bleed much any more. A tiny bubble of blood appeared at one nostril, stayed for a while, and then popped as the last breath slowly left him. The overhead speakers hissed with the no-transmission phenomenon that was called—with grim appropriateness—'dead air'.

Between this and the four lifeless bodies in the room, Mercedes found herself being driven from the studio by an urge that was almost physical. She stepped carefully over Derek, forcing herself to watch him in case this should turn out to be some elaborate and impossible trick to get her within reach, and then she fell thankfully through the outer door and into the low air-conditioned hum of the corridor. The first sight that met her eyes was that of a long trail of yellow papers, scattered around the corridor floor and stretching back and around the corner towards the newsroom; these were all of the bulletin scripts from the last few hours, ripped from the spike and discarded en route to the studio. He must have been pulling them off one at a time, she realized, like the petals from a flower or the legs from a fly.

Her own legs were feeling none too steady, but they held her up well enough as she headed towards the offices. There had to be a phone somewhere, at least one outside line that Derek (or, as she was thinking, the potent force that had expressed itself as Derek) hadn't remembered or managed to block. She wanted to call somebody, it almost didn't matter who anymore . . . the police, the boss, her mother in Bristol, any human voice or contact.

Surely the Director's office would have its own outside line; probably more than one. She expected to find the door locked, but it wasn't. She felt around for the lightswitch before she entered, not wanting to step out into darkness; the lights came on to reveal the quiet expense of executive furnishing. The carpet was thick and soft, the wood panelling warm and mellow. The phone on the desk was ivory-white.

And it rang.

Mercedes lifted the receiver slowly, and listened. The voice that came down the line was a signal now stripped of any pretence at humanity.

'*Men may come, and men may go,*' it quoted softly, '*but I go on forever.*

'*Happy New Year, Mercedes.*'

ACKNOWLEDGMENTS

The Publisher has made every effort to contact the copyright holders of material reproduced in this book, and wishes to apologize to those he has been unable to trace. Grateful acknowledgment is made for permission to reprint the following:

'Jerry Bundler' by W.W. Jacobs, reproduced by permission of the Society of Authors as the literary representative of the Estate of W. W. Jacobs.

'The Crown Derby Plate' by Marjorie Bowen, reproduced by permission of Hilary Long.

'The Stocking' by Nigel Kneale taken from *Tomato Cain*. Copyright Nigel Kneale, 1949. Reproduced with permission from Lemon Unna & Durbridge Ltd.

'The Visiting Star' by Robert Aickman. Copyright © Robert Aickman, 1966. Reproduced by permission of the Aickman Estate, c/o Artellus Ltd.

'The Night Before Christmas' by Robert Bloch. Copyright © 1986 by Robert Bloch. Reproduced by permission of Ralph M. Vicinanza, Ltd.

The following stories are reproduced by permission of the authors: 'Christmas Eve' by Ronald Chetwynd-Hayes; 'The Greater Arcana' © 1992 by Ron Weighell; 'Wish You Were Here' © 1992 by Basil Copper; 'To Dance by the Light of the Moon' by Stephen Gallagher.